A. M. Weston

The Evolution of a Shadow : Or, the Bible Doctrine of Rest

From the Standpoint of a Believer in the Divine Authority and....

A. M. Weston

The Evolution of a Shadow : Or, the Bible Doctrine of Rest
From the Standpoint of a Believer in the Divine Authority and....

ISBN/EAN: 9783337172947

Printed in Europe, USA, Canada, Australia, Japan

Cover: Foto ©Lupo / pixelio.de

More available books at **www.hansebooks.com**

THE EVOLUTION OF A SHADOW:

OR,

THE BIBLE DOCTRINE OF REST.

FROM THE STANDPOINT OF A

BELIEVER IN THE DIVINE AUTHORITY AND PARAMOUNT IMPORTANCE OF THE RELIGIOUS OBSERVANCE OF THE FIRST DAY OF THE WEEK.

BY

A. M. WESTON, A. M.,

Formerly Professor in Hiram College, Ohio, and President of Eureka College, Illinois.

CINCINNATI:
STANDARD PUBLISHING COMPANY.
1886.

Copyright, 1886, by
STANDARD PUBLISHING COMPANY.

TO MY VENERABLE FRIEND,

Hickman New, of Vernon, Indiana,

ALREADY VERY NEAR TO THAT REST WHICH REMAINETH
TO THE PEOPLE OF GOD,

THIS VOLUME,

DEVOTED TO THE MAINTENANCE OF THE
LIKE PRECIOUS FAITH,

IS

RESPECTFULLY INSCRIBED

BY

THE AUTHOR.

PREFACE.

This work is not designed to have a denominational character. That is, it is desirable that the public should not be able to determine the author's religious connection from what he here writes. There are many subjects upon which the majority of religionists will agree as to most of the steps taken and upon the conclusions reached. When this harmony is attainable, the pages of a book should not be embarrassed by anything which would rather awaken prejudice than promote the common object.

No body of religious people is responsible for the sentiments expressed. No such body ever taught them to the author. He derived them from the free exercise of his privileges as an independent investigator of the Word of God. No one is to be charged with them to any detriment or credited with them to any advantage other than he whose name is appended.

They are consigned to the care of an enterprising publishing house, which will issue them as a contribution to the thought of the age. They are confidently given to the public with the certain conviction that the end reached will meet the approval of all religious bodies that delight to worship the Lord on the Lord's day—the first day of the week.

The course of investigation will no doubt appear novel, but on that account the more worthy of notice because more likely to suggest thoughts not already familiar. The great diversity of opinions upon the theme discussed, and the growing tendency to ignore Sunday observance as of divine obligation, to the incalculable injury of the whole country, render it necessary to review the grounds upon which the institution rests.

If, in seeking to develop the true basis, some of the methods of treating this subject, long popular and firmly intrenched in the public mind, be gradually undermined, it is only to establish others, more rational, scriptural, and satisfactory.

The Christian will find nothing here to destroy his faith, but much to strengthen it. To make faith more intelligent is a prime object. He who may have confused ideas as to the teaching of Scripture, will find this fundamental subject drawn out in consistent outline, and rounded into full proportions, with no contradictions to mar its symmetry. With one such "evolution" traced, it is easy to gather therefrom the course of the divine plan in all its parts. An intelligent and inspiring view of the Bible and its one theme is thus acquired. Faith grasps the simple plan. Henceforth it rests secure, because it understands, in a finite sense, of course, what it is called upon to believe.

Many of the thoughts which have guided these investigations, have dwelt for years in the mind of the writer—a well-spring of faith, hope, and joy. May they be the source of like comfort to others.

A. M. WESTON.

Mt. Summit, Ind., June 10, 1884.

CONTENTS.

PREFACE	v., vi.
CONTENTS	vii., viii.
INTRODUCTION	1– 8

CHAPTER I.
At Creation..................................... 9– 15

CHAPTER II.
At Creation—Continued 16– 23

CHAPTER III.
Twenty-Five Hundred Years..................... 24– 34

CHAPTER IV.
The Manna and Sinai 35– 51

CHAPTER V.
Moses' Law.................................... 52– 64

CHAPTER VI.
Historians and Prophets....................... 65– 90

CHAPTER VII.
Types... 91–105

CHAPTER VIII.
The Law Abolished............................ 106–131

CHAPTER IX.
The Lord of the Sabbath...................... 132–152

CHAPTER X.
The Council at Jerusalem..................... 153–170

CHAPTER XI.
The Lordian Day.............................. 171–186

CONTENTS.

CHAPTER XII.
Apostolic Precedent..................................... 187–204

CHAPTER XIII.
The Fathers.. 205–218

CHAPTER XIV.
Constantine and the Popes.............................. 219–233

CHAPTER XV.
Epochs 234–248

CHAPTER XVI.
Comments Here and There............................... 249–268

CHAPTER XVII.
The Weekly Holiday.................................... 269–280

CHAPTER XVIII.
Sabbatismos........................... 281–292

INTRODUCTION.

The historical order is both the natural and the logical. Down the stream is the easier sailing, and yet you arrive at as many places, and as beautiful scenery delights the eye. We are on a broad river in this year of our Lord, 1884. We should never be able to get back to its source but for the book of God. With its radiant pages open before us, we can embark where earth-time begins to flow, and find a channel all along navigable, and never obscured by mist.

If there is one thing for which the author is most of all thankful, it is that in boyhood, when humble circumstances supplied few other books, he read the Bible through many times, from beginning to end, omitting neither the cubits of the Pentateuch nor the horns of prophecy. If there is one thing which considerable experience in the instruction of young men for the ministry has taught him, it is that such a course for them is better than volumes of theological lore, all of one denominational cast, "given from one shepherd," and supposed by such guide of the young to be the infallibly correct interpretation of the inspired record. A fair mind, unbiased by early training, willing to believe and apt to understand, will not readily go astray on any religious subject, if his knowledge of the Bible is acquired from reading it in course. When thus reading, differences in the age, dispensation, circumstances, and others equally apparent, insensibly impress such modifications as lead to correct conclusions not liable to be suggested to the mind of the indiscriminate reader.

False conclusions are just as natural to one who reads wrong as true ones are to him who reads aright. It is believed that there are multitudes of people to whom this thought never occurred. A good deacon of the time to which memory yet reaches was asked by an admiring follower what, in his opinion, was the teaching of the Bible upon a given question. The reply was that the Old Testament contained a pretty equal distribution of the passages on both sides, but that, in the New Testament, a majority was clearly in the affirmative, which, therefore, must be held to be the scriptural doctrine. This was a very sagacious decision, in view of the light which the deacon possessed. If the Bible comes to us, as it did to him, as a book of texts *pro* and *con*, then nothing is left us but to try every subject by their vote, and let the majority of passages rule. But mindful of the fact that the book records the progress and development of a system, such that in one age God may consistently disallow what he has not forbidden in another, apparent antagonisms in the parts begin to appear reconcilable to us. Then the extent and the diversity of circumstance and detail, which mark God's dealings with man, and the vast changes which occur in man, and his language and customs, during these long periods, when considered, as they only can be, by one who acquaints himself with them by following their entire course, explain so many difficulties, that at last clashings are removed, and the whole weight of God's word comes to us on one side of every question upon which it treats.

Thus there is a difference in the attitude of men to God, and of God to men, whether good or bad, in different ages of the world. Hence the necessity of beginning at the origin and tracing the consecutive steps of this progressive scheme which God has inaugurated and carried forward by agencies and under laws as diverse as the times and subjects to which they relate.

There are the fewest number of people in the world who investigate Bible subjects in a broad, dignified and impartial manner. This is as far removed from loose liberalism on the one hand as from narrow bigotry on the other. The world is too large, time too long, and men too shrewd for any other mode to win success of any permanent value. For a time, the man of one idea, giving his whole soul to its advocacy, may advance it rapidly upon the public attention.

All of us who have lived and observed long, have noted that certain measures of public policy, ideas upon education, finance, science, like ephemeral fashions, have come and gone, or at least have retired from prominence, no longer arousing the enthusiasm which once attended them. Happy, indeed, in fame, are their promoters, if even one idea has sufficient value to endure. Practical systems generally grow from such occasional engraftings. The transitoriness of that which is not preëminent in worth, often indeed of that which is useful, is well illustrated by political events now transpiring. A great party has met and made its nominations for President and Vice President. It had been supposed that one name familiar to the nation was sure of a place of honor, but when the time came, lo, a change. It was not even mentioned. His time had passed. His "boom," to use the word of the day, had come and gone. These "booms" do not always signify much of lasting benefit to the race. Everything narrow, all that is false, whatsoever is vain, much that is good, even, shall sink into the sea of the forgotten.

Christianity itself is the marvel of all marvels. It has developed an enthusiasm which has never failed as the ages rolled by. The books of Moses are read vastly more now than in Hezekiah's time. The epistles of Paul, the apostle, to the churches of the first century, are profoundly admired and reverently studied by the saints of the nineteenth. Many usages, which the "fathers of the church" introduced somewhat later, are now never thought of, while their notions are regarded in many instances as silly in the extreme; yet whatever can be traced back to inspired authors stands the test of time. Nothing trifling or impracticable entered into their plans or teaching.

The church itself was organized on a better basis than that of any denomination since formed. We are fast coming to the conclusion that, if religious organizations would be permanent, they must go back to the primitive order. The church must be one, and the same in form as the apostles left it. Its creed must be the Scriptures themselves. Its name, its officers, its worship, its ordinances, its fellowship, its spirit, must be exactly that which apostles have developed in their writings, commanded and illustrated by word and example.

There were narrowness and bigotry among Judaizers, but none among the apostles. They were, as we should be, intensely loyal to Christ, but generous to one another. Theories of the resurrection, as of every other subject, had their intolerant advocates, then as now, who pressed them upon others as though containing the sum of the needful. It is easy to perceive in reading the New Testament that it is possible to be too partisan as well as too loose in religious life. The essential in the Christian system may be dismissed with a " Well, no matter." The non-essential incident may be exalted to undue prominence, held to and enforced with the stubbornness of " grim death " itself.

It is this latter that has generally lighted the fires of persecution, while the true Christian has furnished the victim. The persecuting spirit, which has at times possessed even the church, like the demon of Christ's time, never entered it till, empty of holiness, swept and garnished from all active spiritual life, it had been surrendered to this wicked bigotry. Men who have swung far off to the other extreme, that of unbridled license in faith and deed, have foolishly charged this upon Christianity itself. What a blunder! Or is it an intentional slander, inspired by hatred? Was Christ a persecutor? Can, then, a Christian be one? A sect may. One denomination may treat another with more or less uncharitableness. It may unjustly censure the unbeliever. Poor, weak human nature in the church may have striven to coerce into its fellowship, or punish those who rejected it. But this is not the spirit of Christ. The Saviour, with legions of mighty angels hovering about, went down to the abodes of death. He fulfilled his divine mission with a world-embracing love, an infinite philanthropy that included friends and enemies alike; and yet the fires of heaven, that Elijah once summoned, were at his command to consume forever the Pharisees who traduced and the rulers who crucified him. It is sin that persecutes. It is the devil, in the name of Christ, who has committed every wrong against man that has stained the history of the church.

We must approach the study of God's word in that broad and catholic spirit which will not permit us to be tied to any ungenerous partisanship. There is no act, word or thought too insignificant for our attention, which the Bible inculcates, and none which we dare follow away from its leadings.

In following a subject like the one to which these pages are devoted, we find room for all the impartiality of which we are capable. We dismiss bias, if we can, for it is sure to lead us into bigotry. We must treat our opponents with fairness, for we know they are honest. We must beware of intolerance, for some of them are striking examples of its evil effects. We must carefully consider whatever views they may offer, for we ask like consideration of our opinions from them. Then, too, we shall never be right till we are able to look at all subjects from all angles. Vast changes in appearance, creating decidedly different mental impressions, arise from moving our point of observation from the north to the south. Landscapes shift as we go. Mental and spiritual horizons are like natural ones. What they inclose depends upon where we stand. Take position beside Adam in his primitive purity; then again after the fall, expelled from the garden of delights. Have no ideas, meanwhile, dawned upon the mind, in regard to earth-life and human being? Look again when Noah steps forth upon the regenerated earth, with the arch of promise in the heavens above, and the covenant of God in his heart. What are his ideas compared with those of David the

Psalmist, who long afterwards scans history and breathes prophecy in the poetic utterances of praise? What was Moses at the flaming bush, on glory-crowned Sinai, or at the top of Pisgah? What a difference in the scope of his information at these different times! What vast movements have wrought their changes upon the world, viewed in the aspect of man's relation to God, as we speak the name of John—John the Baptist, John the Beloved Disciple, John the Revelator! Perhaps it is the chief mistake of infidels that they overlook the vast distinctions that truth demands to be considered because of the different epochs brought to view in the divine record. On the other hand, one of the strongest evidences of the truth of the book is the infinite diversity of its contents, which are blended into perfect harmony. No little difficulty may be expected on the part of any conscientious student of the Scriptures, in the same line with that so fatal to the unbeliever. The danger of error should lead to the calmer examination.

It is hoped that the investigation sketched in succeeding chapters will be found to be of this character, and hence worthy the regard of those who desire to understand the great and important subject.

To have read the Bible through often, consecutively, is necessary before undertaking such a work. To be familiar with the sequence of events is indispensable. To have an idea of the intervals of time is important. To read the language as though written for the period and the people when its author lived, and to look at matters with the light which those circumstances permit, have much to do with correct results.

The Sabbath question is necessarily a generalization;

hence the need of such a spirit and preparation to understand it. It is a development, for it treads the course of all the dispensations to the end of time. As, therefore, the dispensations advance from the barest promise of a Redeemer to his full manifestation and coronation, so must this question, constituting one view of the great sacred theme, develop, in harmony with the whole, into the perfection of all that it represents.

THE EVOLUTION OF A SHADOW

CHAPTER I.

AT CREATION.

The opening of our subject in the Bible is one of peculiar interest as well as difficulty. No savage in thoughtful mood—and even to the most uncultured, such mental states will come—has ever looked upon earth, sea, and sky without wonder. As shrewder wits, with closer observation, and the aid of constantly improved appliances for penetrating, analyzing and comprehending, have found time, during the struggle for existence, to cast inquiring glances in the same direction, the same emotion has been overwhelming. Poor Jack Cole, the intrepid seaman, returned from the DeLong Arctic Expedition, one of the few survivors, but a hopeless mental wreck. Lieut. Augur, of the party sent in search of the Jeannette, likewise became insane, and died in that condition. Nature had overpowered them both. Whether you throw yourself against her inexorable laws, gaze with uncovered eyes into the burning sun of her splendors, or search her mysteries with unschooled ardor, you are beaten back, baffled if not destroyed. How often do I remember shrinking with a shudder from such an endeavor. For instance, in contemplating the distance of the stars, as telescope and mathematics have revealed them, a flash of the infinite seemed thrown upon the mind; a feeling, as if I met God suddenly, face to face, in the quiet walk. Let me cast myself veiled at his feet and worship, but let me not try to look upon him. Reason seems to totter on her throne, and I am forced to return to humbler contemplation.

After the greatest minds have studied nature for ages, what is the result? The distance between the known and the unknown has simply increased. The problem investigated, great at first, seems vastly greater now. With every step in advance, multiplied vistas have opened before. When Job inquires, "Canst thou by searching find out God?" now and then a school-boy scientist lifts his hand and cries, "I can." Most, however, at the end of all research, confess their own imbecility. Seeking by our processes, for ages, the origin of things, and finding for the greatest of questions no answers, positively none, weary in mind and sick at heart, how refreshing to sit down and read the few simple sentences in the first chapter of Genesis—the record, by the inspired Moses, of the works that God "created and made." Why, the most of us, should we whittle a pin to fasten a gate, would narrate the achievement in less modest language! Simply, God made the great and mighty wonders that surround us. Through what chemical combinations, furnace heats, mighty upheavals, by what exertion of physical and spiritual forces, we are not informed.

To this sublimest of records addressed to the intelligence of man, we go for our first lesson upon the Sabbath. At this point, too, are found the greatest difficulties that environ the subject. Here is the origin of the greatest mistakes made by those who have sought to understand it. In the nature of things this must be true.

Other things being equal, the lapse of time increases obscurity. Our ancestors of but a few generations past are all unknown to us. Why can we not have the same fond recollections of them as of our fathers and mothers? It may be that in eternity we shall be introduced to them. From the dead and buried past but a few faint rays of intelligence come to us through the medium of history. When we trace these back to their origin, all else is darkness. Unacquainted with the surroundings, any conjectures that we may make are exceedingly liable to be erroneous.

Many imagine that these self-evident facts have no application to the Bible. Why? Because God would not give a revelation to be misunderstood. Indeed! are not men surrounded by darkness upon every matter which intimately concerns them here and hereafter? Are not earth and air filled with untold treasures, some of which even now we are but beginning to grasp, and others we shall never know? We grope about. We feel and we find, but not all. So with revelation. God is infinite, but man is finite, and language, the medium of communication, is finite. We shall know something, but there will ever be far more in the realm of the unknown towards which we shall in this life vainly stretch our dim, earth-born eyes.

The reader, then, is advised, at the outset, on the plainest principles of common sense, to consider the passage found at the beginning of the second chapter of Genesis with caution. Not, of course, with any disposition to reject what it clearly declares, but simply that what is not thus definitely asserted be held under advisement until subsequent lessons drawn from the book shall make it plain.

In the expression of thought by language, written or spoken, the one result most to be desired is to convey or receive the exact idea. Misunderstanding, in many cases, does greater harm than not to hear at all, especially in God's revelation. Men have not heard his voice, or that of his messengers, alike. They have not read his word and received therefrom like impressions and benefits. This is too manifest to need proof. The world is, alas! full of religious differences, among men seemingly equally devoted to the truth. The grand organ of the universe, itself ever in perfect tune, appears to be producing many discords as well as harmonies. At creation and at redemption's birth, nature and grace were in unison. But the performers who are essaying to evoke the symphonies are incompetent. They do not rightly adjust the octave coupler between the Bible and Nature. From the latter we have heard most unmelodious notes of late. But the higher melodies come from the Book. The plain record needs to be struck by more tuneful hands, and the hands of the skillful organist go where the tuneful head and heart prompt.

The inquiry, What is the mind of God? is most pertinent in approaching his word. The candid search for this is not presumptuous. It indicates the highest reverence. It brings from the Father of Mercies, who has sufficiently regarded us as to reveal himself to us in our own methods, and on our own plans, manifestations of his special favor. "For I know the thoughts that I think towards you, saith the Lord, thoughts of peace and not of evil, to give you an expected end. Then shall ye call upon me, and ye shall go and pray unto me, and I will hearken unto you. And ye shall seek me and find, when ye shall search for me with all your heart."

The words which we are thus seeking fitly to approach, that we may at last rightly understand, are found at the beginning of the second chapter of Genesis. "Thus the heavens and the earth were finished, and all the host of them. And on the seventh day God ended his work which he had made. And God blessed the seventh day and sanctified it; because in it he had rested from all his work, which God created and made."

The purpose of God in causing this record to be given must have been consistent with the chief object of the Bible itself. If the book is designed as one of instruction for the sake of that instruction alone, or for the physical, social, national improvement of the race or a part of it, then the extract should be interpreted in the light of such a purpose. The very brevity of the narrative of creation, confined as it is, in the main, to one short chapter, should be held as conclusive that the mere fact of that creation by Jehovah himself, and not the details of it, was regarded as the important thing to be made known. Perhaps, also, the prominence given to the divisions of the time occupied should be attributed to the design to lay proper ground-work for the idea of the Sabbath. Certainly, too, brevity precludes the supposition that any part of God's intention was to give information on scientific subjects. The Bible is a book neither of science, philosophy nor history. Equally true is it that literary excellence, either in prose or poetry, is not one of its objects. And yet, by a coincidence of frequent exemplification, it is, for that very reason, the most remarkable book in existence in all these particulars. It helps us in the study of it to know that these are not at all the ends sought. What we gain of them is exceedingly valuable, but it is only such as is universally incidental to the true and far higher purpose of the book.

Perhaps the great majority of reverent believers in the divine origin of the Scriptures would expect our limitations to cease here. But these preparatory distinctions must be closely drawn. In those which lie near to the line lurk the chief dangers of error in our subject. If the reader will kindly anticipate somewhat, he will perceive that we must hereafter reach that phase of the Sabbath question which assigns to it great moral significance and makes it a part of a great moral law. Hence, if true, the radical statement now made is most important. The Bible is not a book primarily even of morals.

Some qualifications may be necessary. Morals are external. A Pharisee may be moral, though a whited sepulcher, full of all uncleanness within. Regulation of the outward life is rather a necessary incident than a prime object. We have misapprehended the great book if it strikes not deeper than this. The word heart, the center of all being, the inner man, the all in all of his existence, that which when corrupt debases all, when holy renders all pure, sounds the keynote to the whole book so far as man is concerned. What were science, history, philosophy, literature, culture, morals, Eden to dwell in, wealth untold, health perennial, and existence eternal, with a base heart? A curse. An ever-present hell.

When man was created in the image of God he was made infinitely superior to all these as the chief ends of his being. The fall of man was the virtual subversion or destruction of this grand image. Restoration or redemption, therefore, became at once a necessity. Else in an important sense the creation might be regarded as a failure. Hence, from the first, contemporaneous with the fall, with creation, nay, even with the design of creation, including the consequent possibility if not certainty of fall ; in the counsels of the Infinite One, was doubtless, the idea of redemption and a Redeemer. Hence, the phrase, " Lamb slain from the foundation of the world."

Redemption takes rank with creation in importance. Its accomplishment calls into requisition means superhuman, superangelic, even the marvelous and mighty agency of Deity in plural manifestation. Now the creation is an accomplished fact. No Bible is required for that. Redemption, the remaining work, is yet in progress. The plan by which it is undertaken requires a revelation. A patient, careful instruction is needed, such as the Bible furnishes to us, and informs us was given, in earlier ages, to the people, by various personal agents. In this book other purposes than this are not introduced. If any other good results, it is purely incidental. Such additional objects would perplex, mislead, divert attention, and therefore obscure the main purpose. God had but one object in giving the Scriptures, rest assured. Theological writers can name a hundred ; but the more they name, the farther do they get either from agreement with each other or a knowledge of the truth.

Redemption, then, is the main object. If so, the Redeemer is the grand center of it all. He is the bright and morning star, the Sun of Righteousness; in his own expressive words, the Alpha and Omega, the beginning and the end. To give this thought the strongest expression possible, even the Father, the great Jehovah, manifests himself in revelation (it is otherwise, of course, in nature) only so far as properly to prepare the world for the reception of the Redeemer and to introduce the latter to the world.

Let it not be thought that this is a digression. Of two possible interpretations of the Sabbath question which may be easily accepted, two roads upon the subject, widely divergent at a point where the steps of innumerable earnest inquirers have taken the wrong course, this one potent consideration is the sign to guide us aright.

Two conclusions will follow from regarding redemption as the one object of the Bible—first, correct results; second, an increased idea of the importance of our special subject in the divine plan itself.

CHAPTER II.

AT CREATION—CONTINUED.

The time has now arrived for the radical statement, which will not be fully developed till the very concluding chapter of this work. It is this: Though founded on the fact of cessation from the work of creation, and enjoined on man to be observed, with other reasons, because of that fact, yet the true object of the Sabbath points forward to Christ the Redeemer, instead of backward to God the Creator. Its use is to typify rest in Christ, instead of to commemorate the rest of God. It is founded, indeed, as to form, frequency, and outward appearance, upon creation as something tangible after which it could be modeled; its significance refers to Christ, a spiritual idea which the institution itself was to be one of the means of developing before the world. This distinction between the form and meaning of an ordinance should be at all times carefully observed. The form has its use, because it suggests the meaning in which all the value lies. The prophetic pointing of the Sabbath is forward; first, to Christ manifest in the flesh, and the peace to be enjoyed in him by his people on earth; second, and more fully, to the bliss of heaven.

This position, suggested by the view that the Bible is a book of redemption, may properly be enforced by a single argument before the specific investigation is begun. If the Sabbath does not look to Christ for its underlying principle, then it is the one important observance of the Old and New Testament that fails to do so. Nay, more, consider how leading men and events are made to do service in that direction, either primarily or to a subordinate degree. Sacrifice, an institution known and practiced by Cain and Abel, and from that time down to the cross, is acknowledged by the Scriptures themselves as vain and useless, except as referring to the great atonement. It becomes an immense, expensive, burdensome ceremony, without meaning; its animals without spot and unblemished; its white-robed, consecrated, and ceremonially clean priests; its tabernacles and temples, precious in material, exact in plan and construction; its definite forms of service, all enforced with scrupulous exactness; the whole Jewish economy surrounding this one institution of sacrifice; all speak volumes in the light of Christ to come, but otherwise a senseless jargon. Then how beautifully, and with what prophetic clearness, the Jews as a chosen nation represent the Church of Christ. The flesh-pots and the bondage in Egyyt on the one hand, the pleasures and thralldom of sin on the other. The wiles of the wicked and cruel king, the going out of Egypt, the figurative baptism into a new and free nationality, the destruction of the old enemy and all his hosts, by the self-same agency, the wanderings in the wilderness dependent upon the miraculous favors of God for support, the murmurings, backslidings of heart, and numberless vicissitudes of this part of their history, have so clear a counterpart in the progress of the church as to need but the mere mention. Plainer than these, we have learned to speak of the Jordan of death which all Christians must cross, through divided waters, to the Canaan on the other shore, the final inheritance of the saints.

Perhaps the thought would startle the reader, that the history of the Christian Church and matters connected therewith, were more accurately sketched by inspired pen, and God-ordained ritual before it was established than they have ever been by uninspired historians since. You will not understand the object of circumcision, for example, until you look forward through the separated nation to the coming Christ. Priests and prophets become as insignificant as clerks and common school teachers. Christ is the "second Adam," a leader, lawgiver and prophet "like unto Moses," a "priest forever after the order of Melchizedek;" and so everything, great and small, derives its value as it sets forth the Messiah and his mission.

If then the reader is not prepared to answer the question now, it becomes at least reasonable that he should hold it open for further investigation, whether, while the Bible itself as a whole, and in its chief details, refers to Christ, the Sabbath should be considered an exception single and apart, and find its interpretation in the creation.

Entering upon an examination of the passage in Genesis ii., we are reminded of a grammatical principle which will prevent attempting any argument founded on the form of the verbs "ended," "had rested," etc. "In Hebrew one form of the preterit or aorist stands also for the imperfect, perfect and pluperfect."

There are certain things affirmed in the text: first, that God ended his work on the seventh day; second, that he rested on that day; third, that he blessed it; fourth, that he sanctified it; fifth, that he thus honored it because on that day he rested from his work.

There are certain things which, whatever may be true in the case, are not affirmed in the passage, and these are the very points upon which controversy will turn; first, that he blessed or sanctified when he rested; second, that he gave the command to man to observe it; third, that when enjoined as a day of rest it was placed upon all mankind; fourth, that the days were ordinary ones, such as we now use in reckoning time.

As to whether the blessing and sanctifying of the day were synchronous with the rest and with each other, there may be doubt. Though the appearance of the language favors such a view, several circumstances in the nature of the case make it uncertain. To illustrate: Suppose a credible history should contain these words: "The people of the

United States asserted their freedom from the mother country by the Declaration of Independence, which they signed through their representatives on the fourth day of July; therefore they sought to honor the day and perpetuate the memory of it among their children by instituting an immense exhibition of the industries of the world at Philadelphia." Could this exhibition, even if of perpetual observance, be certainly known from the language to have begun at the time of the original signing of the Declaration? Would it recur every year, or how often? As a matter of fact it was held as a centennial in 1876, though it was projected some time before. It is clear that two items may be connected because in import or logically allied, when in the element of time they are widely divergent. Since the divine mind spans all the centuries in an ever-continuing present, this item of time would be especially liable to be overlooked in such a passage as this.

Nor will it escape intelligent observation that this is more likely to be the case in ancient records which were made with far greater difficulty than modern histories. They, too, were far less complete. Scraps traced in one year or century were treasured side by side with those of another. Those of one writer were included with those of another, in later transcriptions or compilations. No intelligent biblical scholar has ever ventured to ignore these weighty considerations, especially in reference to the first books of the Old Testament Scriptures. Authorship is often held to be little more than compilation. The things written were sometimes more and sometimes less the direct origination of the writer. Scribes and priests kept the record of events of public importance. A subsequent Moses or Ezra transcribed, compiled and wrote or dictated or directed the completion of the work.

The first five books of the Bible, called the Pentateuch, are usually referred to Moses, and yet they contain such statements as the following, which he could not or would not have written: "So Moses, the servant of the Lord, died there in the land of Moab," etc., etc. (Deut. xxxiv. 5). "Moreover, the man Moses was very great in the land of Egypt in the sight of Pharaoh's servants and in the sight of the people" (Ex. xi. 3). "Now the man Moses was very meek above all the men which were upon the face of the earth" (Num. xii. 3). It is reasonable to suppose that a subsequent writer inserted the account of his death and commendations of his character.

Upon the book of Genesis, particularly, we can do no better than to quote the thoughtful conclusions of Eichorn: "The early part of the history was composed merely of separate small notices; whilst the family history of the Hebrews runs on in two continuous narratives; these, again, have here and there some passages inserted from other sources." The writer in Smith's Bible Dictionary (Art. Pentateuch) declares: "If without any theory casting its shadow upon us, and without any fear of consequences before our eyes, we read thoughtfully only the book of Genesis, we can hardly escape the conviction that it partakes of the nature of a compilation. It has, indeed, a unity of plan, a coherence of parts, a shapeliness and an order, which satisfy us that, as it stands, it is the creation of a single mind. But it bears also manifest traces of having been based upon an earlier work; and that earlier work itself seems to have imbedded in it fragments of still more ancient documents."

The possible truth of these remarks is nowhere more evident than in the second chapter; and among the seemingly parenthetic portions are those at the beginning, including the teaching in regard to the Sabbath. While it is not desirable to press a possibility of this kind into service as a positive argument in support of any theory, yet it does serve to keep the way open for a discussion based on considerations which are regarded as absolutely conclusive. For many have felt themselves estopped by this very passage, standing as it has appeared to them, in time as well as in logic, at the very threshold of the subject, connected with the sublime scenes of the creation and applied thereto, and hence coming to them with all the force of universality and of supreme authority. But if our readers will give the above consideration and one now to follow, due weight, we may count on their impartial and friendly company throughout the investigation. God, in making a covenant with Noah (Gen. ix. 8-18), and with his posterity through perpetual generations, never again to destroy the earth by water, declares as a token of that covenant, "I do set my bow in the clouds," and "I will look upon it that I may remember the everlasting covenant between God and every living creature of all flesh that is upon the earth."

To the casual reader this appears to be a new creation, that of the rainbow. And yet between sixteen and seventeen centuries had elapsed since the creation of Adam, and (according to the shortest possible view) the arrangement of the seasons with the progress of nature after the present order. There must then have been a miraculous suppression of it up to that time, otherwise it would have appeared by natural laws, at every recurrence of sunshine with falling drops of rain. The true view, warranted by the Hebrew, is that this bow had always existed, but was now appointed by its original creator a token of his promise to all the earth. The attaching of a new significance to a long existing fact is not uncommon in the sacred Scriptures. If it shall transpire that the Sabbath was of even later origin than Noah's time, its being appended to the account of creation will be another instance of the same kind.

The curse pronounced upon Ham, in the same chapter, in the words, "cursed be Canaan," has a somewhat similar underlying principle. Had infidels understood it, it might have saved them much trouble. It is not a case of excessive cruelty, nor of cursing Canaan for his father's fault, nor of destroying nations for the evil deed of a remote ancestor. The punishment in each case fell upon the guilty party, and not another. The overthrow of the Canaanites, as appears in the subsequent history, was brought upon them by their own wickedness and obstinate opposition to the will of God, and not at all by anything their ancestor, Ham, had done. On the other hand, the punishment of Ham was a prophetic declaration to him of these calamities which were to overtake his descendants in that branch of the family which was to spring from his son Canaan. Thus an evil which would occur for other reasons was simply stated to Ham under the title of a curse, to mark by its being attached thereto the enormity of his own act. These blessings in the patriarchal age were simply inspired declarations of good that was to come. They can not be regarded as in any sense bringing to pass that which they declared as though it were subject to the will of the one pronouncing the blessing. Thus Isaac's blessing of Jacob and Esau was simply foretelling the future in regard to them. So of Jacob blessing his sons. Thus we have wide lapses of time brought together, but not with that sort of connection which a reader unacquainted with this method in these early Scriptures would suppose.

Why may not the Sabbath day, in complete accord with such a view, have been instituted long after the creation, for the purpose, as already indicated, of pointing prophetically as a type to the rest in store for the world through the Redeemer, its attachment to the Creator's rest being the foundation of its form, the existing fact, already known, taken to be its sign and pledge? Surely this would not be inconsistent with the scope and purpose of a book of redemption.

Should the question be propounded, Why on the theory of so late an origin is the blessing and sanctifying of the day appended to the account of creation? the answer is plain. The blessing and sanctifying may have been done at creation, or may refer to the time when a Sabbath law was imposed upon men. But if such a law had a later origin than the beginning of the race, all will admit it to have been when given to the children of Israel. But Moses, the great leader and lawgiver of this people under divine guidance, also collected for their use the details of history comprised in the book of Genesis. How natural, then, that, when giving them the history, he should append the verses we are considering explanatory of the Sabbath, and when, on the other hand, giving the law of the Sabbath, he should append to it an explanatory statement of its basis in form, God's cessation from the act of creation. Thus two items logically allied are joined in the narrative of each, though very far separated in time, and all the circumstances of the writer, the time of the writing, as well as parallel instances in the same book, favor the idea.

Nothing being found in the second chapter of Genesis to forbid a later origin of the Sabbath, positive proof one way or the other may be expected soon to appear.

CHAPTER III.

TWENTY-FIVE HUNDRED YEARS.

According to the chronological record found above the page in the common Bible, the second chapter of Genesis is assigned to the year 1, and the sixteenth chapter of Exodus to the year of the world 2513. We now enter upon this period of 2500 years, and a record of over sixty chapters containing nearly two thousand verses. It is worth while to notice that it comprises more than one-half the time from Adam to Christ, is greater by over six centuries than our present date from the Christian era, and is five-twelfths or nearly one-half of all recorded time.

The bearing of this history is evident in view of the creation or commonly accepted theory of the Sabbath, since that requires it to have been observed during all this immense period, by those people who were servants of the Most High; and it was liable, therefore, to be sinfully disregarded by those who transgressed his commandments. A suitable course to pursue will be:

1. To suggest reasons why this period should furnish evidence of the Sabbath if it existed;
2. To ascertain the fact;
3. To consider an attempt, other than the natural, to account for that fact.

The creation theory of the Sabbath would seem to require that greater prominence be given to its observance in the early portion of the earth's history than afterwards. It is to be said in favor of this supposition that such a difference is clearly observable in regard to God's personal manifestation of himself, and also as to those laws which had more especial reference to his power and sovereignty. God is the distinct divine personage and the marked feature of the first part of the Bible; Christ, of the last. God is clearly represented, at the beginning, as making himself known to men by his mighty acts and asserting his right to rule over them. It requires, to do this, not only the revelation of himself as creator, but the exercise of the utmost severity in enforcing his laws. The overthrow of wicked men, cities, armies, and even the entire population of the globe, the extirpation of idolatry, and the personal superintendence of the families of earth, are means to this end. When this is sufficiently accomplished, a gradual change becomes apparent. There is a withdrawal of himself and a substitution of intermediate agencies; while an ultimate object comes to notice, not easily seen at first. The preparation for the Messiah, which was the undoubted purpose of all this divine communication with the race, now assumes such prominence as to be easily recognized, while the personality of God himself gradually fades from view.

As successive steps in this progress, note the antediluvian and the patriarchal ages, the separation of the Jewish nation in which was begun and carried forward a most intricate, comprehensive, and definite outline, in forms and national history, of things in store for the race, to be realized in full when Christ should come. In the progress of that nation also the like change and development is manifest. At first God himself is the more prominent figure. As he reveals himself to Abraham, calls Moses to his special mission, performs the miracles of Egypt and the deliverance, and shadows the mountain in Horeb with the wonders of his glory in the giving of the law, his personality is in wonderful contrast with that time, for example, preceding the call of Samuel, the first of the line of prophets, of which it was said, "the word of the Lord was precious and there was no open vision." Later still, immediately preceding the advent of the Saviour, there were even large intervals between the prophets, and these seem to have spoken by inspiration rather than by open conference with God or his angels. To the most careless reader in course, this gradual withdrawal of direct divine agency, and the substitution of intermediate and organized human means can not fail to be seen. When Christ appears upon the scene, in the New Testament volume, a like arrangement runs through that record to the end.

To make the proper application of these thoughts, recur to the old Testament and direct your attention to either theory in regard to the Sabbath. Is it designed to commemorate the rest of God at creation? Then it should be most frequently noticed and most rigidly enforced at the beginning. Does it have reference to Christ, then expect it to be introduced later and made prominent as that preparation is developed.

The twenty-five centuries, then, commencing with the beginning of Genesis and extending to Moses, will be decisive of the creation theory unless some cause appear to set aside the application of these reasonings to them. Surely the law itself is of such a positive nature, and it so intimately refers to God, has such significance as applied to his creative power, and his consequent supremacy over the so-called gods of earth, and is such a direct test of his authority, that it could not, in such a view of it, be suffered to be disobeyed or in the least neglected. If he should not enforce a law which he had announced at creation's end, and the only one set to mark that event, why should he enforce any other? Why should notice be taken of any other disobedience if not of this? And if this law is of such a leading character as a test of God's authority, any historic record of the times professing to give a narrative of God's dealings with men, will contain numerous allusions to it. Is this the case? Far from it. Nothing whatever is said about it. Indeed, there is not one incidental allusion, by which you would conjecture that the people or any part of them, had ever heard of such a thing as the Sabbath.

Undoubtedly, if, during the early period of 2,500 years now under examination, there had been a clearly marked division of time into weeks in common use, among the people of which the Bible narrative gives account, this might furnish some inferential, though not direct, much less sufficient, proof of its observance. But even this is denied us. The most that can be said is that the number seven is one of special eminence in the book. So are other numbers, though to less extent. This fact in regard to seven is no more true when applied to days than to anything else, otherwise there might be some weight to an inference that an established week led to the use of the division of time into seven days. The word week properly does not occur as month does. True, there is one such translation (Gen. xxix. 27). But it is properly heptade, the sum or number seven. "Fulfill her seven," presumably a seven day's feast, does not necessarily imply a customary division of time into weeks. If it did, what would the service of seven years for Leah and seven for Rachel imply? If Joseph mourning for his father seven days (not heptade this time), (Gen. l. 10), implied a week, what in the same chapter does the fulfilling of forty days for him signify and what the mourning of the Egyptians seventy days? If Noah waiting in the ark the space of seven days proves the existence of a week, what does the introduction into the ark of clean beasts and of fowls of the air by sevens denote? And now that the uses of seven as applied to days is exhausted so far as this portion of Scripture is concerned, suggestions are in order as to the seven fat and seven lean kine, the seven full and the seven shriveled ears of grain of Pharaoh's dream, and the seven years of plenty and the seven of famine. Surely even the most fertile imagination would not see evidences of the existence of a marked division of days by a weekly Sabbath in such scanty data as these.

With confidence, therefore, it is repeated that there is in this Bible record of 2,500 years positively no evidence whatever, of the knowledge of a Sabbath or of the division of time even into weeks. This weakest of all arguments is reinforced, however, by another like unto itself, under the mistaken notion, which sometimes finds lodgment in the brain, that the sum of two or more infinitesimals does really amount to something. We are told that Egyptians and various other ancient people were accustomed to this division of time, in those early days, and so, grounded in indefiniteness and obscurity, the idea is fastened upon the mind and passes for conclusive proof. So far as we have been able to trace any of the points relied on to substantiate this extra biblical addition to an imaginary biblical argument, they have vanished into thin air at first approach.

The one answer to all this blank nothing upon the Sabbath during all this most significant half (so far as a creation Sabbath is concerned) of the world's history, is this: We are told that the fact that no mention is made of it during all this vast period " is not to be wondered at when we consider how very brief that history is." (Nevin's Bib. Antiq. p. 366). Now there are some things which were not likely to be omitted even in so very brief a history, and of these the Sabbath is one provided it had any existence at all at that time. An enthusiastic advocate of the seventh day observance, in a newspaper article now at hand, says that there is no other command so often repeated in the old Testament as the fourth. If this is correct, as probably it is, how shall we account for the fact that previous to Exodus sixteenth, for 2,500 years of history, there is absolutely no allusion to it whatever? Manifestly that it did not exist during that time. If we adopt the statement quoted above referring it to the brevity of the history, Mr. Jahn, another eminent authority, meets us with the declaration (Bib. Arch. p. 386) that " the book of Genesis is abundant in instances of moral discipline."

To answer, in a more satisfactory manner than in the words of any author, however varied the suggestions we may thus derive, the question as to whether brevity of history will account for the omission of so important a matter, an abstract of the topics treated of may be given, in reading which, each is at liberty to judge for himself as to where the truth lies. We shall note simply the salient points.

After the Lord God had planted a garden in Eden, he took the man and put him into it to dress it and to keep it. I once heard it suggested that had the Lord added "Six days shalt thou labor and do all thy work, but the seventh day is the Sabbath of the Lord thy God; in it thou shalt not do any work," this question of antiquity would never have been sprung. The suggestion was perhaps not very reverent. But though an appropriate occasion there is no mention of such a command as given to Adam, but, instead, an injunction against partaking of the fruit of a particular tree, the disobedience to which brought the fall and all our woes.

The account of the fall is somewhat extended, as also that of the condemnation of man, woman, and serpent, and the expulsion of Adam from the garden. The narrative pauses, also, to give prominence to an account of the offerings of Cain and Abel, sons of Adam, in which the existence of sacrifice is noted, under the special observation of the Lord, that of one brother being approved, that of the other rejected. The terrible record of jealousy, hate and murder follows, and God's conference with and punishment of the murderer.

The genealogy of men, the length of their lives, the origin of various trades and arts, the fact that Enoch "walked with God" and that "he was not for God took him" are stated. When men multiplied greatly upon the face of the earth a striking distinction appears. "The sons of God" take wives of the "daughters of men." God's displeasure is awakened by these unnatural alliances. He declares, "My spirit shall not always strive with man," it thus appearing that he has been patiently instructing them and urging them to good. It is here noted that the earth becomes filled with violence, that the wickedness of man is great, and all flesh corrupt. The variety of sins of which the people are guilty should be noted as the summary proceeds, but among them is no record of the desecration of the Sabbath, afterwards to be honored with the title of "My holy day." To such a pass have the inhabitants of the earth come that its destruction is decreed by the Almighty.

Noah's history in the preparation of the ark, and the saving of "eight persons by water," together with representatives of the various kinds of living beings, is given in detail. Upon going out of the ark, an altar is erected and sacrifices offered, the distinction between clean and unclean beasts is for the second time recognized, the law is announced against eating blood, as also against shedding man's blood. Then follow the blessing of God upon Noah and his posterity, the covenant with man not to destroy the earth again by water, and the appointment of the rainbow as a token of that covenant. Next succeed the account of the drunkenness of Noah, the sin of Ham, and the prophetical declaration in the form of a "curse" in regard to the overthrow of the Cananites. It would seem that the history is not so "brief," but that had there been a Sabbath with the importance that was afterward attached to it, some intimation might have found place in regard to it. We find rather with Jahn, that "the Book of Genesis is abundant in instances of moral discipline."

A genealogical record and an account of the Tower of Babel with the confusion of languages bring us to Abraham. The particulars of this faithful man's life are given with such minuteness that he is as well known to us as any man, perhaps, in the entire sacred writings. Among the incidents are the call of Abraham, God's covenant with him, the miraculous gift of a son Isaac, the deception practiced upon Pharaoh and Abimelech, the military expedition against the kings and rescue of Lot, the story of Hagar and Ishmael, the institution of circumcision in connection with a blessing and covenant, the conference in regard to the impending destruction of Sodom, the overthrow of that city and plain following the wicked conduct of its inhabitants, and the rescue of Lot by the angels, the origin of the Moabites and Ammonites, Abraham's prayer, his erection of numerous altars in different places, offering of sacrifices, typical offering of Isaac, securing a wife for Isaac, purchase of a sepulchre and death. It is difficult to see if the Sabbath were observed regularly by this man of God, how there could fail to be some reference to it. God's covenant is renewed with Isaac. He also "built an altar and called upon the name of the Lord," becomes wealthy and powerful, transacts business with Abimelech and others, and blesses his sons Jacob and Esau, the account of which is one of the most remarkable of this period.

Jacob, escaping from his brother Esau, when journeying to seek a wife, on his way to Padan Aran sees the vision by night of the ladder reaching to heaven, while the Lord renews to him also the covenant made with Abraham. He sets up a pillar at that place which he calls Bethel, pours oil upon it and makes a vow, then accomplishes his journey, makes the acquaintance of Laban's household, secures a plurality of wives by a long term of service, becomes very wealthy in flocks and herds, and finally sets out to return to the land of his kindred. On the return occurs the incident of the stolen image, Jacob offers sacrifice upon the mount. When the coming of Esau afflicts him with great fear, during the night he has another vision, wrestling with a man till break of day, and prevailing he secures a blessing and his name is changed to Israel. Under this name he becomes the progenitor of that mighty nation with which the Old Testament scriptures have chiefly to do.

The incidents connected with him and his sons are too numerous to be recounted. Suffice it to say that the practice of the rite of circumcision is carefully recorded; the building of altars, offering of sacrifices, marrying of his sons and grandchildren, the putting away of false gods which have come into their hands from surrounding nations, and many incidents of home life are given in circumstantial detail. The tribes of Israel are now forming; meanwhile an event occurs which prepares the way for all the wondrous history of this people. Joseph has a dream in which the sheaves of his brethren all make obeisance to his, and another in which the sun, moon, and eleven stars make obeisance to him. The significance of these is too evident to his brethren, foreshadowing their inferiority; hence, moved by envy, they cast him into a pit, then sell him into Egypt, where, after a succession of experiences, the Lord being with him, he is exalted to be chief ruler of the kingdom. The circumstances which lead to Joseph's elevation, together with the coming of his brethren to Egypt to buy corn during the years of famine, and all the successive steps in the history, till they remove to the land, Jacob and the patriarchs are dead, and the now extensive tribes under "a Pharaoh that knew not Joseph" are reduced to abject servitude, constitute, in the simple manner in which they are told, one of the most fascinating stories ever recorded by pen. Here, too, their typical significance begins, in bondage, making brick without straw. Still there is no evidence of a Sabbath, notwithstanding details so minute and unimportant are given with a fulness so marked as to render it impossible to suppose that such an institution, being in existence, could escape mention; especially, when we note the great importance that attaches to it elsewhere after it is introduced.

Yet another long train of wonderful events is transacted before us, and with an extended description of them we are brought to the close of the period now under examination. The purpose of God to deliver the oppressed people, in pursuance of the covenant made with Abraham, Isaac and Jacob, comes to view in the call of Moses, the association with him of Aaron, and the series of plagues by which he scourges the land until he compels the reluctant, treacherous, hard-hearted, sordid, cruel, and wicked Pharaoh to let the people go forth. The imposition of exact, distinctive forms now begins, in connection with the saving of the first-born among the Hebrews, and the institution of the Jewish Passover. We shall henceforth notice, in all the details of their worship, the most rigid ritual, in accordance with the most positive commands of God.

With the presence of God manifested in pillar of cloud by day, made luminous by night, as their guide, they pass through the arm of the sea, the waters standing apart on either hand as a wall, while Pharoah and his hosts, following them with impetuous zeal, contending against the angel of the Lord, are thrown into confusion and finally destroyed by the returning water. The rescued Israelites come forth from this baptism "in the cloud and in the sea," a free nation. Singing the song of deliverance, they start upon their career as the chosen people of God.

Thus is completed this review of twenty-five centuries. It is, of course, a digression from our subject, which fact, together with lack of space, has allowed but the barest skeleton abstract of a Bible account singularly full, minute, and satisfactory. Among the instructive details, given in many parts, and with numerous circumstances rounding it into a complete narrative, such as precludes the idea of any important omission, appear altars on every hand; sacrifices are frequent, vows, covenants, prayers, and all the forms in which men of God devoutly worship their creator. Matters of slight importance, incidental allusions, natural indeed, but with no farther recognized bearing, have made the history charming in style as well as instructive in what it relates. We are forced to conclude that whatever belonged to the ages traversed, either of God-imposed or man-adopted, ritual or religious custom has been mentioned. Nothing but a providential interposition could have prevented anything of the kind creeping incidentally, if not otherwise, into the narrative. And yet the Sabbath which, if existing at all, should have held, by the very nature of the case, a most important place, is not mentioned at all. Not one instance, or shadow, or suspicion of a shadow of an instance occurs showing the existence of the Sabbath. No near or remote circumstance which appears to have any possible relation to a Sabbath observance can be recognized. Not even the week, the necessary result of such a day, can be distinguished.

Let him who would impress these facts upon his mind, take his pen and sketch from the Bible such a summary of leading events as is here given, noticing the numerous instances in which Sabbath observance, if such there were, would naturally appear, and then, when he finds absolutely no vestige of it whatever, think of the remarkable prominence into which it hereafter suddenly comes, and then decide, if he can, that it was in existence during this period.

Now that this twenty-five hundred years has passed, a change occurs. Henceforth among this Jewish people which the Almighty has just adopted as peculiarly his own and set free, the Sabbath comes into notice and becomes the most prominent of all institutions. Again and again is it brought to view and kept before us till we are forced to the conclusion that some most important object was had in establishing it, to be accomplished through this peculiar people alone.

CHAPTER IV.

THE MANNA AND SINAI.

The *penchant* of English biographers to commence with William the Conqueror, and thus get a great name for their heroes from ancestral origin before beginning their story proper, has its counterpart in our work. With suitable deference to the reputed antiquity of the Sabbath, we have labored long to bring down its history for twenty-five hundred years, and now, at last, we have only reached its origin. Every history of the institution begins properly when the Red sea was crossed and Pharaoh's hosts overthrown, with the joyful song of deliverance. The ancient chosen people of God, just at that point, put off their bondage and put on their freedom. Their baptism in the cloud, and in the sea, occupies the same relation to this change of condition that baptism now, by the authority of the Lord Jesus Christ, does to the change of the person from sinner to Christian. The remark just made in reference to the sabbath, then, places it at the entrance of the Israelites upon their freedom. It is a rest day peculiar to that typical people, and as their nation represented the church of Christ, so their rest day represents the rest in Christ. As this latter can not be enjoyed outside of his church, so the former, typically, had no place outside of the free Israel. To have kept a sabbath day while in Egypt, would have been as anomalous as for an unrepentant sinner now to claim rest or peace with God from his sins.

Here, then, is a vital point. It is the turning or rather the beginning point in our subject. We should have commenced here at first, but that the mistaken notions of a great multitude of the best people on earth seemed to require of us a long preliminary explanation. Our investigations have heretofore been hypothetical, explanatory, more or less negative; now we have a real, positive subject before us. All will admit that now, at least, undoubtedly, we have reached the institution in full force. We do not, however, logically assign its origin to Sinai nor even to the giving of the manna. Its introduction at the latter event and legal proclamation at the former, are rather incidental, or circumstances of convenience. The crossing of the Red Sea really brought the people to the point when the Sabbath was theirs. Its observance not beginning till afterwards is a fact akin to that of a foreigner who is naturalized on a certain day, but may not vote perhaps for months afterwards. He is entitled to the franchise but has no occasion to exercise it. The Jews were naturalized and made a free people at the Red Sea. God selected his own time for giving them the Sabbath and the formal law. That he should wait nearly a month for the one, and more than that for the other, is easily justified by the fitness of the occasions when they arrive.

Men have made the mistake of supposing that because Sinai was remarkable, therefore it was the beginning. Not so. The crossing of the Red Sea was the beginning of the Israelitish nationality. Till that, they were not rescued from Egyptian thralldom. Till then they were not fully committed to, because safe in, the leadership of Moses. It is the saving of the people that brings the obligation of obedience. It is wonderful, therefore, that men have conceived of the Jewish nationality as beginning at the giving of the law. They have argued that because the Sabbath is mentioned in the sixteenth chapter of Exodus, several weeks before the commandments were issued, it antedated the Jewish nation itself. They have been ready to suggest, if you are required to go back of Sinai to the giving of the manna, and, still further, if you go back of the latter to the crossing of the Red Sea, why not go to creation itself, the second chapter of Genesis?

It was remarked, just above, that after the Israelites crossed the Red Sea, the Sabbath was theirs. The Saviour told the captious Pharisees, in a passage hereafter to be carefully considered, that the Sabbath was made for man and not man for the Sabbath. Whoever else, then, it may have been made for, it at least belongs to the Jews. It was theirs, too, as a privilege and a blessing, and not as a burdensome observance. We could undoubtedly keep one day in seven, or any other portion of our time, as a day of rest from labor, and yet not associate it with Christ or with any forms of worship. So doubtless might they have had a stated time for rest, even had it not been enacted by the command of God. But the Lord's day belongs to Christians especially. The mere man of the world knows not the benefits of it. Even so the Sabbath belonged to the Jews in a far higher sense than as a mere day of rest from labor. In the latter sense they would undoubtedly often have been willing to relinquish it, even as now many are willing to give up the rest which belongs, under common usage and by common law, to Sunday, in order to hunt or fish or gather their harvests. To give up, however, this rest from labor is quite another thing than to give up the Christ which it prefigured, the forgiveness of sin, the restoration from a fallen estate, the eternal blessedness as well as rest in store for the children of God. To the children of Israel was given the high privilege of being the great representative people, chosen of God to show forth in figure, his glorious purposes towards the race of man, which were to be enjoyed by those who should, in like manner, be the liberated people of Christ.

Let it not be forgotten, then, that separate and apart from the mere rest which Sabbath or Lord's day brought or brings, which any one may enjoy, there is a peculiar significance to them in connection with redemption from sin, salvation through the blood of Christ, restoration from a fallen estate, and promises of future glory in heaven, that as indisputably makes the Sabbath the especial right of the free Israel, as it does the Lord's day that of the Christian. Thus Paul says of the Israelites (Rom. ix. 4): "To whom pertaineth the adoption and the glory, and the covenants, and the giving of the law, and the service of God, and the promises, whose are the fathers, and of whom, as concerning the flesh, Christ came, who is over all, God blessed forever." It is thus that the Sabbath belongs to these people as a part of their peculiar heritage.

The emphasis is on the word *free*. The free Israel was made so at the Red Sea. Hence the Red Sea marks the time and the place. The free Israel prefigures the Christian, or, if you please, the church in its true sense. Before the Red Sea was Egypt and bondage, after it freedom; before becoming a Christian is servitude to sin, after it, release therefrom and the favor of God. Before the Red Sea was no Sabbath; before conversion there is no rest from sin which the Sabbath prefigures. "Come unto me," says the Saviour, "and I will give you rest." As after coming to Christ in conversion, one enjoys this rest, so after the Red Sea, coming into their freedom the Israelites came to the Sabbath, the type of the Christian's rest.

How long a time elapsed from the beginning of their freedom, when they became a people suited to observe the Sabbath, to the institution itself? Perhaps three weeks. The thirty-third chapter of Numbers enumerates the stations and encampments, of which there were seven from their starting, after the first passover, until they reached the Wilderness of Sin. The Red Sea was in the fourth of these, or midway. Supposing the times occupied in each to be equal, and dividing what intervened, which is also given, from the passover to their arrival in the wilderness, and then adding the six days of partaking of manna preceding the first Sabbath, something like the length conjectured seems probable.

Were any Sabbath days observed during this interval, as they might have been according to the theory here advocated? Probably not. First, the history does not indicate it. Second, they may have been encamped on those occasions, as they must have been for a considerable portion of their time, thus not in any state of activity requiring it. Third, and most probably, the institution was delayed to a more suitable time for its introduction. This will shortly appear.

It is not supposed that when men or a nation of people enter upon a new history, with a multitude of incoming requirements and experiences, that all of these will become familiar to them at once, or that their leader or lawgiver will bring all of them to their attention at first. Time is required to introduce any system. Hence the Sabbath did not originate for several weeks after the people were fitted to receive it. Hence the more extensive laws of Mt. Sinai, with all the wonderful glory of their announcement, were postponed still longer. And yet, this admitted delay in beginning should not be held to invalidate the position that, at the crossing of the Red Sea, the Israelites entered upon that national existence to which these appropriately belonged.

Why was the Sabbath instituted prior to the giving of the law on Sinai? Because, while the nation was already fitted for both, the most suitable time for instituting the one came before the best occasion for giving the other. In all the Jewish history there never again occurred as favorable a time for imposing the Sabbath observance upon the people as at the giving of the manna. For forty years (Ex. xvi. 35), comprising more than two thousand weeks, they were to subsist upon manna as their daily food. God was to furnish it every day; they were to gather it every day. Thus was presented the opportunity both for God to mark the day and for man to keep it. During all those two thousand weeks God gave them a double supply on the sixth day, and preserved that given on that day fresh for two days instead of one. Two thousand Sabbaths came, but on them no manna. It was vain for them to look for it. Soon they ceased to do so altogether. What a lesson for beginners! The most stupid and the most obdurate alike learned it. Time and the world may be searched for another series of events by which it would be possible to impress the idea of a Sabbath upon the minds of the people as effectually as by this.

The manner in which they set out to keep the Sabbath shows that it was wholly new to them. Some of them put God to the test at once, by attempting to keep manna over and by going out to gather on the day on which it was not to be found. "And Moses said, Let no man leave of it till the morning. Notwithstanding, they hearkened not unto Moses; but some of them left of it until the morning, and it bred worms, and stank; and Moses was wroth with them" (vs. 19, 20). "And it came to pass, that there went out some of the people on the seventh day for to gather, and they found none" (27). Had they been trained in the restraints of the day, they would, doubtless, not have made these early mistakes. There was a perplexity and confusion in their minds, in regard to the observance, strikingly suggestive of unfamiliarity with it.

The form of the announcement of the law in this place, likewise indicates that it was new. The day is declared the Sabbath, not simply referred to as already existing. Had they been acquainted with it, as the creation theory supposes, the language of God would, naturally, have been something like this: "And the people shall go out and gather a certain rate every day, but on the sixth day they shall gather a double portion which shall be to them for the sabbath." Instead of such a statement, which would imply a knowledge of the sabbath as heretofore existing, it is four times explicitly declared the seventh day is the sabbath of the Lord. Why so long and precise declarations in regard to an institution that had always existed! It is clearly a detail of instructions given to beginners. "See, for that the Lord hath given you the Sabbath, therefore he giveth you on the sixth day the bread of two days; abide ye every man in his place, let no man go out of his place on the seventh day. So the people rested on the seventh day" (29, 30). The description, throughout, has so plain an appearance of unfamiliar beginnings on the part of the people, and of definite enactment and careful condescension to the ignorance of the people on the part of God, that nothing but a preconceived notion that the sabbath must have originated either at creation or at Sinai could prevent its impressing the mind of every reader. The creation and Sinai are indeed the two places wherein the Sabbath law comes to us with most startling surroundings, and consequently before we are aware, all our thoughts have arranged themselves with reference to one or the other of these as the necessary initial point. Thus its quiet beginning among an untutored people, under circumstances most wonderfully adapted to the growth of the weakest seminal idea, is overlooked, and the sixteenth chapter of Exodus is strained in interpretation into maladjustment with hypotheses with either of which it is entirely irreconcilable.

In passing, it may be profitable to notice the coincidence, not, however, as having any bearing upon the argument, that as this rest day finds its origin and its constant visible suggestion surrounded by the miraculous gift of food in the wilderness; so also with that which both typify — the rest of the Christian is intimately associated with a constant supply of that spiritual food which is given us from above.

. . . .

In the next month, the third from their departure out of Egypt, the children of Israel reached the base of Mt. Sinai.

Here that law was given to them which is now familiarly known as the Ten Commandments. No one can be regarded as intelligent in the Scriptures who is not familiar with this law and the relation which it bears to other parts of the divine scheme. It has held a prominent place in the catechisms; and, in the time of our boyhood, it was thought indispensable that the child should learn it as soon as the alphabet. A nice little cotton handkerchief, upon which the ten commandments were printed, was regarded as a very appropriate present for a child, in these primitive times. It is to be hoped every reader of this book is as familiar with this law and its connected history as this solicitude of our religious instructors would imply, for in that event we are certain of being understood in the observations to follow.

Right here will be found one of the turning-points of our subject. The ten commandments, found in the twentieth chapter of Exodus, will take rank with the explanatory mention appended to the account of creation (Gen. ii.) and the giving of the manna (Ex. xvi.), as important in any proper examination of the sabbath question. It will be seen much further on in our investigation that controversy grows strong as we linger about the fourth commandment. It will not be prudent, therefore, to delay here long, until the subject is more fully before us. Only let the reader be assured, to whatever position on the main question he may suppose our remarks thus far tend, that we do not propose in the least to undervalue the great law given on Mt. Sinai.

The solemn scenes that attended its proclamation, as well as the stress placed upon it by the Almighty himself, forbid any slighting estimate of it as a part of the divine plan. The people were commanded to be sanctified on two successive days, and washed, and when, at the sounding of the trumpet on the third day, they gathered about, bounds were set, by rigid command, that neither man nor beast should touch the mountain on pain of instant death. And then the thunders and lightnings, the quakings of the mountain, the cloud, smoke, fire, the trembling of the people, the voice of God himself to Moses, and the rehearsal by Moses to the people, all tended to produce an impression in the minds of the people ineffaceable during life and sure to be rehearsed by them to their children and children's children. It seems to have been God's purpose thus to implant in the minds of this infant nation an abiding memory of those things which were most important. Since, therefore, no other scenes in their history were more marked than these, we may infer that in the mind of God nothing was of greater moment to them than this law. Bearing in mind its supreme importance at least to the Jews, and deferring, for the present, the examination of its claims upon other people and other times, one or two suggestions may now be made, based upon the reading of the fourth commandment.

"Remember the sabbath day, to keep it holy. Six days shalt thou labor and do all thy work. But the seventh day is the sabbath of the Lord thy God; in it thou shalt not do any work, thou nor thy son, nor thy daughter, thy man-servant nor thy maid-servant, nor thy cattle, nor thy stranger that is within thy gates. For in six days the Lord made heaven and earth, the sea, and all that in them is, and rested the seventh day, wherefore the Lord blessed the sabbath day and hallowed it" (Ex. xx. 8–11).

It will be acknowledged that there is nothing in this quotation up to the word "gates" to contradict the supposition, already made in this chapter, that the sabbath belongs to Israel freed from bondage by the overthrow of their enemies in the Red Sea, and was first introduced to them at the beginning of the manna, a month before. The injunction "remember" is just such as would be required in view of the confusion shown at that time, and the probability that, being new, in its extension, under this command, to all the phases of their lives, it would likely be neglected.

Again, the statements—"The seventh day is the sabbath of the Lord thy God," "In six days the Lord made heaven and earth, . . . rested the seventh day, . . . the Lord blessed the seventh day," etc.,—are of that declarative form which implies an intention to apprise them of something either wholly unknown, or of so recent origin and so little familiar as to be liable to be forgotten. Such a state of facts is consistent with the view of the introduction of the sabbath with the giving of the manna, and the accepted supposition that the book of Genesis, with the appended notice of the sabbath in the second chapter, had not yet been written by Moses. Imagine, for instance, the Saviour, in his time, when these facts were universally known and recognized, making such declarations. So of the prophets. The requisite knowledge was assumed. Just as we say, "Mr. Smith, I am delighted to see you;" and not, "Your name is Smith, I am delighted to see you." Whatever conclusion, then, we shall ultimately reach, a mere reading of the history will convince all of one thing, namely, that the sabbath was not a well-established and familiar institution at that time. The reader may settle with his own judgment whether it should have been on the theory of its origin at creation and its enforcement on the earth for twenty-five hundred years, with a consequent division of time into weeks by all their ancestors and among all the nations of earth.

The prohibition of labor is here made general. The Jew, to whom this commandment came, was forbidden to work himself, or to employ any agencies in work, whether of his own household, or of his property—animals, etc.—or of the stranger under his influence. Some very able writers have here seen evidences of the necessity of stated rest days, one in seven of course being regarded as more exactly that which nature requires, and they have thought that because of that general necessity, God enacted this sweeping clause in the law for the physical welfare and happiness of all his creatures. It seems hardly probable, however, that the fact of God's rest upon the seventh following his labor for six, indicates any general constitution of nature by which it becomes a physical benefit for any or all animate creatures which labor continuously to rest every seventh day. Experience would rather teach us that the harder the work the more frequent the rest required. Many kinds of employment are so exhaustive that a cessation one day in three would be far better; while, again, others are so light that no perceptible injury would accrue to the physical system were no sabbath whatever observed. Still, we are not disposed to question the general utility of the law, nor that one day in seven is probably the most appropriate proportion, nor, even, further, that God had this in view in the special enactment. His infinite wisdom, shown in innumerable instances, proves that all phases of every question were in his contemplation and provided for in his wonderful creations around us. While the manifold and important spiritual interests of man's highest nature were carefully provided for as ever paramount, we are taught, too, that even the hairs of our head are numbered. When, therefore, a sabbath law was enacted to fulfill the highest purposes, no doubt it was formed so as to confer minor benefits likewise.

Had the physical welfare of the race been the object, by all the analogies known to us, man would have been left to discover the utility and appropriate it himself. How many centuries elapsed before printing, railroads and telegraphs? Even the Jews, under God's own care, worked away with their rude agricultural devices, while in the omniscient mind dwelt, from all eternity, perfect inplements such as the nineteenth century even has not brought into operation. The more reasonable supposition is that the provision in regard to animals, servants, etc., was to make the observance the most perfect possible, to the end that as a shadow or type it might have the greatest significance.

The concluding part of the command brings us again face to face with the creation theory. "For in six days the Lord made heaven and earth, the sea, and all that in them is, and rested the seventh day; wherefore the Lord blessed the sabbath day, and hallowed it." This language is almost identical, in substance, with that in Genesis. Hence the advocates of the theory mentioned have regarded it as establishing their position beyond question. But we must not forget that Zion and Tabor have overshadowed Sinai. It remains to see whether the luster which surrounds the giving of the law in that ancient mount, lends all the brightness that belongs to the sabbath as a divine institution, or whether we may look still forward to the Sun of Righteousness, rising above the beaming summits of Judea, for its supreme glory as well as its just interpretation.

If with this latter view, this passage, like that in Genesis, shall yield to palpable considerations, which, because fundamental, can not be ignored, then no further ground remains for the old theory to rest upon. Let the reader, then, not forget what has already been said in the second chapter, upon the former passage, while with candid mind he follows our suggestions upon this. Fortunately, the evidence is complete. Deuteronomy furnishes it. That word, signifying second law, names the fifth book of the Bible, because in it is repeated the Mosaic law, including the decalogue. At the close of the fourth command, as recorded in the fifth chapter of Deuteronomy, the clause found in the same connection in Exodus is not given, but, instead of it, the following: "And remember that thou wast a servant in the land of Egypt, and that the Lord thy God brought thee out hence, through a mighty hand and by a stretched-out arm: therefore the Lord thy God commanded thee to keep the sabbath day."

Deuteronomy has the same authority as Exodus. The

key to the whole subject may be discovered in a judicious inquiry as to the import of the two clauses. Why is the rest of God on the seventh day after the creation, alleged in Exodus, while in Deuteronomy the rescue from Egypt is stated as the reason for giving the Sabbath law? A superficial and unsatisfactory answer to this leading question is the first obtained. We are informed that Exodus contains the real object of the sabbath itself, as it was first ordained at creation, but that in Deuteronomy is given the reason of its special imposition upon the Israelites. In the former it is declared: "Wherefore the Lord blessed the sabbath day, and hallowed it;" in the latter: "Therefore the Lord commanded thee to keep the sabbath day."

To this explanation there are objections which increase as they are examined, and finally must be admitted to be insuperable. 1. They stand in exactly equal positions, and assume to give equally weighty reasons for the same command, and yet, according to this view, one is as far above the other in importance as it is possible to conceive. For, one is universal, the other limited; one would apply to men, angels, and even God himself, the other only to one race of men—the Israelites; one expresses a grand cause as it exists in the divine mind, the other a mere incentive to act upon the human volition; the one sets forth the basis of the law itself as well as its purpose, wide as the universe, and from its nature applicable to all beings beneath God himself, the other is an appeal to one people only, and to one motive only, that of gratitude for one benefit only, that of deliverance from Egypt.

2. While such an explanation of Exodus has to encounter all the objections heretofore in this work filed against the creation theory, such a view of Deuteronomy is palpably absurd. For, under it, how can we explain its being affixed to the fourth command alone? Would not the deliverance from Egypt apply as a motive to all commands, inspiring

gratitude in the hearts of the Israelites and thus leading to general obedience?

While these objections lie justly against this superficial interpretation, and seem sufficient to overthrow the popular theory of which it is an inseparable part, we shall be able to give a reason, founded in the nature of the case, for affixing this clause in Deuteronomy to the fourth commandment only—one which makes it applicable to the sabbath only, one which is fundamental, and equal in importance to that used in like connection in Exodus, as well as essential to the complete scriptural idea of the sabbath itself.

It is impossible, from the places in which these clauses are found, to consider them otherwise than as giving fundamental reasons, each essential and therefore each equally important to the special command to which only they are joined. Now our supposition that the sabbath is a typical institution, prefiguring rest in Christ, permits of precisely such a consistent interpretation. In our view, as already explained, creation forms the divine model, and constitutes the basis after a divine, unchangeable, and, in every way, impressive form. By it, both form and frequency are forever fixed; and to the model the attention of the Jews was directed, both in one of the two statements of the law, and likewise in the history given to them, at about the same time, of the creation itself. On the other hand, at a later date, when the outward form was already somewhat familiar, and the people were prepared for glimpses of the prophetic indications which the type contained, the clause in Deuteronomy came with the second statement of the law. It contains an idea equally as essential a part of any typical institution.

Why, then, in keeping the sabbath, were they to remember their deliverance from Egypt? Because that event was requisite to the completeness of the type. As the rest enjoyed in the Church of Christ can not come until the soul is delivered from the bondage of sin, so the typical rest of the sabbath among the Jews could not properly be observed till that people were freed from the bondage of Egypt.

To make the expression of this thought perfectly clear, take four items in order: 1. Bondage in Egypt; 2. Deliverance by the power of God; 3. The free nation; 4. The sabbath observance. Then the following in order: 1. Bondage to sin; 2. Deliverance by Christ; 3. The Church; 4. Rest from sin enjoyed in it. Now the members of the former series are respectively set forth as types of the latter. If, therefore, deliverance by Christ is a necessary idea in connection with rest from sin, then, correspondingly, deliverance from Egypt is an essential precedent idea to the Jewish sabbath. Hence the Lord says, "Remember that thou wast a servant in the land of Egypt." Hence this clause, instead of being appended to all commands, a mere incentive to grateful obedience to all, is strikingly affixed to one, and that in the decalogue itself, as an essential part of that one special required observance, the sabbath, a fundamental part of it alone. When, therefore, it was remarked in a previous part of this chapter that the emphasis is on the word "free," in any true statement of the purpose of the sabbath, it was in view of absolute proof furnished by the fifteenth verse of the fifth chapter of Deuteronomy.

The typical importance of the Jewish nation extends to all the chief points in its history. The law, especially the ten commandments, to which particular prominence is given, represents its like in the Christian Church. There is also a law which every follower of Christ is required to observe. The ten commands " were written and graven in stone;" the Christian law, as foretold by the prophet Jeremiah, was to be written in "the fleshly tablets of the heart," by which reference is made to the fact that the religion of Christ was more especially to be spiritual, whereas that of Moses was external and formal, or in a more limited and definite sense, to that inspiration by the Holy Spirit which led apostles and early Christian teachers into the utterance of all needed truth.   Further, the law of Christ which the church now observes has its ordinances as well as its moral precepts. So the ten commandments had, in the midst of moral enactments, this one, the fourth, relating to the sabbath day, which was purely and simply an ordinance.

If the inquiry be made, why the ten particular items, rather than any others out of the great mass of Jewish laws, were accorded the preëminence of being included in the decalogue, and engraven by the finger of God upon tables of stone, no clearly-defined and definite answer perhaps can be given. And yet some thoughts suggest themselves founded in the nature of the case. 1. The most important would doubtless be thus assigned. 2. The briefer items. 3. Those of more general application. For example, "Thou shalt not seethe a kid in its mother's milk," and "Thou shalt have no other gods before me," differ so greatly in importance that the latter heads the decalogue, while the former sinks into the common mass. Again, of sacrifice and sabbath observance, the former has such an immense abundance of details and variety of form and occasion, that, though equally if not more important, both alike also being ceremonial, it is unsuited for such a place, and occupies, instead, page after page in the outside record. "Thou shalt not kill" and "Thou shalt not steal," are not only brief in terms, but, with others, are so necessary to the existence of the nation itself, so essential to good order, that, unless observed, no other law could be enforced; nor would the Almighty, who once destroyed the earth when it became corrupt and filled with violence, give any other laws, or deign his presence and blessing to any people who did not first observe these. Strange to say, writers have been found to overlook these plain and natural distinctions, and, instead, to create one without any warrant in Scripture — namely, that the decalogue consists exclusively of moral laws, to which in this way there has been given preëminence and authority over all people for all time, while the remainder is purely ceremonial, and passed away with the Jewish nation at the coming of Christ. To this position proper attention will be given in a more appropriate place.

CHAPTER V.

MOSES' LAW.

We have seen that after the children of Israel, in the enjoyment of their freedom from the oppressions of Egypt, had marched, under the guidance of the Almighty, a little way from the Red Sea, they came to the place which God had selected as suitable, and received the law, under most impressive circumstances, from the burning summit of Horeb. Immediately after this, while yet encamped about the base of Sinai, all those other arrangements were made, which were necessary that as a nation, fully equipped in order, government, and religion, they might go forth to accomplish the real object of their exodus, the occupation of the land of Canaan. The construction of the tabernacle, an immense number of laws civil and ecclesiastical, the preparation of priests for their sacred office, of the Levites for theirs, the collection and provision for the preservation of the sacred archives, of the pot of manna, Aaron's rod that budded, the tables of the law, and the public records up to this time, all of these, in extensive detail, fill up the Scripture pages, until in the tenth chapter of the book of Numbers, very near a full year after their encampment, it is said, "the cloud was taken up from off the tabernacle of testimony, and the children of Israel took their journeys out of the wilderness of Sinai."

Among these details we have now to search for whatever scraps of information may be found to assist us in this investigation. Exodus, Leviticus, Numbers, and Deuteronomy are the books. Law rather than history predominates. It was the most elaborate system ever, in the space of one year, imposed upon a nation, beginning an independent existence. They were comparatively rude and inexperienced. The taint of heathenish customs and superstition was about them. But the watchful eye of Jehovah was upon them. His chosen and qualified minister, Moses, was their leader. Hence, though at first probably better acquainted with the gods of Egypt whence they came than with the God of their fathers, Abraham, Isaac and Jacob, and rather disposed, at the coming of privations, to wish themselves back in Egypt, and to trust a golden calf as a god than to remember the God whose "mighty hand and stretched out arm" had delivered them, and who now stood ready to hear their cry and to verify his most gracious promises to them; they were brought, nevertheless, under the most perfect discipline, compelled to observe the most minute requirements, and finally trained, as a people, to such supreme faith in the great Jehovah, as to be the wonder of the world.

To one who should, for the first time, and without the necessary preparation for an intelligent understanding of this history, read this mass of forms, so entirely different from our own customs, it would be the merest rubbish. Indeed it requires a very thoughtful man and one already well versed in the mysteries of the divine volume, to extract interest, much less enthusiasm, from these pages. The common mind will make little out of them, without a guide —with a blind guide much less. He is likely to be bewildered and wearied with the copious stream of seemingly worthless forms. A young person, ordinarily, would as soon read old patent office reports, or the various city directories, as the laws of Moses.

Strange indeed is it that out of such unpromising materials such grand results should flow; that here should be contained a system, capable, on the one hand, of guiding a rude people to national greatness, and, on the other, of embodying, in definite symbol—exact type—the full and perfect likeness of a coming spiritual kingdom with the Messiah of God as its founder. Considering how much of divine philosophy is combined in this code of laws, it is not remarkable, after all, that to one who has reached that degree of proficiency which enables him to gather its hidden pearls, its study becomes extremely fascinating and richly remunerative.

Without making any very complete analysis, it appears on the surface, that by far the largest part is taken up with ceremonial observances. These being more particularly the typical portions, the fact is in keeping with our general view. Sacrifice, the most important type of all, has perhaps the fullest development. Then the priesthood, ceremonial cleanness and uncleanness, purification, the tabernacle and the Sabbath. Sacrifice, simply known, probably, in previous periods of the world's history, and hitherto single in form and observance, now expands into a complicated system. The Sabbath day likewise has its expansion. A system of Sabbaths is developed, all, however, according to the general pattern, and adding to the original significance of the seventh day observance.

Having already sufficiently noted the institution of the Sabbath day at the giving of the manna, and its further enforcement in the law of ten commandments made on Sinai, recorded in Exodus and repeated in Deuteronomy, it remains to examine further legislation in regard to it, before considering other enactments of like nature. Other passages relating to the Sabbath day occur as follows:

1. "Ye shall keep the Sabbath therefore; for it is holy unto you. Every one that defileth it shall surely be put to death; for whosoever doeth any work therein, that soul shall be cut off from among his people.

"Six days may work be done; but in the seventh is the Sabbath of rest, holy to the Lord: whosoever doeth any work in the Sabbath day, he shall surely be put to death. Wherefore the children of Israel shall keep the Sabbath, to observe the Sabbath throughout their generations, for a perpetual covenant.

"It is a sign between me and the children of Israel for ever: for in six days the Lord made heaven and earth, and on the seventh day he rested and was refreshed" (Ex. xxxi. 14-17).

2. "Six days thou shalt work, but on the seventh day thou shalt rest: in earing time and in harvest thou shalt rest" (Ex. xxxiv. 21).

3. "Six days shall work be done, but on the seventh day there shall be to you a holy day, a Sabbath of rest to the Lord: whosoever doeth work therein shall be put to death.

"Ye shall kindle no fire throughout your habitations upon the Sabbath day" (Ex. xxxv. 2, 3).

4. "Concerning the feasts of the Lord, which ye shall proclaim to be holy convocations, even these are my feasts. Six days shall work be done: but the seventh day is the Sabbath of rest, a holy convocation; ye shall do no work therein: it is the Sabbath of the Lord in all your dwellings" (Lev. xxiii. 2, 3).

5. "Every Sabbath he shall set it before the Lord continually, being taken from the children of Israel by an everlasting covenant" (Lev. xxiv. 8).

6. "And while the children of Israel were in the wilderness, they found a man that gathered sticks upon the Sabbath day.

"And they that found him gathering sticks brought him unto Moses and Aaron, and unto all the congregation.

"And they put him in ward, because it was not declared what should be done to him.

"And the Lord said unto Moses, the man shall surely be put to death: all the congregation shall stone him with stones without the camp.

"And all the congregation brought him without the camp,

and stoned him with stones, and he died; as the Lord commanded Moses" (Num. xv. 32-36).

7. "And on the Sabbath day two lambs of the first year without spot, and two tenth deals of flour for a meat offering, mingled with oil, and the drink offering thereof.

"This is the burnt offering of every Sabbath, beside the continual burnt offering, and his drink offering" (Num. xxviii. 9, 10).

For convenience' sake the passages will be referred to by number. Only a few others having reference to the weekly Sabbath, remain to be noted separately, including a clause preceding the first quotation.

As to the observance of the Sabbath day, it is here (1, 3, 6,) distinctly specified that they should do no work therein, that they should kindle no fire throughout their habitations, and that he who was found gathering sticks on that day, must receive the full penalty of the law. It is also declared that he who should transgress these commands, should "be cut off from among the people," or should " be put to death," which appears to be the same thing, at least in this instance, and to have been accomplished, under the law, by the offender being stoned to death by the whole congregation outside the camp. This fearful penalty, attached to disobedience, must be regarded as evidence of the high rank of the law and of the day in the Jewish economy. Side by side with idolatry (naturally in a theocracy the highest crime,) with desecration of the sanctuary, pollution of the priestly office, the offering of impure sacrifices, murder, and the vilest lust, Sabbath-breaking stands as an offense against Jehovah himself of the greatest enormity. No wonder then, if, in the future, we shall find these people neglectful of this law, that God, through his prophets, shall denounce them and bring his judgments upon the nation itself.

The fact is, it stands with most of the others just mentioned, as a foul blot cast upon the fair page upon which

God is showing forth, in advance, to the world, his Son who in the fulness of time, after type and law and a trained people and prophets have made the necessary preparation, is to appear, the actual antitype which these in different ways prefigure. Surely he that would pollute the sacrifice most solemnly enjoined by Jehovah, would contemn the cross itself; he who would defile the sanctuary in the wilderness, would corrupt the church of Christ as well; and he who would refuse to keep holy the typical rest day in the free Israel, would spurn the rest to the weary, sin-laden, sin-enthralled soul which Christ the Saviour, with divine benignity was coming to give. "He that despised Moses' law died without mercy under two or three witnesses; of how much sorer punishment, suppose ye, he shall be thought worthy who hath trodden under foot the Son of God, and hath counted the blood of the covenant wherewith he was sanctified, an unholy thing, and hath done despite unto the Spirit of grace" (Heb. x. 28, 29).

Some have supposed the Sabbath to have been instituted for the physical refreshment of the toil-worn race of men. To such does not the infliction of death for gathering sticks on that day seem an extreme penalty? Others again have thought its object, (not its form merely,) to have chief reference to God as a creator. Upon such the task will devolve to show why its observance was so especially and so minutely enjoined upon the Israelites alone. Either the extreme of its keeping or the punishment of its violation can not so well be explained on that hypothesis.

But if in the study of the wonderful scheme of redemption, we regard this, as indeed it is, to be one of the most striking points in that picture which God was painting in advance, by which he could show to the world, in furtherance of the grand object for which alone his revelation of himself was undertaken, salvation through the Christ his well beloved Son; then one readily perceives that it would not be possible for God to allow the law to be broken. To break a law so important in that picture as that of the Sabbath, would disfigure the whole and thwart thus much of God's purpose. It could not then be tolerated. Thus the correctness of this view is shown in the precision, minuteness, and severity which characterize the various parts of the Mosaic system.

While the strictness of the law is under consideration in connection with the various sabbath theories, we inquire, Why should the creation be commemorated at all? Answer: to testify the power of Jehovah. Surely its testimony would not be conclusive upon this point. The miracles at the Red Sea, at Sinai, and all along their journey; the continuing witness of his glory above the tabernacle, and the numerous calamities brought upon the people for their transgressions, would teach them far more in regard to God's power than any observance of a sabbath which men might keep then as they do now, without believing that God created the world at all. One might well pause to inquire why so weak a witness should be upheld by such extreme penalties.

The repetition of the clause (1) in regard to the creation, coming immediately after the ten commandments, gives no added significance. All the instances of its use—this, that in the command, and that in Genesis—were undoubtedly written at about the same time, namely, when the sabbath law was first announced, and the statement was dropped after the people became acquainted with it as the model for the sabbath. The word sign in the connection favors the same idea. The Lord established a visible rite, circumcision, as a sign or pledge of his covenant with Abraham. He took an existing phenomenon in nature, the rainbow, as the sign of his pledge or covenant with Noah. He took an existing fact, the creation in six days and cessation therefrom on the seventh, represented it before the people by the institution of the Sabbath day, as a sign or pledge of his covenant, as he here declares, with the Israelites. Which is greater, the sign or the covenant? In seeking the object of a sign, do we find it in its form or model, or rather in the covenant of which it is a pledge. Was circumcision to be considered valuable on its own account, or was the value in the covenant of future prosperity to the nation? Was the value in the rainbow, or in the preservation of the earth from floods? Is the utility in the sabbath itself, whether in the creation model or in the weekly observance, or in the covenanted blessedness of future rest to a sin-enslaved world? It is evident that the word sign in connection with the sabbath bids us look forward and not backward, to the promise and not to the outward form of the pledge. The creation was wonderful in itself, and well worthy to be the basis of the sign of the most glorious covenant that God ever gave to man. But that covenanted blessing, when it should expand from its Israelitish restriction to "all the families of the earth," when still further it should rise above an earthly Canaan to a heavenly, and reach beyond mortality to eternal life, was soul-inspiring enough to fix the eye of the Jew, who might perchance gain some faint conception of it from his position among the "shadows," in the vestibule of the primary school of the ages, and certainly ought to draw our thoughts, since we have the light of their experience and a more perfect revelation, upon its future glory, as the sum of all that man could wish or God could give.

When the record (1, 5) speaks of this as a "perpetual covenant" to be observed by the Jews "throughout their generations," and refers it particularly to the children of Israel, it is easy to perceive that that nation, at least, were to observe it while their theocracy lasted, and that the covenanted mercies were to endure forever.

The religious rites (5, 7) enjoined on this day, namely, the setting the shew bread in order before the Lord continually, as mentioned in the quotation from Leviticus, and the offering, besides the daily sacrifice, of the burnt, a meat, and a drink offering, not to speak of temple service introduced at a later date, are all in themselves significant.

God instituted a rest day and guarded it jealously against the most trivial infractions, and yet enjoined work upon it, in the performance of religious rites, in excess of that required on other days. As before, we look forward for the reason. The Christian who has accepted the gracious offer of Christ and found rest to his soul, is relieved from the servitude of sin, but has at the same time taken upon himself the obligations of a holy life. His activities are increased, but they are sanctified. He is a diligent worker still, but not for worldly and temporal ends. Worship, religious duty, employs his powers in this life, and the glimpses which the Bible has given him into the next, reveals its continuance. Hence the rest of the type, like that of the antitype, was the most rigid abstinence from toil or anything that might represent it, but at the same time, as indicated by the double offerings on that day, an increase of religious activities. The faithful Israelite, then, could look forward through the sabbath rest and ceremonies to a time when cares and toils, pilgrimages, poverty and oppression should cease and he should enter upon the covenanted blessings of God, hold sweet communion with and offering grateful worship to him, while he had the pledge of creation itself given for its fulfillment. The present Sunday observance among Christians resembles that of the ancient sign.

The phrases as connected with the sabbath (1, 3, 4), "of the Lord," "to the Lord," "holy to the Lord," "holy unto you," and "to you a holy day," simply imply that the day is to be kept holy by the people, which would be done by implicit obedience to the command, and furthermore that this was to be done in deference to the Lord's rightful authority.

The occurrence of the phrase, "holy convocation" (4), as applied to the weekly sabbath, leads to the consideration of a new list of passages. Further use of it may be found in the following chapters, too long to admit of full quotation: Ex. xii., Lev. xxiii., Num. xxviii., xxix. The chapters in Numbers or that in Leviticus will be sufficient to verify most of our observations. The great annual feasts established by the Lord to be observed by the people are here named, together with the other occasions on which there were to be holy convocations of the people. Two of the feasts lasted a full week, with two holy convocations, one on the first and the other on the last day. These holy convocations were as follows: two at the Passover, one at Pentecost, one at the feast of Trumpets, one on the day of Atonement, two at the feast of Tabernacles, making seven in all.

It is distinctly stated in regard to each of these days that there shall be no work, or "servile work," done therein, thus constituting them, what they are sometimes distinctly called, sabbaths. They should be distinguished from the weekly institution, however.

The twelfth chapter of Exodus presents a seeming difficulty, from the fact that it mentions these days previous to the crossing of the Red Sea, at which date a sabbath became possible. Two facts, however, fully remove this objection: 1. These convocations were not, as from the nature of the case they could not be, observed in the first Egyptian passover. 2. The law of the passover in full, as here announced, is declared to have a future application. "And it shall come to pass [ver. 25] when ye be come to the land which the Lord will give you, according as he hath promised, that ye shall keep this service." There is, then, here no sabbath previous to the crossing of the Red Sea, and though, as at the creation, it is mentioned in connection with appropriate historic facts in advance, forty years are to pass before the condition will be fulfilled.

This investigation is not concerned with the object of these several occasions. It is sufficient to know that they had, connected with them by explicit command, sabbaths, occurring generally on other days than the seventh, each of them requiring special offerings. The obvious purpose of connecting sabbaths with these great national festivals was to emphasize the idea of rest, just as the connection of sacrifice with them must have been to inculcate the idea of an atonement by blood. Thus sabbaths and sacrifices went together side by side, impressing their silent lessons upon the chosen people and preparing the way for the Messiah to come. Every noted national event, and the recurrence of every prominent annual blessing, was marked by these significant festivals, which brought the pledge of God, by all the wonderful providences which they commemorated, to give them both that redemption and that consequent rest which sacrifice and sabbath distinctly promised to them.

But we need to discriminate. Is it the rest or the seventh day that is important? If the latter, then these sabbaths are strangely bewildering, for they could occur, like our Fourth of July, on any day of the week. To illustrate: if God, at the institution of sacrifice, had ordered simply the slaying of a bullock and nothing more, the inquiry might have been whether the significance lay chiefly in that particular animal, or in the deed connected with it. If, however, afterwards it should appear that God enjoined the killing, in like manner, of a great variety of other animals, kids, goats, lambs, heifers, pigeons, we should begin to think the significance rather attached to the slaying. So likewise when he appoints the seventh day as a day of rest, choosing it especially because in it he himself rested from creation, it is easy to magnify the seventh day as being the chief thing in view. When, however, rest comes to be enjoined upon divers other days, falling at different times upon every day in the week, and even appointed upon years, we conclude that rest is the idea sought to be emphasized. And when, further, we see so many institutions, the most prominent in the Israelitish system, pointing forward, as notably sacrifice does, to the central figure of the Bible, the Lamb of God, we very naturally, certainly, as well as truthfully, refer the Sabbath to that same coming one, "the lamb slain from the foundation of the world," and hear him say: "Come unto me, all ye that labor and are heavy laden, and I will give you rest." Furthermore, when in the case of the Passover, two days, one beginning and one ending the protracted occasion, mark the idea of rest first and last, it should be understood that the promised blessing thus made prominent, conveyed to us through that representative and typical people, the Jews, is pledged in this sign by the most wonderful events of their history—those that marked the slaying of the first born of all Egypt, the saving of every Israelitish first born and the rescue of their nation from slavery.

We are highly satisfied with the pledge of our government to pay our bonds in gold, or to do anything else to which it has agreed. How should we rejoice in a pledge witnessed by the whole world, from one who never broke his covenant, and who has solemnly marked the deliverance of a poor, enslaved, representative race, themselves but passive agents in their own release, with a vow to confer the richest blessings. And, further, when all the chief events of this nation's history, its dwelling in tents, its reaping of rich harvests, its gathering of daily food (manna), are pledges of the same thing from the same mighty hand; and when, chief of all, every observance of a weekly day by that same representative people is a sign conveying a pledge on the part of him who created the worlds, of a rest to come, how diligently ought these people to keep the appointed sabbaths in faith, looking forward to and rejoicing in the blessing promised thus, and prefigured not to themselves alone but to all the world through him.

The twenty-fifth chapter of Leviticus contains the law of the sabbatical year and that of Jubilee. It is as interesting as it is instructive. Both this and the chapter following will well repay reading in this connection. Six years they were to sow the land and prune their vineyards. This they were not to do in the seventh year, which was to be "a sabbath of rest to the land, a sabbath for the Lord." The fiftieth year was to be a year of jubilee, like the other a year of rest. On this year there was to be a release of servants, who were to go free, of debtors; and land sold was to return to the original possessor. As punishment for disobedience of the statutes of the Lord, the prophetic declaration is made of the captivity of the people and the desolation of the land, to the astonishment of their enemies. "Then shall the land enjoy her sabbaths as long as it lieth desolate, and ye be in your enemies' land; . . . because it did not rest in your sabbaths when ye dwelt upon it." The year preceding a sabbatical year had a special blessing pronounced upon it, making it so fruitful as to bring forth the harvests of three. Aside from the benefits that might accrue to the land in this, as well as to the Jewish state in all the different national observances, it is impossible to overlook the significance for the future. Release and rest! Words of joyous import! "Oh, where shall rest be found, rest for the weary soul!" "Then said Jesus to those Jews that believed on him, If ye continue in my word, then are ye my disciples indeed; and ye shall know the truth, and the truth shall make you free." "Search the Scriptures; for in them ye think ye have eternal life: and they are they which testify of me." "There is one that accuseth you, even Moses, in whom ye trust. For had ye believed Moses, ye would have believed me, for he wrote of me." "If they hear not Moses and the prophets, neither will they be persuaded, though one rose from the dead."

CHAPTER VI.

HISTORIANS AND PROPHETS.

A great change has come over the nation of Israel. An equal difference appears in the divine record. This has been in part gradual. But one single point occurs that marks a decided epoch in their history. This is the crossing of the Jordan, which brings them into the promised land. Here the type changes. No subject running, like ours, through the entire scope of the Jewish history, can be understood without a knowledge of the varying situation of the people. The difference in their attitude towards the divine law of necessity caused a corresponding change in the manifestations of God towards them.

During the lifetime of Moses, their first leader, "Moses' Law" occupied the chief part of their attention. In the wilderness they had not to till the land, since food was provided for them in the daily manna for forty years. They had little really to do, it would seem, but to learn the law and to keep such part of it as was not inapplicable on account of their wandering life. With this they were, we may suppose, gradually growing familiar, and as they became prepared to keep it of their own knowledge, God's communications to them through Moses were less frequent. It has already been remarked that the Bible indicates throughout that God's purpose has been not to continue his personal manifestations longer than they were absolutely necessary, and to withdraw himself by degrees from association with men, leaving his law to be executed by subordinate agencies. When, therefore, the infancy of this chosen nation was passed, on rare and exceptional occasions only did he himself communicate with them at all.

When they reached the Jordan and were ready to go over to possess the land, the ministration of the pacific Moses ceased, at his death, and Joshua, the military leader, guided the people. The first striking change noticeable is, that war with the Canaanites assumes the chief prominence in the record. All that variety of incident appears which belongs to an active and victorious people, surrounded by hostile nations, among which they are making their way to secure a permanent homestead. God's special assistance as the Lord of Hosts, in miraculous ways, is often shown. Still, in the midst of these wars, they slowly became settled as a people, and the customs and manners of a fixed nation crystallized about them. The judges who ruled Israel for a time gave way to the more settled form of a monarchy. When this reached the acme of its military glory under David, and a more peaceful sovereign, the wise and wealthy Solomon, took his place, a magnificent temple for the national worship was reared at Jerusalem, after the typical likeness of the tabernacle. As the religious worship thus became developed into a permanent system, under the reign of the kings, we find very few traces of God's interference with the national procedure.

A succession of prophets sprang up at this time, beginning with Samuel, who supplemented the kings, giving to the history that religious and theocratic cast which otherwise would have been entirely lost. These were among the most remarkable personages known even to the inspired volume. They seem to have filled a place, considering the difference in the age and dispensation to which they belonged, not unlike that of the apostles. If Peter, James, John and Paul were dissimilar in personal character, not less so were Samuel, Elijah, Isaiah, Jeremiah and Daniel. These prophets foretold events, warned the kings and people, were the inspired teachers and preachers of the day.

Most wonderful miracles attested their divine commission. While God had withdrawn from personal communication with the people, these prophets, however, failed not to inform them that his providences were still over them; that he was angry with them for violating his law, and that he failed not to recognize their obedience; that his punishments followed continued wickedness, and his blessings were sure to result from their righteousness. Thus an unseen presence, strong in authority, irresistibly attested to be the Jehovah of their fathers, guided them, under the increasing sway of the principles of faith and free will—the cardinal principles of perfect divine government. After the nation was divided into two kingdoms, and they rapidly degenerated under inefficient and wicked monarchs, we are shut up to the testimony of these prophets almost entirely for indications such as are of service to us in this investigation. We desire the reader to note that a long time has elapsed, and great changes have occurred in the Jewish nation, such as we have just partially described, since we last examined the record of sabbath law in the wildernsss under Moses.

Such passages as may refer to the sabbath in the historic books of the Kings, Chronicles, and Nehemiah, and in the various prophecies, are well worthy our attention. Most allusions to the subject in the former are merely incidental, and are cited to show first that at this time the sabbaths were regularly observed, or at least were recognized as regularly existing institutions among the people.

Thus, in reference to the visit of the Shunammite woman to the prophet Elisha, her husband says (II. Kings iv. 23): "Wherefore wilt thou go to him to-day? it is neither new moon nor sabbath." It is said (xvi. 18) of King Ahaz: "And the covert (*i. e.*, covered inclosure) for the sabbath that they had built in the house, and the king's entry without, turned he from the house of the Lord for the king of Assyria." The duties of certain Levites are thus specified

(I. Chronicles ix. 32): "And other of their brethren of the sons of the Kohathites were over the shew bread to prepare it every sabbath." And still further, in regard to the Levites as helpers of the priests (xxiii. 31): "And to offer all burnt sacrifices unto the Lord in the sabbaths, in the new moons, and on the set feasts, by number, according to the order commanded unto them, continually before the Lord." This same association of sabbaths, new moons, and set or solemn feasts, occurs several times in II. Chronicles, in Nehemiah, and in one or two of the prophets. They are mentioned, in these instances, chiefly in connection with burnt offerings, which were common to them all.

We have already seen that these set feasts, each occurring annually, had sabbaths engrafted upon them, and from the manner in which they are placed side by side in the references, it is difficult to see that the weekly sabbath held its place by any tenure different from theirs, or that one was regarded as more important than the others. And yet writers upon the sabbath are found who make a very broad distinction; all, except the weekly sabbath, being, in their view, temporary, limited in their authority, and soon to be abolished. The time has not arrived to consider this idea in full; we are only watching, as we go along, for indications that may bear upon it. So far nothing is found. The significant fact should also be noted, that no reference is made anywhere in connection with the sabbath to the rest of God at creation; nor in any of the books of the Bible where creation is referred to, as, for instance, in the Psalms, do we find any statement of the institution, at that time, of the rest on the seventh day.

It will ever be a prime object, in the investigation of this subject, to determine its proper limitations. As its different phases pass in review before us, the inquiry for these must never be omitted. Was the sabbath imposed upon Gentiles? The books now up for examination must be allowed to present their testimony. The quotations already made in this chapter have express application to the Jews in every instance. So also do a number of references found in Nehemiah (chaps. ix., x., xiii.). That book is largely devoted to the history of the restoration of the temple and temple worship, which had greatly degenerated under preceding kings. Next come the prophets, as a part of these are the only remaining books of the Old Testament which make any reference to it whatever. Isaiah, Jeremiah, Lamentations, Ezekiel, Hosea and Amos contain all that is to be found upon the subject, and we shall be careful that none be omitted.

The first chapter of Isaiah — a part of his "vision concerning Judah and Jerusalem" — upbraids the people for their degeneracy. It shows that they were still observing the numerous forms of the law, but so great was their wickedness that even these had become an abomination to the Lord. "To what purpose is the multitude of your sacrifices unto me, saith the Lord: I am full of the burnt offerings of rams, and the fat of fed beasts; and I delight not in the blood of bullocks, or of lambs, or of he goats. When ye come to appear before me who hath required this at your hands, to tread my courts? Bring no more vain oblations; incense is an abomination unto me; the new moons and sabbaths, the calling of assemblies, I can not away with; it is iniquity, even the solemn meeting. Your new moons and your appointed feasts my soul hateth; they are a trouble unto me; I am weary to bear them. And when ye spread forth your hands, I will hide mine eyes from you; yea, when ye make many prayers, I will not hear; your hands are full of blood."

This passage, quoted thus at length, may be taken as a sample of much that is found in the prophets, who, as the inspired messengers of God, devoted a large share of their utterances to warning the people of their growing sins. Idolatry, covetousness and oppression were perhaps the leading ones. These and numerous other wrongs were corrupting the worship itself, alienating the people from God. It was evidently the purpose of God to train his people — the Israelites — progressively, through the later prophets and inspired teachers, adding the higher principles of morality to the more exclusive forms, which had been imposed upon them in their infancy as a nation. There should have been a growth, a pure and holy development, with the flight of years; but, instead, kings and people alike became corrupt, exceedingly wicked in the sight of God. Hence the numerous reproaches, warnings, threatenings, and exhortations. Hence were foretold, and afterwards brought to pass, captivities, national reverses, destruction of temple and city, dispersion and loss of ten tribes, and all the calamities which have rendered their wonderful history famous forever. The fact must not be overlooked, however, that through all this there gleams the promise of the Messiah to come, of a remnant that should be saved, a restoration, a delivery, the wrath of God against their oppressors, and finally through them the coming blessing to all the families of earth. Even now God was remembering his covenant with their fathers, and his design through them of salvation for all races of men.

The last quotation so evidently refers to the Israelites alone, that we may pass at once to the next, where this fact is not probably so clear. The fifty-sixth chapter of Isaiah has been supposed by many to contain evidence that the sabbath was binding on Gentiles likewise. It would be well for the reader to have this passage open before him, that he may judge correctly of the impartiality of the remarks we shall make upon it. The argument turns upon the words "stranger" and "eunuch." It is necessary to observe, also, the logical sequence of the passage. In this respect, Adam Clarke* upon this chapter affords a familiar example

---

* It is our object in this book to refer to as few authors as possible, and to those supposed to be most familiar to the common reader, that all references may be easily verified.

of mistaken comment. He not only styles the sons of the stranger, in verse sixth, Gentiles, but he applies the whole connection to the Christian and not to the Jewish dispensation. Christ and acceptance of him as the Saviour is made the underlying substance of it all. Clearly this is unpardonable. A single glance will show. The preceding chapter contains a Messianic prophecy. It is a declaration that God will fulfill all his covenants. His word shall surely be accomplished. The Holy One shall come to bless the nations. In connection with these promised blessings are exhortations to present obedience.

This is the character, the natural style, of the prophecies. To apply the exhortations and warnings to as remote a time as the fulfillment of the promises is to leave the people without a share in the lesson actually addressed to them. This is an egregious blunder, often made, however. When John the Baptist came in the wilderness of Judea, saying, "Repent ye, for the kingdom of heaven is at hand," who fails to understand that the repentance was urged as a present duty, while the kingdom of heaven was promised or declared in the near future. So in the prophets universally. Duty was enjoined upon the people as present. "Ye" or "you," and not coming generations, were commanded to turn from wickedness, to keep the law, to refrain from polluting the Sabbath, while the blessings promised as a sure consequence of their obedience, were of two kinds, almost invariably connected and generally merging into each other; first, immediate national restoration and prosperity; and second, the glories of the Messiah to come. Not only do these two merge into each other almost imperceptibly, so that it is sometimes difficult to determine, in a given instance, which is meant, but also the conditional warning is often somewhat obscurely blended with one or both of them.

Applying these principles it will be perceived that the passage opening the fifty-sixth chapter of Isaiah is addressed to the people of that day. "Keep ye judgment, and do justice; for my salvation is near to come," clearly includes the present command and the future promise. To any man and the son of man (a poetical phraseology) "that doeth this [present duty], that layeth hold on it; that keepeth the Sabbath from polluting it, and keepeth his hand from doing any evil";—blessing. "Neither let the son of the stranger [of that day], that hath joined himself to the Lord speak, saying, the Lord hath utterly separated me from his people; neither let the eunuch say, behold I am a dry tree. For thus saith the Lord unto the eunuchs that keep my Sabbaths, ... even unto them will I give in my house and within my walls a place and a name better than of sons and of daughters. ... Also the sons of the stranger that join themselves to the Lord to serve him, ... every one that keepeth the Sabbath from polluting it, and taketh hold of my covenant, even them will I bring to my holy mountain." The preceding suggestions will enable any one to perceive that while the prophecies in this connection are largely Messianic, in the element of promise, yet the "sons of the stranger" and the "eunuchs" were of that day while the prophet was himself living, and upon them was urged the keeping of the Sabbath as a then present duty.

It yet remains to determine the status at that day of the parties styled "sons of the stranger" and "eunuchs." In the decalogue itself (Ex. xx.) it is commanded in reference to the Sabbath day, "in it thou shalt not do any work, thou, nor thy son, nor thy daughter, thy manservant, nor thy maidservant, nor thy cattle, nor thy stranger that is within thy gates." So then the Sabbath, under the original law, was bound upon these strangers. Not only so; very many others of the laws of Moses were imposed upon them. And, with justice, too. If a man comes and abides at my house, surely I may expect of him that he will treat with proper respect such religious observances as I may regard as of authority over myself. There were many of these strangers dwelling among the Israelites, from the very first; and it was proper to require of them that they should do no violence to the national religion. The proper keeping of the law by the Israelites themselves called for this much at least from a stranger.

The exact status of these strangers it may be difficult to determine. But this, at least, they were—non-Israelitish residents among the Israelites, incorporated with them in their national polity, though foreigners not belonging to any other government, and not mere visitors or travelers. Casting in their lots with the Israelites, their interests were largely identical with theirs, and it was reasonable that in many things they should even be required to conform to the law. And yet that they were forbidden in the law to work on the Sabbath day, and were exhorted by the prophet to keep it, is no proof whatever that the institution was bound upon the Gentiles of the earth. They seem to have been introduced here to give point and pertinency to the promises of Messianic blessing, in this view of it, namely, that it was to extend far beyond the limits of the Jewish nation alone. So also of the eunuchs. They were referred to by way of giving emphasis to "the everlasting name that should not be cut off," better than that "of sons and daughters" of which they were deprived. These, though probably mostly of foreign origin, were clearly incorporated with and bound in fortune and lives with the Jewish nation which they served.

The last paragraph of the fifty-eighth chapter reads: "If thou turn away thy foot from the Sabbath, from doing thy pleasure on my holy day; and call the Sabbath a delight, the holy ot the Lord, honorable; and shalt honor him not doing thine own way, nor finding thine own pleasure, nor speaking thine own words. Then shalt thou delight thyself in the Lord, and I will cause thee to ride upon the high places of the earth, and feed thee with this heritage of Jacob thy father; for the mouth of the Lord hath spoken it." It would be impugning the intelligence of any ordinary reader to suppose that he does not recognize at once that this is addressed directly to the Jewish family in a body, as is clearly shown in the use of the phrase " Jacob thy father," as well as in the first verse of the chapter; and that the blessings consequent upon their ceasing to violate the Sabbath would be national aggrandizement; and that the passage has no application whatever to any other people.

What shall be said then of the preachers belonging to a certain religious persuasion of the present day, who compass both sea and land to make one proselyte to the observance now of the seventh day, or Saturday, as a Sabbath under the law, of binding authority over all Christians, and who quote this passage as addressed by the prophet to us. When these preachers, presuming, no doubt, upon the non-acquaintance of most of their auditors with the Scriptures, and particularly with the prophecies, cry out unto the ordinary orthodox Sunday observer, " Take your feet off the Lord's Sabbath," as the author of this book has heard them time and again; when with a presumption, impudence and hypocrisy unparalleled by any class calling themselves ministers of the word of God, they thus distort and misapply the sacred oracles; the only words that seem adequate in reply are those of Michael the archangel, " The Lord rebuke thee."

Just in the final chapter of Isaiah a vision of future glory to the people of the Lord is revealed. The imagery of the passage exceeds that in common use by the prophet, and it will hardly be supposed by any one that the statement is throughout to be taken in a literal sense. When therefore it is declared, " They shall bring all your brethren for an offering unto the Lord out of all nations upon horses, and in chariots, and in litters, and upon mules, and upon swift beasts, to my holy mountain Jerusalem ;" when the expressions are employed, " a new heaven and a new earth," " they shall look upon the carcasses of men that have transgressed against me, for their worm shall not die, neither shall their fire be quenched ;" doubtless all discerning Bible-readers will regard the descriptions as figurative. So also in portraying the constant worship of the Lord which his people will offer in that coming day, the prophet sets forth its frequency figuratively by the use of language well known then. In glowing terms he declares: "And it shall come to pass that from one new moon to another, and from one Sabbath to another, shall all flesh come to worship before me, saith the Lord."

A literalist will call this prose, and understand from it that in the halcyon Christian age new moons are to be observed as by the Jews, Sabbaths as by the Sabbatarians, and all mankind without exception are to be Christians as held by the Universalists. A judicious interpreter, however, will recognize it as prophecy clothed in poetic imagery and rightly perceive that it simply and only means that in the Christian age, then future, now present, God's people were to come, not from the Jewish nation alone, but from all the families and tribes of earth, as promised in the covenant with Abraham, to worship before him, regularly, constantly and frequently, on any and all appointed or suitable occasions. All Christian worship of to-day, whenever held, is in exact fulfillment of these words.

The seventeenth chapter of Jeremiah, in the latter part thereof, presents to the "kings of Judah and all Judah and all the inhabitants of Jerusalem," who are the parties specially addressed, a slightly different phase of the Sabbath question. From this it would seem that the law of the day had been, in a measure, violated in the carrying of burdens. The exhortation to cease this transgression is accompanied by the usual promises of glory to the city itself. On the other hand, if they would not hearken, the Lord declares by the mouth of the prophet: "I will kindle a fire in the gates thereof, and it shall devour the palaces of Jerusalem, and it shall not be quenched." This is another case of limited application.

Passing to the Lamentations, ascribed to the same

prophet, passages are found (i. 7 and ii. 6) referring to the Sabbath as belonging to the Jews only; in the one case their enemies mocking at their Sabbaths, and in the other the Lord causing them to be forgotten in Zion.

Next examine Ezekiel (chapters xx., xxii., xxiii). It will be here observed that the Lord by the prophet goes back to recount to certain of the elders of Israel, who "came to inquire of the Lord," the history of their fathers, and among other things the giving to them of his Sabbaths, as he declares in the twelfth verse, to be "a sign between me and them." The rebellion of the fathers against the Lord in the wilderness, their failure to keep his statutes, the pollution of his Sabbaths, are mentioned among the continued violations which were followed by fresh reverses through all the checkered vicissitudes of their national history. The prophet (chapter xxii.) speaks directly to the people of his own time. Idolatry, shedding of blood, oppression, extortion, and uncleanness are alleged against them. "Thou hast despised mine holy things and hast profaned my Sabbaths" (ver. 8). "Her priests have profaned mine holy things, and have hid their eyes from my Sabbaths" (ver. 26). "Moreover, this they have done unto me, they have defiled my sanctuary in the same day and have profaned my Sabbaths" (xxiii. 38).

Ezekiel furnishes no evidence against the limited Israelitish view when he returns to the subject again near the close of the book. The reader will gain a sufficient idea if he will begin at the fortieth chapter and glance at the printed headings to the end of the book. He may then examine the special allusions to the Sabbath (chaps. xliv., xlv., and xlvi). Ezekiel, like the other prophets, had before him the present instruction of the people and also visions of the future. The last nine chapters constitute a grand finale of the whole—a consummation of future glory. The vision was witnessed during the captivity, and looked to a future restoration, the rebuilding of the temple destroyed, and the reappearance in it of the Shechinah, or glory of the Lord, which had been denied to the second. Connected with this vision of a city and temple, and the Messianic glories which were foreshadowed in it, was a synopsis of more or less of the ritual, apportionment, and other similar matters. In this portion we find references to the Sabbath. That these, in their special character, look backward for their exact counterpart and not forward, is evident from the fact that the exact measurements, whatever they might indefinitely teach as to the future, were like those of the previous temple, and everything else was also in keeping with previously existing institutions. Thus these passages afford no evidence of Sabbath observance outside of the Jews or in the coming Christian age (xliv. 24; xlv. 17; xlvi. 1, 3, 4, 12.)

In the condemnation of the people by the prophet Hosea, the Lord declares (ii. 11), "I will also cause all her mirth to cease, her feast days, her new moons, and her Sabbaths and all her solemn feasts." This is spoken of the Israelites, and Amos (viii. 5) represents Israel as saying: "When will the new moon be gone, that we may sell corn? and the Sabbath, that we may set forth wheat, making the ephah [measure] small, and the shekel [price] great, and falsifying the balances by deceit?"

Recognizing the fact that the general reader is not sufficiently familiar with the Scriptures to understand fully the discussion of such a subject as this without refreshing his memory upon the passages bearing upon it, and that it is extremely irksome to look them up when perusing the book, they have been quoted at length or accurate descriptions given of them. All of them have thus been brought out with the exception of one in Kings and its repetition in Chronicles (II. Kings xi.; II. Chr. xxiii.) having reference to the crowning of Joash as king, and having no bearing upon any of the points embraced in our inquiry. We shall return shortly to a very few that were passed by in the law of Moses, and thus endeavor to give a fair examination to everything which might be supposed to belong to the discussion. Finally, it may be well to repeat the point just established, that no references to the Sabbath by either the historians or prophets, indicate that it was intended to be binding upon the gentiles at any period in the world's history.

A new line of investigation now opens before us. The Old Testament is by no means a small book. There is so much in it that he who attempts to read it through, word for word, will find that it requires a great many sittings. There are the fewest number of people even in Christian lands, unfortunate for them as it is, who have done so. Had the intention been to impose the obligation of the Sabbath upon Gentiles, there was ample opportunity for this to appear. Nothing short of a studied attempt could have prevented some allusion to such a fact even had a direct statement been omitted. First the Gentiles themselves are much discoursed of in the book, both those who feared and served God and those who did not. Why should it not have appeared, for instance, in the long personal history of Job, called of the Lord himself "my servant," that he was a Sabbath observer. Second, the Old Testament itself, was designed ultimately to be for the instruction of all the nations of the earth; hence if the Sabbath were intended for the Gentiles it would have been in some way clearly shown. As the case stands to-day, Gentiles are required to keep the Sabbath, if at all, by virtue of the fourth commandment of the decalogue, and yet there is no statement whatever that it was ever from the first imposed upon one of them.

Passing more particularly to the prophets, considerable interest attaches to their treatment of foreign nations. From one-fourth to one-third of their utterances have directly to do with them. Their sins of all kinds are again and again brought up for condemnation. Surely if Sabbath breaking be one it will appear. The nations joining the

Israelites, such as had more or less to do with them, contended against them in wars, and corrupted them by their proximity. Allusion to these various people in the prophetic writings is rather in the form of declarations in regard to their future, in more or less symbolic language, than such reproof or exhortation as largely constitutes that pertaining to the Israelites. Successive prophets repeated the story of coming calamity to the same nation, each however in his peculiar way, and with such variations as were necessary, owing to the different times in which they spoke. There is a striking uniformity of reasons given for these visitations of the Almighty. There is an almost unvarying recurrence of two chief offenses. First, idolatry or reliance upon their own gods as superior to the God of Israel, and consequently, pride, exaltation and confidence in themselves. Second, the setting of themselves to do harm to Israel, the Lord's chosen people. "Verily the Lord God is a jealous God" is written on every page. He would neither allow himself to be degraded in the eyes of Israel in comparison with heathen idols, nor the people of his choice to come to disadvantage with neighboring peoples.

Isaiah, the first in order, is a case in point. He represents Assyria as saying, "By the strength of my hand I have done it." Now though Assyria had been made the instrument in the hand of God for the affliction of Israel for their sins, her own thought had been self-aggrandizement, pride and hatred to God's people. Hence punishment was pronounced against her for the very act in which she had been used to punish others. "Shall the axe boast against him that heweth therewith?" "For thou hast said in thy heart, I will ascend into heaven, I will exalt my throne above the stars of God." It was this proud exaltation of herself over the God of heaven directly or as manifested in her treatment of God's people, that brought upon Assyria, as upon other nations, the divine wrath. Rabshekeh, the Assyrian general, is represented as taunting the inhabitants of Jerusalem, by declaring to them that their God could not save.

In like manner the other prophets follow Isaiah. Jeremiah describes Moab as magnifying himself against the Lord and deriding Israel. Ezekiel in seven chapters directed against as many foreign nations, declares "the Ammonites said Aha! against my sanctuary when it was profaned, and against the land of Israel when it was destroyed, and against the house of Judah when they went into captivity." Moab and Seir do say, "Behold the house of Judah is like unto all the heathen." "Because that Edom hath dealt against the house of Judah by taking vengeance, and hath greatly offended and revenged himself upon them," "Because the Philistines have dealt by revenge," "Because Sidon was a prickly brier, a grieving thorn to Israel, despising her," because "the heart of Egypt was lifted up," saying, "my river is mine own, I have made it for myself," because "Mt. Seir had perpetual hatred and had shed the blood of the children of Israel, by the force of the sword, and in the time of their calamity;" because "thou hast said, these two nations [Israel and Judah] and these two countries shall be mine and we will possess it; when the Lord was there." "And the heathen shall know that the house of Israel went into captivity for their iniquity; because they transgressed against me, therefore I hid my face from them, and gave them into the hands of their enemies."

In Daniel, when the king spake and said "Is not this great Babylon that I have built for the house of the kingdom, by the might of my power and for the honor of my majesty," and "while the word was in the king's mouth, there fell a voice from heaven, saying: O king Nebuchadnezzar, to thee it is spoken, the kingdom is departed from thee," and that terrible calamity of loss of reason, and degradation to eat grass with the beasts of the field, came upon him. And when, under Belshazzar, they brought the golden vessels taken from the temple, and the king, princes, wives, and concubines drank wine and praised the gods of gold, of silver, of brass, of iron, of wood, and of stone," the height of blasphemy was reached, and the terrible hand-writing upon the wall foretold the doom of the kingdom.

Amos, in successive declarations against Syria, Philistia, Tyre, Edom, Ammon and Moab uses one formula: " Thus saith the Lord, for three transgressions [of Damascus] and for four, I will not turn off the punishment thereof;" because " they have done evil against my people." Edom is denounced by Obadiah because of violence against his brother (Jacob), and rejoicing in the day of destruction of Judah. Zephaniah represents the nations against which he prophesies as "reviling and reproaching my people," as "magnified against my people;" and thus while all of them, with perhaps the exception of Micah and Malachi, denounce these nations, the leading and unvarying causes of the Lord's wrath against them are twofold, evincing their contempt for himself, first, in their self-pride, and second, in their abuse of the two houses of Israel who were the Lord's people. True there are some additional reasons, given here and there throughout the sacred record, for their overthrow. These are: sorceries, witchcraft, enchantments, idolatry, greed, covetousness, drunkenness, cruelty, violence, robbery, selling of nations, lies, etc.

If now the Sabbath is a moral institution, and has from creation belonged to all Gentile nations, why should not its neglect have appeared in this list of offenses. Especially, if, in addition to its moral and universal character, the Sabbath commemorates the creation, its desecration by heathen would be to impugn the power and authority of the God who made the heavens and the earth, which is without exception chief of all sins in the sight of Jehovah. The thought is worth a moment's pause.

Surely the reader has not failed to observe the key to Old Testament sins and punishments in the words "The Lord thy God is a jealous God" (Ex. xx. 5). His reputation as creator, lying at the basis of all his authority, must be maintained, not only among the Israelites, but before all the nations of earth. Through the Israelites, of whose cause he was the champion, he forced this supreme fact upon the knowledge of the unwilling heathen. How often were nations overthrown because they insulted the God of heaven by denying his power, recognizing graven images instead. How often is God's power in creation reiterated from Genesis to Malachi. And yet the one institution, claimed to be set for the commemoration of that idea, claimed to belong, too, to these very Gentiles, was utterly disregarded by them without punishment or even rebuke. But the children of Israel who both recognized God as creator and kept the (commemorative) Sabbath were punished even with death for the slightest infraction. It is believed to be impossible for any fair-minded man to examine carefully the record on these points and not conclude that God never did impose the Sabbath upon the Gentiles, which alone will satisfactorily explain why he never punished them for profaning it. We can not pass to another point in the inquiry without expressing surprise, unfeigned and unlimited, that so many people of critical acumen, profound scholarship, and undoubted piety have passed over the total silence of the Bible as to the Sabbath for 2,500 years, from Adam to Moses, and its equally perfect silence, so far as pertains to Gentile nations, for still 1,500 years more, up to the very time of the advent of Christ, and not recognize it as limited to the Jewish nation alone.

The lesson taught or rather confirmed by the historians and prophets may be summarized in two statements, thus: The recognition of God's supremacy over men and all gods was required of Gentile nations, and any slight cast by them upon the chosen people of God was punished as an offense against himself. On the other hand, of the Jews there was demanded in addition to increased strictness in the preceding regard, that they should preserve intact that national polity in which was embodied in type the only clear advance presentment of Messiah and his kingdom. The Sabbath, as one of the important features of the latter, setting forth rest in Christ, must of course be rigidly observed by the people exhibiting that kingdom, the Jews, and hence historians and prophets agree with all portions of the sacred writings in connecting the day with them only.

As a foundation of much of the sophistry upon the Sabbath question, and an easy means of escape from some of the entanglements of a false theory, an effort has been made to distinguish the weekly or seventh day—Sabbath—from those which were observed on other days, which indeed in different years might occur upon any day of the week whatever. Thus a prominence and significance has been attached to the seventh day which was denied to the others, and while it was held to be of universal and everlasting obligation they were admitted to be limited to the Jews only. The objections to this view will be found on examination to multiply and magnify. There is no foundation for it either in the nature of the Sabbath or in the teaching of Scripture. The distinction which it makes is this: The weekly Sabbath is held to be referred to in the use of all such expressions as " the Sabbath," " the Lord's Sabbath," and " my Sabbath," while the minor Sabbaths are said to be indicated in the phrase "your Sabbaths" and the like.

Now either there must be a declaration decisive of the truth of this distinction, or a clear line of demarkation must be observed between them in their use, such as would justify it, else the interpreter does violence to Scripture in making it. Neither of these can be shown. The whole is a mere escape from difficulty and nothing else. Having seen that the Lord at the giving of the manna instituted the weekly Sabbath which he subsequently confirmed in the decalogue on Mt. Sinai, it is evident that " the Sabbath," " the Lord's Sabbath " and " my Sabbaths " would at least include that. Having seen also that before the children of Israel removed from the base of Sinai the Lord established great national convocations, also called Sabbaths, in the keeping of which he required all the abstinence from labor, and all the ceremonies and sacrifices which he had previously attached to the seventh day, it is easy to believe that these also might be included under the above terms. And still further, when the Lord enacted a Sabbath of a year's duration for the land, and imposed this upon the people under the severest penalties, it is easy to believe that this also is one of the Lord's Sabbaths included under the same names.

On the other hand, not having seen that the people of their own accord instituted any Sabbaths for themselves which they observed of their own volition, and knowing as we do that neither Scripture, their tradition, nor credible profane history mentions such, it is impossible to find any different days designated by the phrase "your Sabbaths." True the Israelites kept other feasts which originated at a later date, marking special events of great national importance. But these had not Sabbath days engrafted upon them as had those recorded in Moses' law. There are not, then, let it be distinctly understood, two sets of Sabbaths, one of which God instituted, and calls his Sabbaths, and the other originating with the people, which he calls their Sabbaths. This would be a plain distinction if it were true, which it is not. Nor, in justice to those who affirm such a division, is it known that any of them believe in the human origin of either. The more unaccountable, then, is the distinction. There is left no rational basis for it. There is, however, an explanation for these varying terms so natural as to be self-evident. God gave the Sabbaths, the Israelites kept them. They were then his Sabbaths as well as theirs : his as instituting them ; theirs as observing them. In full view of all the passages in which these designations occur, we confidently declare that this key unlocks the whole mystery ; whereas, the theory mentioned demands great credulity, and flourishes best when in line with the support of some preconceived system, especially when not questioned by any critical reader.

The writer once heard a speaker in debate say that "your sabbaths" was never used in the Scriptures to include the weekly sabbath. On the same occasion, a chart was exhibited, wherein the seventh day sabbath was represented as beginning at creation, and coming down with uninterrupted force through all ages, on to the final consummation of all things. It was a very fine chart, reaching from creation to heaven. Sinai, the cross of Christ, and other events usually regarded by the Bible student as important, were mere episodes. The great sabbath stream, with all nations, tribes, and tongues on its bosom, went coursing on past them all. I could not but see that the chart was as broad and the ink as bright, for the 2500 years during which the Scriptures say nothing whatever of the sabbath, as at any other time. And for the 1500 years thereafter, while the Israelites were held subject to the law of the fourth commandment, the stream was still wide as ever, sufficiently so to include, not the Jews alone, but all nations of earth, and still on from Christ to the present time, and thence indefinitely to that day and hour which no man knoweth, when time shall be swallowed up in eternity, the stream kept on all the same, though the whole Christian world, with an insignificant exception, observe another day. In other words, the sabbath authority was represented to be as long and wide as the stream of time. I thought then, what the maturest reflection aided by the closest investigation now confirms, that if the chart as there drawn, commensurate with the human race, had been cut off at the present time, while the past was divided into twelve equal sections, each representing five hundred years, a hair breadth line of some light color, beginning at the end of the fifth and reaching to the end of the eighth division, would have represented justly and scripturally the extent of seventh day sabbath authority. In other words, what the Jews were, in extent, to the whole human race, and what fifteen hundred years are to the whole of humanity's time, past and present, that is the true seventh day sabbath to the magnified misrepresentation of it by modern sabbatarians.

On the chart, underneath the representation just described, was another, showing the constructor's idea of "your sabbaths" to include all except the weekly and to pertain to the Jewish economy alone, beginning with Moses and ending with the cross of Christ.

To show that the distinction, illustrated by these two pictures, is entirely unauthorized, note the use of the terms themselves. Thus in Leviticus. A foot-note under the article "Sabbath," in Smith's Bible Dictionary, remarks: "It is obvious from the whole scope of the chapter that the words, 'Ye shall keep my sabbaths' (xxvi. 2), related to all these. In the ensuing threat of judgment, in case of neglect or violation of the law, the sabbatical year would seem to be mainly referred to." By what authority, then, does any one affirm that "my sabbaths" refers to the seventh day only?

God had been giving, in the preceding chapters, some detailed instructions to his people in regard to the sabbath of the seventh year, and then of the year of jubilee, and the liberation from servitude which should be granted on that year, closing (though the division by chapters is not important), with the declaration, " I am the Lord." The next chapter opens with the same idea, prohibiting graven images, "for I am the Lord your God," then, "ye shall keep my sabbaths and reverence my sanctuary. I am the Lord. If ye walk in my statutes, and keep my commandments and do them, then I will give you rain in due season," etc. The remainder of the chapter is a continued discourse, setting forth the blessings which God would confer upon them if they kept his commands, and the punishments to follow a contrary course. The closing passage from the thirty-third verse onward, relating to the sabbath to the land which it should enjoy while it lay desolate, because it did not rest while they dwelt upon it, shows that this coming desolation was to be, in part at least, (1) punishment for neglecting this particular (year or land) sabbath. Hence (2) the land sabbath was included among the statutes of the whole discourse referred to in verse third, and consequently (3) in the "my sabbaths" of the second verse; a conclusion in direct contradiction of the supposed distinction. On the other hand, to suppose the "my sabbaths" of the second verse to refer to the seventh day only, shows an interpolation of a new subject and a going back to the matter of the decalogue, which had been passed, while other subjects were being developed in detail. Also the clause, "and reverence my sanctuary," joined directly to the words in question, treats of a subject not mentioned in the decalogue, thus rendering the idea of "my sabbaths" in the passage referring to the seventh day only well nigh impossible. Thus we have already found the same thing styled "her (the land's) sabbaths" (ver. 34), " your sabbaths" (35), and included under the probably more general term "my sabbaths" (2). Where, then, is the fancied distinction?

Upon this absurd theory we are to understand when Jeremiah declares (Lam i. 7) of Jerusalem, that her enemies "did mock at her sabbaths," that, though heathen, they carefully abstained from deriding the seventh day, though its observance was exactly like that of the others and much the more frequent; since "her sabbaths" never includes that day. Quite expert sabbatarians, indeed, these heathen! Well versed in nice distinctions! Or was it because from creation down, being Gentiles, they had themselves kept and reverenced the seventh day?

In the next chapter it is declared of the Lord himself, that " he hath violently taken away his tabernacles . . . the Lord hath caused the solemn feasts and sabbaths to be forgotten in Zion, . . . he hath cast off his altar, he hath abhorred his sanctuary." Thus he styles the tabernacle "his," the altar and the sanctuary "his," though these are not institutions of the decalogue, but belong to that later Mosaic law in which those other sabbaths are found.

When (Isaiah i. 13) the Lord says: "Bring no more vain oblations; incense is an abomination unto me; the new moons and sabbaths, the calling of assemblies I can not away with; it is iniquity even the solemn meeting. Your new moons and your appointed feasts my soul hateth," are we to understand that he is offended at these institutions of his own appointment, or only at the corrupt and unworthy observance of them? Even in the New Testament we are taught that an institution so important as the Lord's Supper may be observed unworthily, and bring condemnation upon the partaker. These were all of divine appointment, but rejected and loathed of God because of their unholy observance. Hence, in such connection, they were wont to be spoken of as "your solemn assemblies," etc.

Ezekiel declares (xliv. 24): "They shall keep my laws and my statutes in all mine assemblies, and they shall hallow my sabbaths." Now it should be observed that the "holy convocations" or assemblies which the Lord here calls "mine," occurred on all the sabbath days. Why then should the phrase "my sabbaths" be limited to any less number? Or, if "my" applies to all, why should "your" include only a part? The laws and statutes referred to above confessedly include all the Mosaic, whether moral or ceremonial. Why, then, limit "my sabbaths" to the decalogue?

The Lord says by Hosea (ii. 11): "I will also cause all her mirth to cease, her feast days, her new moons, and her sabbaths, and all her solemn feasts." Compare this with Lamentations, quoted above, wherein he affirms substantially the same thing, using the pronoun "his" (the Lord's) instead, and discover if you can any ground for the fancied distinction persistently insisted upon because essential to the false theory of the seventh day sabbath preëminence. How simple the explanation that these—"his" because he instituted them, "hers" because she observed them—became an abomination to the Lord by being perverted, and therefore by his providences he caused them to cease altogether.

The twentieth chapter of Ezekiel must not be passed without referring to its convincing testimony upon the limited origin and authority of all sabbath observances. "Wherefore [ver. 10] I caused them to go forth out of the land of Egypt, and brought them into the wilderness. And I gave them my statutes and showed them my judgments, which, if a man do, he shall even live in them. Moreover, also, I gave them my sabbaths, to be a sign between me and them, that they might know that I am the Lord that sanctify them. But the house of Israel rebelled against me in the wilderness; they walked not in my statutes, and they despised my judgments, which, if a man do, he shall even live in them; and my sabbaths they greatly polluted; then I said, I would pour out my fury upon them in the wilderness, to consume them."

Observe the Lord first brought the people out of Egypt. It was after this, after they had crossed the Red Sea, where their former oppressors were overthrown, and they baptized into a new, free life, and had entered the wilderness, that God gave them his statutes, his judgments and his sabbaths. Whether the phrase "my sabbaths" means the seventh day only, which it does not, or includes all the various sabbaths, which it undoubtedly does, in either case one and all of these were given after the crossing of the Red Sea. As a consecutive narrative, it can not be understood otherwise. If their fathers, Abraham, Isaac, Jacob, Joseph, Judah, and the first descendants of these, had observed the seventh day by divine command, then these people already had it, and no matter how much they had degenerated, it had not to be given anew to them. "I gave them my statutes," "I gave them my sabbaths." These statements are exactly alike in form. We are certain the statutes were given at Sinai originally; we must, then, be equally sure that the sabbaths were given, for the first time, according to the narrative in Exodus—the weekly a few days before, and the others after reaching Sinai.

Not only does this chapter fix the time, but it also equally limits the persons to whom they were given. The people, as a nation, who were brought out of the land of Egypt, the Israelites, and they alone, had these statutes and sabbaths imposed upon them. Still further, the sabbaths were given to them as a sign between God and them. We have already seen that it was a sign or pledge of a covenant which God made with them. They were to keep it, and all his statutes, accepting him as their God; he pledged to them the rest, under his own peculiar favor, which such an institution, founded in its similitude on his rest after creation, would properly typify. Of that rest we shall attempt some explanation in the final chapter.

CHAPTER VII.

TYPES.

The types are an interesting study. Types are poetry. Since drawn by the Master's hand, they are masterpieces of poetry — perfect figures, sketching transcendent ideas. Do you admire Shakespeare or Scott, Tennyson or Browning? Have you learned to apprehend and comprehend? Do the chords of a refined sensibility within you vibrate responsive to every echo through the corridors of fancy? Does your "imagination body forth the forms of things unknown?" Does it fly away on wings of its own, to taste the sweets and enjoy the delights that a poet has sketched as existing far off in the land of the ideal? Do its dreams seem real, its representations lifelike and true? Yet, after all, its suggestions are often delusive. Its enchantments captivate without benefit. We invite you, however, to as enticing scenes, with a basis of infallible truth. We summon you to the wedding of the ideal and the real, the union of poetry, painting and art, with the definite certainties of an age to come. Would you examine pictures such as are nowhere else to be found? It is but the paltry paint of common words, of every-day deeds of drudgery, and the usual forms of toil, that represent ideas such as never before it had entered into the heart of man to conceive; such, indeed, as the Divine One alone could bring, and has since brought, into realization—delightful, ecstatic, heavenly, yet human and within finite comprehension and experience. Go with me to the types. Study them. Strange that, in dull forms, in the routine of daily personal and national life, should be represented spiritual exaltations so high!

I think we need a few words on the types just here. To show that they exist; to explain what they are; to draw lines distinctly bounding their province; to cut off the indefinite surmises of many eminent writers in regard to them. An illustration shall start us. We have no faith in baptism as "an outward sign of an inward washing." It is difficult to perceive the use of such a sign to any one. It can not assure the subject himself of the change, nor prove it to others. We do not think such a view satisfactorily explains the purpose and value of the ordinance. Besides, Christ gives a better sign, namely, good works: " By their fruits ye shall know them."

Even so, a type is not a mere symbol of some grace before given or then in possession. We believe that types had a definite purpose for their use. They prefigure important coming events. In combination, they outline a future state. They as accurately describe that to which they refer as can be done in advance. Their language is simple, like that of our Lord's parables. They inculcate their lessons silently. They stand an everlasting monument of the truth they teach. They require no learned linguists to translate them. Theologians can not twist them very far from their correct place. They are beautiful, comforting, and instructive. When apprehended, being more easily understood than much of the prophecies, they confirm the force of the latter as an evidence of the truth of revelation.

Adam Clarke says: " In ancient times almost everything was typical, or representative of things which were to come." This statement is exactly true. The greater pity is it that a commentator so well known, and so universally read, should not have had a clear understanding of this important subject.

Jahn is much less satisfactory, in short, strangely ignorant of the plainest facts. Speaking of a time when among writers prophetical types were too greatly multiplied, and condemning the other extreme which had come to prevail in denying so many of them, he suggests that while "express and insulated types of Christ or the Christian Church might not be known to be such by the Hebrews, yet it is important to inquire as to God's ordering, through Moses, certain events and ceremonies, so that they should be discovered to be typical at the coming of Christ, and in this way facilitate the conversion of the Jews to the Christian system." The characteristics of this statement are weakness and timidity. If this were the place to enter upon the subject, we would pledge ourselves to show very many important results, aside from their effect upon the Jews, and admitting even that they never knew of them at all. Their value, when understood, is incalculable to us at the present day; nay, even when not understood. Familiarity with one system assists in the understanding of another similar one, even though the likeness may not have been recognized, nor any of the items of resemblance pointed out. For instance, the God of Nature being the author of revelation, and there being harmony between them, the ignorant savage has, so far as he has learned nature, prepared himself to understand God's moral government. Thus, then, was and is a typical system beneficial. An *a priori* argument for a system of types is founded upon this principle.

But let us hear at least one more author. Nevin, in his Biblical Antiquities, while treating of the provisions of the Mosaic law in regard to the day of Atonement, remarks: "The whole institution of sacrifice was a shadowy representation of the Redeemer's death, and the whole priestly service had respect to his mediatorial work. They presented, in common cases, however, only some particular features of these mysteries in any single view, without bringing the scattered sketches at any time together, or supplying, even in this separate way, all that were wanting for filling up the general representation. But in the case before us, there was, as it were, an orderly and complete concentration of typical images, into a single, full, and striking exhibition of the whole at once; such as, the more narrowly it is contemplated, can not fail to excite the highest admiration, and to display the more convincingly, in all its coloring, the inimitable touches of a divine pencil."

The article "Tabernacle," in the Bible Dictionary, represents the different materials of which that structure was made, the accurate measurements which gave it definite form, the richness of its elaborate workmanship, all, as having a meaning. "The structure of the tabernacle was obviously determined by a complex and profound symbolism."

In the line of indirect evidence of the existence of prophetical types may be mentioned the symbolism employed in prophecy. Here the Scriptures themselves place the whole matter beyond the reach of controversy. Joseph's dreams wherein his brethren's sheaves all made obeisance to his, and the sun and eleven stars made obeisance to him, were so intelligible that they moved his brethren to his attempted destruction and his sale into Egypt. Pharaoh's, of the seven fat and the seven lean kine, and of the seven full and the seven shriveled ears, are declared to have betokened the approach of seven years of plenty followed by seven years of famine. Nebuchadnezzar's image, as interpreted by Daniel, whereof the different parts were composed of different materials, each representing successive universal kingdoms, the peculiarities of which were indicated by the particular material named, showed, as the prophet told the king, "what must shortly come to pass." Thus taking the idea from these inspired interpretations, Biblical scholars of all ages have, with substantial unanimity, agreed, if not upon events symbolized, at least upon the fact that some were thus set forth, future at the time of the utterance, and of great importance in the divine plan, whether those events were political, religious, or whatever their nature, and that Ezekiel, Daniel, parts of other Old Testament prophets, as well as the final book of the entire Bible, are largely made up of such figurative prophetic imagery.

Even the Saviour's parables taken together are chiefly valuable to us as constituting an extended revelation of the nature of events which had not at the time transpired. Could prophecy, that which is presented in imagery, too, be lost from the Bible, it would be an incalculable injury to the book. We can hardly realize the comparatively barren state in which the glowing pages of Scripture would be left. Now when we think of Christ in his multiplied offices, and Christianity in all its varied phases, of plan, of organization, of development, as set forth in its essential parts, the spiritual by the physical, in an elaborate system of types; and consider how vastly such representations would assist the world to the comprehension of spiritual ideas with which it had been before entirely unacquainted; when we further regard such a system, properly apprehended, as confirming by its coincidences, deductions derived through direct means; and still further, when we regard the beauty which adequate pictorial representation gives to the whole scheme, with the added strength of human faith which the constant discovery of such beautiful divine forethought, cast in the mold of prophecy, and accurately fulfilled before our eyes, and in our very heart's experience, induces; then indeed the typical character of the Old Testament greatly enhances our appreciation of its value.

A portion of the direct Scriptural evidence as to the existence of types may be adduced. Thus:

Hebrews x. 1: "The law having a shadow of good things to come and not the very image of the things."

Heb. ix. 9: "Which was a figure for the time then present."

Heb. ix. 23: "And almost all things are by the law purged with blood, and without shedding of blood is no remission. It was therefore necessary that the patterns of things in the heavens should be purified with these, but the heavenly things themselves with better sacrifices than these."

Heb. ix. 24: "For Christ is not entered into the holy places made with hands, which are the figure of the true; but into heaven itself, now to appear in the presence of God for us."

Heb. viii. 5: "There are priests that offer gifts according to the law; who serve under the example and shadow of heavenly things."

Rom. v. 14: "Nevertheless death reigned from Adam to Moses, even over them that had not sinned after the similitude of Adam's transgression, who is the figure of him that was to come."

Col. ii. 16: "Let no man therefore judge you in meat or in drink, or in respect of a holy day, or of the new moon, or of the Sabbath days, which are a shadow of things to come, but the body is of Christ."

I. Pet. iii. 21: "The like figure whereunto even baptism doth also now save us."

I. Cor. x. 1: "Moreover, brethren, I would not that ye should be ignorant how that all our fathers were under the cloud and all passed through the sea; and were all baptized unto Moses in the cloud and in the sea; and did all eat the same spiritual meat; and did all drink the same spiritual drink; for they drank of that spiritual rock that followed them; and that rock was Christ."

These passages are thus placed in juxtaposition, that they may be compared and analyzed together. Note then that the types indicated therein, include not only the law and the subjects of which it treats, but also men, things, and incidents pertaining to the history preceding. Thus Adam is declared a type of Christ; the ark and the crossing of the Red Sea of baptism; the manna, the miraculous food provided for the Israelites, of the spiritual food, likewise divine, furnished to the Christian; the water miraculously drawn from the rock, of the Christian's spiritual drink; the rock itself, the source of the one, of Christ the source of the other. So in the law, the tabernacle is stated to have been a figure, and the shutting up of its most holy place from all except the high priest once a year under the most rigid requirements, significant that the way into the heavenly places was not yet made manifest. We are told that under the law almost all things were purified with blood, but their antitypes, the heavenly, with better things. Thus are we taught that everything was typical with which blood was employed. Again, the priests themselves served under the example and shadow of heavenly things. Again, even meat, drink (ceremonial), holy days, new moons, and Sabbaths were a shadow of things to come.

Surely where so numerous, varied, and often apparently insignificant items of the Jewish law are referred to as emblematic of things to come in Christ or in his spiritual kingdom, it is not unreasonable to suppose that many, if not all, of those not thus mentioned, are nevertheless thus typical. In treating prophecies no one classes everything as literal which is not said to be figurative. We are left, in the exercise of our own God-given judgment, to determine for ourselves which are figurative and what the import may be. But a small fraction of the whole number of prophetic images are asserted in the divine record to be such. So doubtless it is with the types. We are not then in sympathy with the rule adopted by Ernesti's translator and endorsed by the cautious Jahn, namely: "Just those things should be regarded as types and only those which in the Scriptures are declared to be." Types are not so limited, but a comprehensive department of prophecy, as wide in its range, varied in its character, and valuable in its lessons as the rest. Especially is the whole Mosaic system typical of the Christian, however difficult it may be to trace the details accurately. This fact is manifest throughout the Epistle to the Hebrews, as well as definitely affirmed in the first of the tenth chapter quoted above, "For the law having a shadow of good things to come, and not the very image of the things."

If the law be not "the very image of the things," nor the "good things" themselves which God had in store for the race — if, on the other hand, they are (" to come ") yet future, and the law, not having them, does have their shadow—it is difficult to see how the passage can be understood in any other way than that the whole Mosaic law is a type of blessing to the world in Christ, and this not simply as a unit, but that the parts, the contents of the entire system, are separately thus typical of parts of a new and better scheme. For these were the only good things to come. And what is a shadow but an exact representation in form, not in substance—the very idea expressed by the word "type." If it should be suggested that all this would be beyond doubt had the Bible so stated in plain terms, the answer is ready. So might nearly every other matter of equal importance. It would have been quite easy for inspired writers to say that at a certain exact date Christ should come, and to describe with precision his contemplated mission. Or, instead of using such vague language as this, "The voice of one crying in the wilderness, Prepare ye the way of the Lord, make his paths straight," why not inform the ancient Jew that at a fixed date a man called John the Baptist should arise, and describe his appearance and actions with the same minuteness that history records them. Such is not the style of prophecy, however we may reason about it. Still, it may be safely assumed that the Messiah and his mission are the kernel of all the Old Testament forms, and that in every possible way the testimony as to Christ is imbedded in those forms.

The well-known allusions of the Saviour to the testimony of Moses as to his Messiahship, lead us to look to that source for far greater evidence than is contained in the few obscure prophecies in the Pentateuch. If these were all, it would seem unlikely that the Jews would be able to understand them. And yet our Lord implies a culpable negligence or blindness on their part, in not having learned from

Moses that he was the Christ of God. If we regard the system of types as a prominent feature of that history, and an inwrought typical nature as the predominant characteristic of that legal dispensation, this difficulty is removed. For surely the Jews, of all nations which ever inhabited the globe, have been most familiar with symbolic institutions. So often had things been done with this very idea in view, and distinctly explained to them, that their minds should ever have been alert to discover the hidden lesson of every form, especially when it had no direct practical utility otherwise. When, therefore, the Saviour insists upon the Jews recognizing him in Moses and the law quite as positively as in the later prophets themselves, we are strongly inclined to regard this obligation as resting prominently upon a clear, definite, typical symbolism, with which in all their history they were familiar, and which, when the antitype appeared, himself directing their attention to it and explaining it, they should at once have seen and acknowledged.

However we may reason upon the necessity of revelation being plain, the fact still confronts us that all of it is not easily understood. In the descent of God to man, shown in the incarnation and in redemption, and in the rise of man to God as the beneficent result, there is such a commingling of the divine with the human, that much of mystery is to be expected. This of itself requires every plan of instruction that can be employed, to bring ineffable ideas, as near as may be, within our mental and spiritual grasp. For such a purpose, typical sketches are vastly more effective than verbal descriptions. The delineations of the law, through habitual observance, produce a familiarity in kind and degree, unlike and superior to that effected by words, without the use, too, of that mental energy which many people are loth to exert. The whole line of biblical scholars, from Origen to Lange, with incredible labor, have evolved from doctrinal texts far less information as to the church of Christ than is contained in the simple imagery of the tabernacle. The latter, too, impressed itself upon the common mind, so that every Jew had the image formed within, according to which the church was to be modeled. There was an infinite advance made, but no sudden, abrupt, or violent transition; no contradictions, or reversals; nothing to be unlearned in the introduction of the new order.

That the book of nature was never entirely read by the untutored savage is not alleged in proof that it has defects; nor even that the brightest science has failed to interpret the greatest share of its cabalistic signs. Reason asserts that it is better so; that new mysteries should unfold every hour; that new discoveries should reward each successive investigation; that age after age, and learning superadded to learning, should gradually develop its hidden laws, and utilize its unlimited resources. So with the Bible. Laid up in that great store-house of spiritual wealth are ideas now hidden, but sometime to be revealed. While humble faith finds its food on the surface, profound wisdom dives in vain to reach the bottom.

If objections should then be urged against the existence of types, as insisted upon in these pages, and essential to our treatment of the main subject, on the ground that, if actual, they are often hidden, we may point in confidence to the book of nature, the work of the same Almighty author, whose mysteries seem also to have been intentionally stored away, to the end that in successive ages they may be brought to light. No doubt a kind providence superintends these developments and causes them to be made when necessary. This diversity in kind; these simplicities; these intricacies; this milk for babes; this meat for strong men; these lessons of duty, these unspeakable ecstasies! This book of yesterday, to-day, and forever, adapted to the slave Uncle Tom and to the learned critic, will always have untold treasures for every age. If these types be imperfectly understood to-day, the next generation may be able to appropriate their teachings to greater profit.

As much space as practicable has perhaps been given to the general argument. Three separate examples will be examined by way of illustration; the passover, the priesthood, and the nation itself.

The passover has been aptly styled the Birthday feast of the Jews. It was instituted in Egypt, and that celebration alone, and not the subsequent ones, is considered in this comparison. We shall endeavor to present in this, as in the other examples, not an exhaustive view, but such a one as seems most conclusive in proof of our proposition, as to the existence and object of types.

1. The initial point of Jewish history is placed in fact, (the covenant and promise had been made long before with Abraham) when God, by Moses, undertook to bring the children of Israel out of Egyptian bondage and take them into freedom and to the promised land.

1. The initial point of the Christian Church, in its actual organization, is fixed on the day of Pentecost, (Acts ii.) when God by Christ undertook to bring man out of "the bondage of sin into the glorious liberty of the children of God."

2. Moses the Leader.

2. Christ the Leader.

3. This original passover (not as celebrated after reaching the land of Canaan) entirely preceded the deliverance of the Israelites from bondage.

3. The antitype of the original passover entirely preceded, (1) in a national sense, the organization of the church at the Pentecost above referred to, and (2) in an individual sense, the completed change of the sinner to a Christian.

4. The passover was founded upon the danger to the first born of destruction by the angel of God. This class among both Egyptians and Israelites represented, (as first fruits did afterwards the whole harvest,) the entire people.

4. While in sin and subject to sinners, all are under condemnation to death, and unless provision be made to avert it, will be lost.

5. On the principle of blood for blood, the provision which seemed, in a representative way, adequate to meet the case, was the slaying of the paschal lamb. This was to be without blemish.

5. Paul writes (I. Cor. v. 7,) "Christ our passover (paschal lamb,) is sacrificed for us." A pure and holy sacrifice.

6. The blood of the offering was to be sprinkled upon the lintels and door-posts of every house. Though slain for all, it did not save all without the use in each case as required.

6. Though Christ tasted death for every man (Heb. ii. 9,) his blood must have an individual application, and would not save without subsequent appropriation.

7. The flesh of the sacrifice was to be eaten.

7. Jesus said: "I am the living bread which came down from heaven; if any man eat of this bread, he shall live forever" (John vi. 51).

8. Unleavened bread was required to be eaten.

8. Paul speaks of "the unleavened bread of sincerity and truth" (I. Cor. v. 8). Such is the spirit that must characterize sinners in all their movements towards the church, holiness and heaven.

9. Their loins were to be girt and their sandals on their feet.

9. So also according to Paul "having your loins girt about with truth and your feet shod with the preparation of the gospel of peace" (Eph. vi. 14).

The adaptability of many of the statements made in the second column to the condition of the Christian is evident. Hence the feast itself was to be observed through the existence of the Jewish nationality.

As to the priests, the epistle to the Hebrews informs us that the high priest represented Christ, who entered not, as did those under the law into the most holy place once a year, but once for all into its antitype, heaven, where he made an offering for his people. It is otherwise affirmed of him that he is of a higher order than the Levitical, being represented rather by Melchisedec, to whom the former were shown to be subordinate in that by their representative, Abraham, father of the race, they paid tithes to him of a tenth.

As to the ordinary priests, they represent all Christians. In the religious life the whole body, all Christians, are to perform spiritual priestly functions. They are represented as consecrated priests in Revelations (i. 5) "Unto him that loved us, and washed us from our sins in his own blood, and hath made us kings and priests unto God." So also in the offering of "spiritual sacrifices," (Rom. xii. 1,) and in the complete typical consecration and exercise of priestly duties (Heb. x. 19, etc.)

The regular national Levitical priesthood, with Aaron as first high priest, was not organized, (Ex. xxviii,) though Aaron had been an assistant of Moses from the first, until after the first fruits of the law, the decalogue, were promulgated (Ex. xx.) and the tabernacle, type of the church itself, was constructed (Ex. xxv). So in the antitype at pentecost (Acts ii.), the first fruits of the new law pertaining to the new covenant were given, and in accordance therewith, the church was constituted or first announced as existing, after which the individual members of the Church of Christ entered in that capacity upon the exercise of their legitimate priestly functions. But the completion of the whole legal system followed the establishment of the priesthood; and the completed law, including the decalogue, was placed under their care and by them was preserved and given to the people (Heb. vii. 11). So also, after the initiatory law was announced by Peter at Pentecost, and obedient disciples pressed into the church at Jerusalem, thence onward so long as inspiration continued, other regulations were added governing their conduct, the sum of which is now on record in the Acts and the Epistles. This complete Christian law, while it guides the Christian priesthood, is also in their charge as the means by which to instruct one another and to evangelize the world.

In the constitution of the Hebrew theocracy, which is

the type of the Christian commonwealth, there is a regular order of leading events, which we shall place side by side with their antitypical counterparts, for the purpose of discovering whether there be any such coincidence, apparent and undeniable on its face, as the theory of types asserts. The promise of both was given long before the actual events occurred: To Abraham that he should be the father of a great nation, and to Adam, " The seed of the woman shall bruise the serpent's head."

1. A people — Israelites in Egypt in bondage.

1. A people — the "world lying in wickedness," "sold under sin."

2. Confiding in God they start under his direction to gain freedom. Moses their leader. They celebrate the passover.

2. Confiding in God (faith,) they start (repentance,) acknowledging Christ as their leader (confession). They appropriate the blood of Christ, partake of his life, and by their conduct show themselves prepared for a speedy and effectual departure from sin.

3. Arriving at the Red Sea, the waters miraculously divide, they are "baptized unto Moses in the cloud and in the sea." Their enemies are overthrown. They come forth free. They chant the song of deliverance.

3. They are baptized into Christ, their former enemies are destroyed, and they become free from sin. Having had all done for them, and done all for themselves that was necessary, they are Christians and chant their glad songs of praise.

4. The Sabbath is instituted.

4. Christians enjoy rest from sin.

5. The law is instituted and delivered to them while sojourning about Sinai. Old covenant.

5. Christians study the Scriptures and are taught of God. Knowledge of him increases. His law is written in their hearts. New covenant.

6. They wander in the wilderness for forty years. They are subject to rigid law, often sin, often complain, sometimes rebel, are often severely punished. They are fed on manna from

6. Christians live still in the world, are subject to the law of Christ, often sin, often complain, sometimes rebel, suffer, look forward to future punishment. They are fed on spiritual food, have

heaven, drink water miraculously brought from a rock.

7. At last they pass the divided waters of the Jordan, the ark of the covenant going before.

8. They enter upon their inheritance — the promised land. They rise into a higher nationality; worship in a grand temple, with the most imposing ritual; keep now the national feasts. The types simply expand into a more perfect form. The Sabbath.

spiritual drink from the rock which is Christ.

7. Christians reach at last the Jordan of death, comforted and sustained by the divine presence.

8. They have reached their heavenly home, and now enjoy in its fulness that whereof they had heretofore received but an earnest, complete and perfect rest.

We can not forbear quoting some very just remarks of Fairbairn upon this subject, although his view of the identity of the church appears to differ from our own. "There was required as a proper accompaniment to the intimations of prophecy, the training of preparatory dispensations, that the past history and established experience of the church might run, though on a lower level, yet in the same direction with her future prospects. And what her circumstances in this respect required, the wisdom and foresight of God provided. He so skillfully modeled for her the institutions of worship, and so wisely arranged the dealings of his providence, that there was constantly presented to her view, in the outward and earthly things with which she was conversant, the cardinal truths and principles of the coming dispensation. In every thing she saw and handled, there was something to attemper her spirit to a measure of conformity with the realities of the gospel; so that if she could not be said to live directly under 'the powers of the world to come,' she yet shared their secondary influence, being placed amid the signs and shadows of the true, and conducted through earthly transactions, that bore on them the image of the heavenly."

CHAPTER VIII.

THE LAW ABOLISHED.

There are many moral precepts, contained in the law, that all admit to be in force by divine authority at the present day. And yet few, if any, standard writers, representing what may be called orthodox religious sentiment, will object to the statement that the Jewish law, as such, is abolished. The exact point, therefore, upon which it may be difficult to formulate a statement to which all these writers would subscribe, is, What is the tenure of authority which these precepts have over us? How have they come down to us through the shifting scenes that have displaced Moses, the Levitical priesthood, and a national Israel by the Lord Jesus Christ, and both priesthood and church drawn by individual accessions from every nation under heaven?

There are three leading views. First, that the law which was abolished was really only the ceremonial law, leaving these precepts, including all the ten commandments, unabrogated. Under this view, we still go to the decalogue as a source of authority. Second, these precepts are in their nature eternal and universal. They belonged to all mankind, existed before the law was given on Mt. Sinai, and, though included in the Jewish law, could not, in the nature of the case, be abrogated with it. Third, the whole Mosaic law, including the ten commandments, has been abolished and new authority instituted transcending immeasurably the old law.

Now, if by these three paths men arrive at precisely the same destination, namely, the present obligation of these precepts, surely one ought not to be intolerant of another because his process of reasoning, merely, has been different. In class first, however, there is a divergence, arising from two interpretations of the fourth commandment, the one party holding that it still imposes the obligation of keeping the seventh day, the other that its authority has been transferred to the first day, or Sunday, according to the present general practice among Christians. It is of course incumbent upon the latter, without chance of mistake, to determine whether such a change of day has been made.

The Scripture passages wherein is set forth, as admitted by all, the abolition of the Jewish law, either in whole or in some phase or part, when examined fairly, may be relied upon to reveal the true nature and extent of that abolition. One objection meets us at the outset, standing in the nature of a prejudice, opposed to any candid inquiry, which ought, therefore, to be removed. "It is," say some, "in the nature of the case, clearly impossible to repeal the ten commandments. Could God, consistently with his holy character, abolish the prohibition of murder, or theft, or coveting? He who advocates the view that the entire law, including the ten commandments, is removed, arrays himself against a sound morality, an orthodox view of the holiness of God. His position, consequently, is inadmissible. We will not listen calmly to him, since, in truth, whether professedly or not, he saps the very foundation upon which have been securely built those principles and rules of action which, most of all, good men have ever cherished. We fear he is an enemy in disguise, assailing covertly what he dare not openly oppose."

Jealous care is indeed a good quality in a guardian of the truth, but let the objector be sure, at least, that he does not repel the truth's best friend, for such, assuredly, is he who establishes it upon its just ground. The foundation should be as firm as the superstructure. To rear an edifice of right upon a false basis is, like erecting a beautiful mansion upon shifting sands. If these precepts rest now upon the authority of the decalogue, well and good, if upon a new law we wish to know the fact. Only this do we positively refuse to admit, namely, that they have passed away entirely.

Suppose a society of some kind having among its by-laws this: "No member is permitted to quarrel or fight," should displace it by another; "no member shall seek to injure another either in thought, word, or deed." Has there been any loss in order or morality from the change? Has there not been rather a decided gain? Suppose one teacher has a long list of rules. "No chewing of tobacco, no swearing, no whispering, no defacing of school property." Another says: "My pupils, I am certain you already know what good conduct is; I shall not lay down any rules, but expect only the best order and behavior, such as are always necessary and creditable in a school." The question is not which of these teachers pursues the wiser course? which is the more practical—specific regulations or general precepts? but which is the more comprehensive?

As man advances from the barbarous and selfish state he becomes more subject to general precepts. Gentlemanly courtesies and worthy instincts largely supersede definite prohibitions compelled by brute force. And surely the Christian law ought to be a still farther advance in the same direction. Even the ten commandments, firmly intrenched as they are in the respect of the good of all ages, standing without higher interpretation, are in a majority of the items, better adapted to a heathen than a Christian country. It needs that higher interpretation to interdict an inordinate love of self. Without it covetousness is not idolatry; nor hatred, murder; nor impure desire, adultery. The difficulty of enforcing the higher general precepts is, moreover, inherent in human systems of a lower order. The law of Christ professedly grapples with the sinful instincts of the heart, and, by that method, reaches the infinite diversities of the outward life. This being the nature of the Christian system, not only can no just prejudice adhere to him who believes in the abrogation of the entire Jewish law and the substitution therefor of a more comprehensive and heart-controlling system, but the argument from the nature of the case is in his favor.

It could not be supposed that a few, even many, specific enactments would meet all the requirements that would arise. They can not cover the ground. The "golden rule" could not be expressed in libraries of such codes. Solon, Lycurgus and Moses might combine in the futile attempt. When Jesus declared that upon love to God and love to man "hang all the law and the prophets," when Paul wrote to the Romans, "Love is the fulfilling of the law," they both expressed the genius of the new system, the supplanting of the partial by the complete, of the weak and ineffectual by the all-sufficient, of the preparatory by the ultimate, of the type by the antitype, of the human which grasps man on earth by the divine which lifts him to heaven. In a subsequent chapter the "higher interpretation" of the Mosaic code will receive attention in its proper place. It remains simply to assert that every single precept contained in the decalogue, except the sacred obligation of the seventh day as such, is expressed many times in the New Testament, both specifically and under general forms, with such a variety and wealth of illustration and application, accompanied by heart-searching motives and such stirring exhortations as to win obedience. He who reads will respect. He who reads carefully and often, will learn to love, and obey because he loves.

Note an illustration: "Without faith it is impossible to please him, for he that cometh to God must believe that he is, and that he is a rewarder of them that diligently seek him" (Heb. xi. 6). Now these words are not an intended substitute for the first and second commandments, yet they are not only better adapted to the present age, but they include all that the former contained and much more. One whose mind does not yield ready assent to the point before us, could read with profit, in reference to this thought, the 12th and 13th chapters of Romans, the 6th chapter of First Corinthians, the 5th of Galatians, and the like. While there are very many respects in which the Old Testament is of incalculable value to us, this is equally the fact whether the ten commandments be abolished or not.

Practically the case stands thus: A code of laws is repealed, but every principle of present value comes to us in the new code. Where then is the loss? The State of Indiana calls a convention, forms and adopts a new constitution. What becomes of the old? It is abolished, good and bad features going alike with it. A law is enacted against murder superseding an old one. Does crime acquire any license by the change? Not if the latter law is as stringent as the former. Let us have the faith to believe, that if the sequel shall prove incontestably that the entire Mosaic law as such was repealed, the outcome of the investigation will prove the divine wisdom of the abrogation and that righteousness and holiness will be enhanced thereby.

Among the passages indicating the abolition of the law are those which represent it as in various senses subordinate to the law of Christ. Such are those by which we have proved it, in whole and in various parts, the "shadow of good things to come," that is, typical of the gospel. The types expired by limitation when the glorious antitype appeared. Such also are those which declare the inefficiency of the law. "It was weak through the flesh" (Rom. viii. 3). "It can never make the comers thereunto perfect" (Heb. x. 1). "That no man is justified by the law in the sight of God is evident" (Gal. iii. 11). "If there had been a law which could have given life, verily righteousness should have been by the law" (Gal. iii. 21). "It was added because of transgressions till the seed [Christ] should come" (Gal. iii. 19). "Avoid foolish questions and genealogies and contentions and strivings about the law; for they are unprofitable and vain" (Titus iii. 9).

Such are those which represent it as a barrier between Jew and Gentile. When God made to Abraham the promise of the Christ to spring from his seed (Gal. iii. 16), saying, "in thee and in thy seed shall all the families of the earth be blessed;" when the prophet Isaiah, voicing the sentiment expressed over and over again by his brethren in the holy office, declared of "the mountain of the Lord's house" which should be "established in the top of the mountains," that "all nations should flow unto it," it became necessary for the fulfillment of these promises of universal blessing, through the Jewish people to all peoples, that the restrictions of their peculiar law should be broken down, to the end that all, whether "Jew or Gentile, bond or free, barbarian or Scythian," might be gathered under one government, "the perfect law of liberty," the law of Christ. When circumcision, the national sign, the passover, the Sabbath, all alike having been strictly Jewish rites, were removed, then, without prejudice, could Gentiles of all nations come under the inspiring sentiment of faith, and, by willing obedience to whatever the new law might require of Jew and Gentile alike, into the kingdom of Christ.

Paul writes to the Ephesians (ii. 11, etc.): "Wherefore remember that ye being in time past Gentiles in the flesh, . . . being aliens from the commonwealth of Israel, and strangers from the covenants of promise, . . . but now are made nigh by the blood of Christ. For he is our peace who hath made both one, and hath broken down the middle wall of partition between us, having abolished in his flesh the enmity, even the law of commandments contained in ordinances, for to make in himself of twain one new man, so making peace: And that he might reconcile both unto God in one body by the cross, having slain the enmity thereby. . . . Now therefore ye are no more strangers and foreigners, but fellow citizens with the saints, and of the household of God." In like manner the same apostle (Col. ii. 14) refers to Christ as "Blotting out the handwriting of ordinances that was against us, which was contrary to us, and took it out of the way, nailing it to his cross."

It will be here objected that "ordinances" and ceremonial laws, not moral precepts such as are found in the decalogue, are the barrier between Jew and Gentile which is declared to be removed. The answer is plain. True, moral principles were not the parts obnoxious to other nations, since they are universally recognized as just; hence when the Mosaic code was removed, these find a place in the new law infinitely magnified, multiplied and exalted. True, it was those peculiar observances of the Jewish people called ordinances, against which the Gentile nations had set themselves with an ineradicable prejudice, and which had raised an insuperable barrier between them and the Jews. It is safe to say that for these they had a supreme contempt, and that under them they could never be brought. Hence when Paul, having this difficulty in view, refers to the abolition of the whole law, he names specifically this part or feature of it which was in the way, the part thus, according to very frequent usage in such cases, standing for the whole. "The handwriting of ordinances," "the law of commandments contained in ordinances," are undoubtedly expressions referring to the whole law.

Moreover it is evident that the Sabbath, especially the Sabbath day, was the most obnoxious of all to the Gentiles, unless circumcision be excepted. Does not the life of Christ show that the Jews were more bigoted, exclusive, intolerant and exacting upon the observance of the Sabbath day than anything else. Assuredly then this ordinance went with the rest in the "blotting out," for otherwise no peaceful union could have been effected. We shall hereafter see that with all of these abrogated, still sufficient difficulty remained upon this point to cause the primitive church a vast amount of factious trouble.

Paul declares (Heb. vii. 11) that the people "received the law under the Levitical priesthood" and that "the priesthood being changed, there is made of necessity also a change of the law." When was this change of priesthood? When the Christian church superseded the Jewish economy. The apostle to the Gentiles exhorts the Christians in Galatia (vi. 2) to bear one another's burdens and so fulfill the law of Christ. He sets in opposition to the old law grace (or favor), declaring (Rom. vi. 15) "Ye are not under the law but under grace," and that (Gal. v. 4) "whosoever of you are justified by the law, ye are fallen from grace," and that from this source salvation is derived (Titus ii. 11). "The grace of God that bringeth salvation." He places in opposition to the law, also, faith, setting in sharp contrast the righteousness of each (Rom. x), "that I may win Christ and be found in him, not having mine own righteousness, which is of the law, but that which is through the faith of Christ, the righteousness which is of God by faith" (Phil. iii. 9), averring (Rom. iv. 14) "if they which are of the law be heirs, faith is made void, and the promise of none effect," inquiring of the Galatians (ch. iii.) "received ye the spirit by the works of the law, or the hearing of faith?" saying, (ver. 23) "before faith came we were kept under the law, shut up unto the faith that should afterwards be revealed, wherefore the law was our schoolmaster to bring us unto Christ that we might be justified by faith. But after that faith is come we are no longer under a schoolmaster." He has, also, in numerous passages, presented the gospel as the means of salvation, (Eph. i. 13), declaring (II. Tim i. 10) that Jesus Christ had "brought life and immortality to light through the gospel," and (Rom. i. 16) "I am not ashamed of the gospel of Christ, for it is the power of God unto salvation to every one that believeth."

Thus grace, the divine favor displayed in the gift of redemption, the gospel proclaiming the advent of that gift, and faith the first and chief subjective act of man by which that gift is appropriated, are taken, by the inspired writers in the passages quoted, as each including or representing the whole scheme, and, in this view, held up as superseding the entire Mosaic system, which is comprehensively included under the term law.

It should be noticed that the term law is sometimes used in its general, not limited (Mosaic), sense, in which case the argument is equally conclusive. From the nature of the case the inefficiency of any and all law to secure salvation is evident. For to that end the law must evidently be perfect, and it is certain fallible man would not be able fully to obey a perfect law. Let him then rejoice in the fact that he is not under law, but under grace, and render unceasing thanksgiving to God for the gift of his love. Clearly, the old law which speaketh in this wise, "If a man do he shall even live in them," was "a ministration of death," a "law of sin and death," transgression and its penalty coming in sure and inevitable succession. The Scriptures quoted clearly teach the abrogation of the entire system. (II. Cor. iii. 7–11) "But if the ministration of death, written and engraven in stones, was glorious, so that the children of Israel could not steadfastly behold the face of Moses for the glory of his countenance, . . . how shall not the ministration of the spirit be rather glorious. For if that which was done away was glorious, much more that which remaineth is glorious." No wonder, then, that Paul exhorted the Galatians in reference to this very matter: "Stand fast, therefore, in the liberty wherewith Christ hath made us free, and be not entangled again with the yoke of bondage," and that (iv. 24) he declares, speaking of the two, old and new, covenants, that "the one from the Mt. Sinai gendereth to bondage," and that it "answereth to Jerusalem which now is, and is in bondage with her children," alluding to the Jewish nation clinging to the law instead of accepting Christ.

Christians are declared (Eph. ii. 20, and iii. 5) " to be built upon the foundation of the apostles and prophets, Jesus Christ himself being the chief corner-stone," and that it is " now revealed unto his holy apostles and prophets by the Spirit." The word " now " shows that the apostles and prophets were of Paul's time, hence Christians are built upon the foundation of New and not Old Testament inspired teachers.

Immediately after his baptism, when he was entering upon his active personal ministry, our Saviour was introduced in a formal manner to the world by the Father, when the voice came from heaven : " This is my beloved son in whom I am well pleased." Each of the three synoptic gospels records this event. They also unite in relating another, not so public but equally impressive, (Matt. xvii. 5): Taking Peter, James and John, he goeth up " into a high mountain apart, and was transfigured before them. And his face did shine as the sun, and his raiment was white as the light. And behold there appeared unto them Moses and Elias talking with him, speaking (Luke ix. 31) of the decease which he should accomplish at Jerusalem. . . And behold a bright cloud overshadowed them, and a voice out of the cloud, which said, This is my beloved son in whom I am well pleased, hear ye him." Verse 9 adds, " Jesus charged them, saying, Tell the vision to no man, until the Son of Man is risen again from the dead."

A more instructive and conclusive passage than this could not be imagined. These pages have all along insisted upon the prominence which is given to imagery in conveying truth throughout the Bible. To the Jew, believing, as he did implicitly, the story of the glory of the Lord on Sinai, above the ark of the covenant during the wanderings in the wilderness, in the tabernacle and Solomon's temple, this transfiguration was an emphatic announcement of the divine personality of Christ. Not that he was a prophet, an angel, a " teacher sent from God," but that he was God. The same fact is expressed from heaven in words, " This is my beloved son." Thus two declarations, one symbolic and one verbal, announced his divinity—not only divine, but the representative divine one. His actions should have the divine seal of authority; so also should his words. To make this more emphatic it is declared, "Hear ye him." Hide his words in your hearts. Obey his commands. But some Jew is prepared to respond, Moses is our lawgiver. We know he spoke with God's authority, and his commands we can not forsake. The prophets, too, for centuries spoke to our fathers, whose words are treasured among our sacred oracles. They, too, commanded us to observe Moses' law under promises of wonderful blessings, while with terrible denunciations they condemned all disobedience. We know too well the history of the past, the overthrows, destructions, captivities and calamities that have written in our hearts, with pens of steel and ink of fire, the lesson of obedience.

But, O Jewish objector, observe that on this mountain both Moses and Elijah appear, lawgiver and mighty prophet, that in their presence heaven commands "Hear ye my son." Think you Moses did not understand that he was superseded? Think you Elijah did not, like John the Baptist, feel that "he must increase but I must decrease"? Think you, when they conversed with him of the decease that he must accomplish at Jerusalem that they did not look to that event as the consummation of all the law and the prophecies? Thus by a heavenly symbolism and declaration is announced the near abolition of the old system and the inauguration of the new.

"Quite a private affair," continues the Jewish objector. " I thought you apostles were wont to boast, 'these things were not done in a corner,' and now I am expected to believe in the abrogation of our time-honored system upon the evidence of an event which Peter tells me he saw and was required not to mention till after the resurrection." Well, there were evident reasons (see next chapter) for this injunction of secrecy, and consequently for the private nature of the scene itself. But, O Jew, do you remember that your law itself declares that "at the mouth of two or three witnesses every word shall be established"? (Deut. xix. 15). It is even "written in your law the testimony of two men is true." Now Matthew, Mark and Luke record these events, hence they are true. Peter, James and John repeat them by word of mouth, hence again your law, by its own judgment, is superseded. And that the three disciples were taken upon the mountain to be witnesses, for that definite purpose alone, is further evident because of the phrase " before them " twice written, as if the panoramic view were for their special observation, and the time when they should give their testimony, namely, after the resurrection, definitely appointed.

(Jer. xxxi. 31): " Behold the days come, saith the Lord, that I will make a new covenant with the house of Israel, and with the house of Judah: Not according to the covenant that I made with their fathers, in the day that I took them by the hand to bring them out of the land of Egypt: which my covenant they brake, although I was a husband unto them, saith the Lord: But this shall be the covenant that I will make with the house of Israel: After those days, saith the Lord, I will put my law in their inward parts, and write it in their hearts, and will be their God and they shall be my people. And they shall teach no more every man his neighbor, and every man his brother, saying know the Lord; for they shall all know me, from the least of them unto the greatest of them, saith the Lord: for I will forgive their iniquity, and I will remember their sin no more."

To the superficial observer, even, it would appear that the covenant "made with their fathers in the day when I took them by the hand to bring them out of the land of Egypt," included the entire Mosaic economy, to deliver which to them under the most impressive circumstances, God caused them, at the beginning of their wandering in the wilderness, to linger many days at the base of Mt. Sinai. It would seem further, that the new covenant, being yet future in the time of Jeremiah, as also from the peculiar terms in which it is described, must refer to the gospel of Christ. This also teaches that the old was to be done away when the new should be instituted. These conjectures are confirmed in the eighth chapter of Hebrews, in which the whole is quoted with that unmistakable meaning and the added statement (vs. 13) "In that he saith a new covenant, he hath made the first old. Now that which decayeth and waxeth old is ready to vanish away."

The favorite method of eluding the force of the foregoing arguments is that of the partialists, chiefly those who strive to rescue the Sabbath of the law from the sentence of abrogation. These have little or no ground for making distinctions, but they sedulously cultivate what they think they have. The contributors to Smith's Bible Dictionary are conspicuously candid writers. The following is from the article "Law of Moses:" "That we are not under law; that we are dead to law, redeemed from under law, etc., etc., is not only stated without any limitation or exception, but in many places is made the prominent feature of the contrast between the earlier and later covenants. It is impossible, therefore, to make distinctions, in this respect, between the various parts of the law, or to avoid the conclusion that the formal code, promulgated by Moses and sealed with the prediction of the blessing and the curse, can not, *as a law*, be binding on the Christian." This quotation is made not for its weight of authority, but to disarm any possible prejudice, by showing that our position is the one to which impartial scholars, favoring the present Sunday observance, are necessarily drawn. And it may be added that, standing on this ground, their advocacy of the Christians' day can not be successfully opposed.

It is noted, just above, that an old covenant has been removed and a new covenant has supplied its place. To that old covenant belonged all the Mosaic law, Decalogue engraven on tables of stone, moral precepts or ceremonial enactments, whether uttered by Moses or written by him, the entire mass of commands and observances which the children of Israel recognized as binding upon them as a people. With that old covenant these all passed away. We unhesitatingly deny that there exists any divine authority for dividing the Mosaic law into parts. We believe that (Luke xvi. 16) "the law and the prophets were until John; since that time the kingdom of God is preached, and every man presseth into it," meaning thereby that at the preaching of John the Harbinger, for the first time, men, all men, were to look forward. They were in sight of another shore, and for it they were to strike out boldly. By this the law does not "fail," but reaches its supreme and perfect accomplishment.

Immediately succeeding the passage from Hebrews, quoted above, which declares the first covenant old and ready to vanish away, it is said (ix. 1) that it "had ordinances of divine service and a worldly sanctuary." These, then, passed away with it. Further, when (Col. ii. 14) Christ is spoken of as "blotting out the handwriting of ordinances," etc., "nailing it to his cross," it is universally admitted that the ceremonial part of the law is abolished. It remains, then, to examine the supposition that the decalogue is not thus removed.

That the decalogue was done away with the old covenant is evident from the fact that it is itself called the covenant. The "Ark of the Covenant" which was ever borne before the children of Israel, and which found its place in the innermost recess of tabernacle and temple, contained only the tables of stone with the decalogue written upon them. In the ninth chapter of Deuteronomy these are thrice called the "tables of the covenant." They were broken by Moses, on descending from the mount, when the iniquity of the children of Israel in the making of the golden calf was discovered. Therefore, at the beginning of the tenth chapter, the Lord directs Moses to hew out two other tables of stone like the first, upon which God declares, "I will write the words that were in the first tables which thou brakest, and thou shalt put them in the ark." And Moses states (ver. 4), "He wrote on the tables according to the first writing, the ten commandments, which the Lord spake unto you in the mount, out of the midst of the fire, in the day of the assembly; and the Lord gave them to me. And I turned myself and came down from the mount, and put the tables in the ark which I had made, and there they be as the Lord commanded me." Here, then, the ten commandments constitute the "covenant," the tables upon which they were written the "tables of the covenant," and the ark in which the tables were placed the "ark of the covenant." Again we read (Ex. xxxiv. 27): "And the Lord said unto Moses, Write thou these words: for after the tenor of these words I have made a covenant with thee and with Israel. And he was there with the Lord forty days and forty nights; he did neither eat bread nor drink water. And he wrote upon the tables the words of the covenant, the ten commandments."

From the instruction of this scripture, we are prepared to say that the old covenant, in its most limited sense, was simply the ten commandments. Whatever, therefore, passed away with it they did. In a broader sense, all the institutions and forms that gathered around the decalogue were included in the covenant, and they, too, went with the rest. But we pray you do not lose sight of the primacy, so to speak, of the decalogue in this matter, and the certainty that it was abrogated, if anything was. Nor should one forget that the essential element of a divine covenant is law. God gives no law without promises in some way connected with it, either expressed or understood. When man undertakes to keep that law in view of the consequent blessing, a divine covenant is in full operation. We can conceive of no possible meaning in the statement that God removes an old and establishes a new covenant, except by removing the old law, the nucleus and essential part of it, and at the same time so modifying the accompanying promises as to adapt them to the change. The law is the chief matter. To get that obeyed is the thing sought. From creation, so far as sacred history teaches, he has repeatedly changed his laws as he desired man to do this or that or to refrain from any thing.

The opposing view, advocated especially by a sermon now at hand, labors to prove that the covenant was the mere agreement between the parties, God and Israel, independent of the law to be obeyed. Webster's definitions are quoted and grossly falsified to that end. They are (1), "A mutual consent or agreement of two or more persons;" (2) "A writing containing the terms of agreement or contract." What Webster means is this: The first is simply the agreement itself, no matter how made; the second is a document. The latter, of course, expresses precisely what the former is. A says to B, "I will build you a certain kind of a house for a thousand dollars." B says to A, "Agreed." All the laws of God and man require A to build the house and B to pay the thousand dollars. It is a covenant, complete in every respect. A week after, C goes to a depository of public records, and finds on file, or transcribed in the books of the office, a paper written upon "Covenant"; he reads it, and then knows just exactly what A and B understood a week before, namely, that A agreed to build a certain kind of a house for B, and in return B promised to pay A a thousand dollars. Those are Webster's definitions, the one the agreement proper, the other the document setting it (the very same agreement) forth.

Apply these definitions to the old covenant of God with Israel. God having announced a certain law with promises, Israel consents to keep it, in view of the blessings to follow. This is according to the first definition. The tables of stone upon which this is written constitute the documentary covenant, according to the second definition. Now these were both somewhat incomplete in comparison with such a transaction between man and man. The authority of one party overawed in a measure the volition of the other; and in proportion as it does, so does a divine covenant approximate simply divine law. Into what depository of records, into the hands of what third party should this documentary covenant between God and man be placed? Are there courts competent to enforce the observance of God's part of it? In short, what is needed to secure the safety of a divine covenant? Why, chiefly, if not alone, the preservation of the law; for if men keep that, all else is secure. We assert, then, in consonance with plainest reason, that the decalogue was the essential part of the formal covenant, while the entire Mosaic law and the prophets constituted the essential part of the full covenant of God with Israel.

The attempt to find the covenant entirely outside of the law, in order that the latter may remain when the former shall, according to the prophecy, be changed, is a failure, since that which the sermon would retain in the great reconstruction, is so conspicuously the chief part as to have occupied the place of the whole and given the name to it. Again we say, the law must have been done away in the change of covenant, if anything was.

The sermon alluded to distinctly admits that the decalogue is called the covenant, and yet proceeds to explain that it can not be the covenant. Its definition thus becomes a mere abstraction. It was the concrete and not the abstract that was abolished. Exodus xxiv. 8 will not sustain the abstract view. "Behold the blood of the covenant, which the Lord hath made with you *concerning all these words.*" Why so far from "all these words" "concerning" which the covenant was made, being out of it, they constituted the essential part of it. The house is white. This is a sentence "concerning the house." Leave that out and what have you? Even so with the covenant concerning the law, when the law is left out. There may be enough of it left for sabbatarian sophistry, but that is all.

Our sermon assumes that the Israelites weakened and finally destroyed the covenant, because Paul and Jeremiah assert that they broke it. Hence, it reasons, the covenant could not have been the commandments, for it would be impossible to destroy the law of God. Well, if to break the covenant destroyed it, why might not breaking the law destroy that, also? for the Scriptures and the sermon assert that they did break the law. The fact is, they destroyed neither covenant nor law. They broke both. They broke the covenant by breaking the law. And yet we are told the law was no part of it. A covenant is a singular thing, in that you can break, weaken and destroy it by breaking that which is no part of it. If the sermonizer will show how it was possible to break the covenant without breaking the law, we will admit that the latter was no part of the former.

Now suppose the formalities attending the ratification of the covenant were extensive. Are they, therefore, the covenant itself? Do they not rather serve to mark and emphasize the importance of the law, which, if kept, the covenant is fulfilled; if broken, the covenant is broken also; if changed, the covenant is changed; if abolished, the covenant is abolished also? Suppose the formalities attending the future giving of the law, as foretold by Jeremiah, were different. Suppose teaching, spiritual influence, inspiration, were to be the methods adopted instead of writing upon tables of stone. Would that constitute a new covenant, or a new giving of the old? Suppose you do tear up a contract and place the same conditions in a new blank form. Is it a new transaction? No. A new transaction consists of new conditions. A new sentence must have a different subject or predicate. A new covenant must have new law or new promises; and to suit one to the other, probably both; especially a new law, if that has been considered so prominent a part of the whole as to have itself alone taken the name of the whole.

Mr. Andrews, our Sabbatarian sermonizer, triumphantly catechises in reference to Jeremiah's prophecy, "I will put my law in their inward parts." "Is it, I will abolish my law? No. Is it, I will change my law? No. Is it, I will supersede my law by a better code? No." Similarly we imagine C, when A informs him that he has made a new contract with B, inquires "Is it that you have changed the plan of your house? Is it that you are not going to build a house? Is it that you are to build a better house?" To which A stupidly responds: "No. I have destroyed the old written contract and we are simply going to remember the conditions."

The sermon distinguishes between the Levitical law and the ten commandments as the Scriptures do not. With them the law of God is the law of God, to be obeyed alike by all who are under it, obedience bringing God's blessing and violation his punishment. It was only when modern system builders divided it to suit their schemes that we hear of the Levitical law, ceremonial law, moral law, etc. When it is declared (Heb. vii. 11,) that the people received the law under the Levitical priesthood, the sermon asserts that the ten commandments could not have been included for they were not received under that priesthood. On the contrary, we assert that they were. Aaron, the head of that priesthood, was associated with Moses from the start. For the entire fifteen hundred years, until indeed the Epistle to the Hebrews was written, none but the Levitical priesthood existed both over and under the law. They were indeed established and regulated according to its provisions, but they were also placed in charge of it as its custodians through whom the people always received a knowledge of it. In short they were by the law recognized as its ministers, and either the people received the whole law of Moses under the Levitical priesthood or under none. They were given together in close succession. It does not matter which was established first. When the people entered upon the full observance of the law, they had the Levitical priests to guide them. When the priests entered upon their duties, they had the law to direct them. The ark of the covenant containing the ten commandments was ever in charge of the children of Levi. The Scriptures say "the law;" Mr. Andrews informs us that it is the Levitical law. Again the Scriptures say "the law" and Mr. Andrews informs us it is the ten commandments. By this judicious assignment of different significations to the same term, a system is sustained. But is it true?

In a previous part of this book, some reasons were given evidently determining the assignment of certain specific commands to the honorable position in the decalogue rather than in the body of the Mosaic code. We now give a reason why the decalogue itself was separated from the rest at all, announced from Sinai, included in the ceremony of the ratification of the covenant, and preserved in the archives on tables of stone. The tendency to formalities in the Mosaic economy is one of its most striking features. That types were imbedded in these forms has already been shown. But more than that, God intended that they should be impressive. Solemnity, glory, power, majesty, appeared on every hand. The least defect was an insuperable barrier, the smallest item of immense importance. The dedication of the sanctuary, ordaining and sanctifying of the priesthood, the solemnities of the great national feasts, are familiar instances. Hence when God gave a law, he surrounded it with the most impressive circumstances. A formal covenant was entered into with the people binding them to keep it. Hence the thunderings and lightnings and quakings of Sinai, the terrible voice and the awful presence, hence the blood of the covenant, the sprinkling thereof, the divine announcement through Moses, the unanimous response of the people. Now the law was the objective, the essential part of it all. God would impress upon these people, steeped in the degradations of heathenism, surrounded by idolatrous nations, himself, his right, his authority, and would do this in giving his law.

The Mosaic law in all its parts was very extensive and could not be given to them in one lesson, nor legibly engraven on one set of tables of stone. God therefore took a sample. That sample, a representative of the whole, he used in the marked formalities of the mountain, in the impressive pledges of the covenant, had it carried by consecrated carriers in the inmost recesses of the sacred ark, placed in symbolic situation under the protecting ægis of the cherubim, under the shadow of the mercy-seat. Thus it was laid away as a memorial and kept throughout all their generations. Its weight must have been considerable. Four Levites usually carried the ark. At one time (II. Sam. vi. 6) it was drawn on a cart by oxen. The addition of the number of tables necessary to contain the whole law would have been unwieldy and burdensome. Nor was it necessary, since the idea of representing the whole by a part was perfectly familiar to the Israelites. Two tables and ten commandments were amply sufficient to represent the whole Mosaic code, in the establishment of the covenant at Sinai, and for preservation in the ark of the covenant afterwards. Instances in which the Israelitish mind must have recognized this thought, might be mentioned indefinitely. Thus, " the twelve pillars according to the twelve tribes" (Ex. xxiv. 4), the twelve stones of the breast-plate, the twelve cakes or loaves of the tabernacle, the twelve stones of Jordan. But, omitting all others, we may consider the first fruits as especially adapted to our purpose. From the time that the first born were saved from the destroying angel in Egypt, these were ever after, whether of man or beast, except as redeemed, devoted to the Lord. " The first sheaf of barley, on the second day of the passover, and the first loaves of Pentecost were presented to God as offerings for the whole nation. But besides these, offerings of all sorts of first fruits were required to be made, year after year, by individuals; first fruits of the harvest and the vintage, from the threshing floor, the wine press, the oil press, and the honey crowned hive, from the first baked bread of the new crop also, and from the fleecy treasures gathered at every time of shearing from the flock " (Nevins' Bib. Ant. p. 335). These have always been understood as a formal recognition that the whole crop of which they were the first fruits came from the Lord and belonged to him. On the great national feasts particularly, they were offered in expression of joy and thanksgiving to God for all which he, as Lord of the harvest, had bestowed.

Now that the ten commandments were a sort of representative first fruits, selected to represent the whole law, and in other respects not necessarily superior to the rest, is evident from the following facts: 1. They were first given. 2. They are separated from the rest in certain formal ways, but are not otherwise distinguished from the general Mosaic code. 3. The first formal laws of the new covenant (antitype of the decalogue), which were given with the special seal and witness of the Holy Spirit (Acts ii.) were given when "pentecost was fully come," the very day of first fruits. 4. The decalogue contains duties to God, duties to man, national, individual, ceremonial, moral, with and without promise, regulations of outward conduct and of the feelings of the hearts of the relations of man to man, of man to his servant, of man to his brute property. When these representative first fruits of the law are gathered and surrounded with proper ceremonies to add dignity and solemnity to the giving, and impress the supreme authority of the giver; the whole code like a bountiful harvest ripening in rich profusion comes at once thereafter ready to guide the children of Israel in its early struggles in national life.

Any separation of the ten commandments from the rest

of the law, except in the manner and for the purpose just indicated, runs counter to many passages of Scripture, and must be ultimately abandoned as purely fanciful. That the use of the decalogue alone in the formality of the covenant about Sinai, was purely representative, is evident from the fact that the pledges of that covenant were often renewed and when so, included the entire law. (See Dent. xxix., xxx., xxxi.; Josh. xxiv). Thus God commanded the Book of the Law, which included all, to be placed beside " the ark of the covenant of the Lord your God, that it may be there for a witness against thee." And afterwards when under Asa, Josiah, Hezekiah, Ezra and Nehemiah, a renewal of the covenant was made in more or less emphatic and complete form, no distinction of parts or kind was made, but the whole law included in the pledge of obedience.

So then it is impossible to separate the ten commandments from the former covenant, and thereby rescue it from the sentence of waxing old and vanishing away. It is equally impossible to distinguish it from the rest of the law and thus save it from the general abrogation, or to take it from out the guardianship of the children of Levi, and consequently from the condemnation of Paul (Heb. vii. 12). " For the priesthood being changed there is made of necessity also a change of the law."

That the entire law, and not the decalogue alone, is included in the actual (not formal) covenant, is evident from the fact that the promises in it are complete. It is logically absurd to suppose that God would pledge the fulfillment of his promises on the condition of obedience to only a part of his law. For then, what would be the inducement to obey the rest? A Jew might say: " God has made very valuable pledges, I will keep the decalogue, then I shall receive the blessings, for it is ' concerning the ten commandments' only that the covenant is made." The daily sacrifice, the service of the sanctuary, and numerous commands, ten times as many as the decalogue itself contains, may be thus despised, and yet according to this theory, God is absolutely bound by his own covenant, to bestow the blessings promised. The Israelite knew better than this. He well understood that all the formalities were representative, and that in agreeing to the covenant he was pledging himself to obey every command of God, in or out of the decalogue, whether they had yet been given or not. He was aware that to transgress wilfully any part of God's law, would incur the divine displeasure, and that he would be cut off from among the people.

Even so under the new covenant, Christians are required to keep the entire law of Christ. Persistently, wilfully, and knowingly transgressing any part of the law of life in Christ Jesus, they forfeit the promised salvation. Provision is indeed made for their restoration, but the disobedience is not overlooked.

In this argument we have but caught the inspiration of Paul. He declares (Gal. v. 3): "For I testify again to every man that is circumcised, that he is a debtor to do the whole law." Similarly, James (ii. 10) makes an offender in one point guilty of all. Thus are the several parts of each code, Jewish and Christian, linked together.

We have reason to believe that an immense pressure, rather political in its nature, was brought to bear, at that time, upon Gentile Christians, for the purpose of subordinating the whole church to Jewish control. Had it succeeded, there might have come down, even to us, a Jewish instead of a Roman papacy. The point at issue was, at first and chiefly, circumcision. But there can be no doubt that any other item of the law, sought to be imposed in like manner, would have met the same stern resistance from the apostle. They were given to understand (these disciples who had not from birth been placed under Jewish national control), that they were not now to take a single step in that direction by conformity to one demand of that religion. Not that the law was anything. A principle was at stake. The least enactment of Moses, obeyed as coming from him, would have been the humiliation of Christ before an inferior lawgiver. As the Lord God had been a jealous God, and suffered not the idolatry of the ancients, so the Christian commonwealth was jealous of its supremacy.

With this principle involved, submission to one Mosaic enactment was a deliberate surrender to an authority no longer divinely sanctioned, and, therefore, the act was sinful. Hence, he who made this choice, was, by Paul, turned over to the tender mercies of that law which required perfect compliance with every precept, and which became to him a law of sin and death because perfect obedience was impossible. A precept thus obeyed became, therefore, a representative of the whole, just as James counted one sin a transgression of the whole. In this way was it and is it impossible to select any part of the old code, whether that engraven on the tables of the testimony, or that denied such representative preëminence, yielding obedience thereto, without invoking upon your head the authority of all.

The representative character of the ten commandments is instructive in another regard. We are often referred to the fact that these are more frequently quoted than any others, and that, too, by the writers of the New Covenant itself. This is done on the principle that it is easier to reach a people through its officials, or any aggregate whole through its representative part. For this purpose was it that these commandments were selected at first; and the intrinsic excellence of the precepts, as well as other points of merit, fully justifies the choice. Even when James would illustrate to Jewish Christians the principle above stated, he employs as examples some of the familiar ten, such only, however, as from the very quality were well known to belong to the new code, and might well be made representative in it, as they had formerly been in the old. They greatly err, however, who presume, from such use, to take the Sabbath, or any ordinance, rite, or supposed moral law or observance, not assuredly fully involved in the genius of the new institution, to be, by those examples, taught as Christian law.

There are some who think the moral precepts of the ten commandments not repealed, because, by their nature, the principles of right involved in them must always be in force. The distinction we would draw now becomes plain. When the Mosaic law is repealed, these go with the rest. A man freed from Moses is not, however, released from the obligations of human nature. He takes those obligations with him from one system to another, and any rightful government will be, of necessity, in accordance with them. But when the authority of Mahomet, Pope Leo, or Joe Smith, forbids me to steal, I repudiate that authority. I fall back upon natural right, justice, and the common weal. If I am a Christian, I say, Away with Moses, and the decalogue, with the entire code that follows in its train, and give me Christ. Whatever of Moses' law, in or out of the decalogue, is involved in the Christian, directly declared or unmistakably inferred, has been repealed and yet is in force—repealed with Moses, but divinely sanctioned in Christ. Whatever has not thus been renewed is gone forever. Has the Sabbath thus been brought across the chasm of abrogation, assigned to another day of the week, or has a different institution been established?

CHAPTER IX.

THE LORD OF THE SABBATH.

The relation of Christ to the whole Mosaic law—more definitely, to the Sabbath—in both person and teachings, will now be considered. The keynote to the first is conveyed in his own words (Matt. v. 17) : "Think not that I am come to destroy the law, or the prophets : I am not come to destroy, but to fulfill." The very fact that both the law and the prophets are mentioned forbids the limited application of either. We can not suppose only the decalogue intended, but all the law and the prophets find their fulfillment in the mission of Christ. Not in Christ's advent alone, for his coming did not fulfill; but he came for that purpose—that, at least, was to be one end or result of his mission. So, likewise, it would be equally incorrect to assume any other definite time, as, for instance, his baptism, or even his crucifixion, as a point of time at which was suddenly accomplished what is indicated by the word "fulfill."

A correct idea of the term itself will doubtless lead to right conclusions as to the time and manner of its action. The word "destroy" may assist us rightly to interpret the other, for they are evidently designed to be set in opposition to each other, or nearly so. To destroy the law would be to remove it by both violating it and breaking down its just authority. To disobey merely is not to destroy; to obey is not entirely to fulfill. To take it away contrary to its design, rendering it ineffective when it should control, would be to destroy. To obey it if he were really a subject of it, to modify or remove it if he were the Lord of it, and if at the same time it had accomplished its purpose, might be to fulfill. Prophecy is fulfilled when that occurs which has been foretold.

Jesus, on one occasion (Luke iv.), in Nazareth, on the Sabbath day, stood up in the synagogue to read. He found the passage in Isaiah: "The spirit of the Lord is upon me, because he hath anointed me to preach the gospel to the poor; he hath sent me to heal the broken hearted, to preach deliverance to the captives, and recovery of sight to the blind, to set at liberty them that are bruised, to preach the acceptable year of the Lord." And he began to say unto them: "This day is this scripture fulfilled in your ears." Now all his personal ministry in teaching the people was in fulfillment of that prophecy, and when his career on earth had been concluded, then the words of Isaiah had no further future significance. A promise, like a prophecy, refers to the future, and when one does, at the right time and in the proper way, exactly what he agreed, his promise is fulfilled.

So with the law. We have already found Paul speaking of it as "having a shadow of good things to come." That is, the law was not a mere rigid rule of life; it promised certain good things. Now when Jesus said that he came to fulfill the law, he must have meant in part that he came to bring the things promised by the law. This he doubtless did by giving, in his teachings, his example, his benefactions, his atonement, his church, what the law had typically set forth. In himself, his surroundings, and his gifts to men, were realized what the law had promised.

To fulfill means, primarily, as both the English and its translated equivalent imply, to fill up. We have seen how he did this with his promises. He did the same in obeying it. When the Saviour says fulfill, we are not permitted to understand the word in any limited or incomplete sense. A man may promise me a cord of wood and claim to have fulfilled his promise, though the quality be poor and the measure scant. Not so with Christ. If he fulfilled the law, he did it perfectly in every part, and in every intimation or idea which it contained.

He fulfilled it by obeying it. Never had it been so obeyed before. Not according to outward form but to inward intent. Not with mental reservations, in a stingy, half-hearted way, but willingly, generously, gladly, completely. He was its perfect expositor. At twelve years of age, sitting with the doctors in the temple, he was a prodigy. But in mature manhood, with " the spirit of the Lord upon him," he "spake as one having authority," as one who had himself given it, perfectly understood it, and might modify, abrogate it, or place upon it a higher interpretation.

He fulfilled it by bringing such a state of affairs that it became no longer necessary. If it were adapted to the former state of the nation, it would naturally be inadequate to its changed condition. If he were the son of God and came on a mission of infinite importance to man, when that was accomplished something different from the former law might be required. Thus common sense would suggest. When, then, he fulfilled, he might also abolish. To illustrate: A man lives to be nearly one hundred years of age and dies, not of disease, but his natural powers have matured, declined, and finally worn out and faded away. He sinks into the grave as into a bed of rest. His earthly life is fulfilled though he dies.

So with the Mosaic law. It had a part in the great work which God was doing for man. We speak advisedly—*for man*. The whole Jewish economy was to direct that nation only. But that system, yea, the nation itself, was part of a great scheme that looked toward the whole human race. In the course of time the partial must give place to the universal. The Jewish race, as a favored people, was superseded by an eclectic nationality, freely open to the citizenship of all the tribes of earth. At the same time a law equally expansive came in room of the old. The Son of Man came to gather such a people, to introduce such a law.

He came neither to destroy the nation nor the law. Had it conducted as a nation should, it would doubtless have had a local habitation and a name to-day; as much so as has France or England. Had a large part of its people accepted the Messiah, it would have been a Christian nation, and hence, while it remained so, indestructible. The old laws of circumcision and the like, sacrifices and great feast days, they would doubtless as Christian people soon have seen the propriety of abrogating from their national procedure, as Christ abolished them from his church. With these modifications, their government, supported by the strong national spirit which pervaded them, and the high moral and enlightened sentiments which Christianity ever inspires, might have become one of the best on earth.

But let it be remembered that with this Christ did not come to interfere. He came to obey the Jewish as he did the Roman law. But he came also to distinguish from both the principles which should guide his spiritual kingdom, his holy church. "Render, therefore, unto Cæsar the things which are Cæsar's; and unto God the things that are God's" (Matt. xxii. 21) was his oracle upon this point. Understand, then, that Christ did not come to abolish the Jewish law for the Jewish nation. He came to accomplish it, to perfect, to fulfill, to supersede it, having in view not the Jews at all as a nation alone, but his church, and upon that "peculiar people" no Jewish law as such was ever imposed. The personal guidance of the Jewish nation was now abandoned. They were left to compete with the nations of earth as they saw fit. Their law as preparatory to the Christian was finished, fulfilled and consequently ended. Henceforth they went their own way. As a rule for Christians the law would not be serviceable. It expired by limitation. In religious government it had become old and "was ready to vanish away," as Paul expresses it. It gave way to a "new" and "better covenant," "founded on better promises" and given by the hands of a "perfect mediator."

The relation of Christ to the law and to the Sabbath will be still better investigated when we bear in mind the time when this work was accomplished. From John the Baptist—"the voice of one crying in the wilderness, prepare ye the way of the Lord,"—to Peter's preaching in the household of Cornelius, prophecies in relation to him were fulfilling. He was fulfilling the law during all his lifework, but there came a time when it was done. Then the Christian church was in existence under its own peculiar law, the perfect law of liberty, and in the manner which had been indicated by Jeremiah's prophecy. The national law of the Jews, however, was such as they chose to keep it, and on general principles any Christian who was a Jewish subject would obey it as he would any other worldly code.

The fulfillment of the law, as purely a religious guide, may rightly be considered as to the life of Christ, his crucifixion, his resurrection, or the first preaching of his gospel by his accredited ambassadors, the apostles, beginning on the day of Pentecost. Jesus himself on the mount of transfiguration, as we found in the last chapter, charged his three chosen witnesses not to give their testimony as to that event until "after his resurrection," simply because the Christian kingdom was not to be inaugurated till then. To have proclaimed the supersedure of Moses at the time would have left so momentous a doctrine dependent upon Christ alone, when as yet nothing, aside from his direct declarations, manifested him to be more than "a teacher sent from God," whose claims to absolute divinity were not yet recognized, and not understood even by his personal disciples. To have announced the same after his crucifixion would have been to involve it in the shadows of the grave, ever till that hour the annihilator of man's hopes and pretenses alike. But to "tell no man till after his resurrection" clothed it with divine authority, with another sanction from heaven even more wonderful than that under which it first came.

But how hear him, instead of Moses and Elias, after he, as well as they, had departed from the scene of earthly labors? Hear him by his words which still lingered in their memories, by the chosen disciples who had been his witnesses, by the Spirit which brought all things to their remembrance, by that same spirit of truth that guided the apostles and prophets of the new dispensation. Upon the foundation of these, Christians were builded. It was not till after the resurrection that the new doctrine in its completed form could or would supersede the old.

From these suggestions the reader will gather a correct idea of the word "fulfill" as used by the Saviour in reference to the law of Moses. It is a deceptive course of reasoning that applies that word in all cases alike. Like its part, and in some cases near equivalent, fill, it varies somewhat with the object. A bucket may be filled with water, not so a basket. The mind requires thought, the stomach food. The argument, therefore, that fulfilling love, or fulfilling righteousness, does not put an end to those inestimable qualities, fails to prove that fulfilling the law does not so accomplish it as to render it ever after inoperative and void, for the purpose (a religious rule) under contemplation. A note is a written promise, and, when paid, that promise is both fulfilled and forever annulled.

The so-called "higher interpretation" placed upon the law, by the Saviour, in the same connection, in the fifth chapter of Matthew, can now be readily understood. The people soon discovered, too, that he was not following the beaten path of the scribes, but that his utterances were original and radical, in short that he spoke "as one having authority." The evident showing from the Sermon on the Mount, a name significant in view of the Sinaitic origin of the law which he commented on, is that the old law, as it stood, was entirely insufficient to meet the wants of the coming order of things. The kingdom of heaven would require a new law. He himself was the authorized lawgiver. "I say unto you" was a phraseology which no living man would have dared to employ in announcing radical changes of the law of Moses. It was equally as strong in its self-assertion as Jehovah himself had used upon the former mount.

And the people heard his words, "astonished at his doctrine," but not incensed. For in all these sayings there was no destruction, no violation proposed of any of the statutes of Moses. They were new principles indeed, such as constituted an earnest of those to be promulgated in the coming "kingdom of heaven," which John the Baptist had declared to be at hand. But they were principles superior to the former, and mostly including them as the greater includes the less. If upon the law of love had hung all the law and the prophets, surely in announcing the fact he would not offend any Jew devoted to the less comprehensive system. Nor would he, even to declare for his spiritual kingdom, love to enemies, instead of the rigid *lex talionis* which Moses' law exacted. It was after all somewhat similar to the high morality which their later prophets urged; and so long as he said nothing derogatory to Moses, and proposed no destruction of his system, they listened patiently. No doubt, too, his precepts commended themselves to their minds as pure and beneficent; possibly they thought them too utopian to be harmful.

The man partial in all the Mosaic code to the ten commandments, should not neglect to observe that our Lord here did not make distinction between the "tables of the covenant" and "the book of the covenant," in selecting the items for his comment, but each alike passed under review, some of each were amended. As well have said at once that "thou shalt not kill" is not sufficient, as to append to it, "but I say unto you that whosoever is angry with his brother without a cause shall be in danger of the judgment," and upon the whole, it may be gathered from the Sermon on the Mount, that Christ in setting forth the general nature of his coming kingdom, foreshadowed the supersedure of the imperfect Mosaic law, even in the matter of what are called moral principles, by another infinitely higher and more comprehensive.

If, finally, it should be objected, that Jesus declares: "Whosoever therefore shall break one of the least of these commandments, and shall teach men so, he shall be called the least in the kingdom of heaven," we reply: Certainly, this must be so while they are in force. And he said: "Verily I say unto you, till heaven and earth pass, one jot or one tittle shall in no wise pass from the law, till all be fulfilled." And he also said of the same law: "I came not to destroy but to fulfill." There was a fulfillment then which he was to accomplish, after which the law might pass away, at least as an authoritative rule for the guidance of those in the kingdom of heaven. Previous to that event, while he might announce the coming better day and more perfect law, he would neither break the latter himself nor justify its being broken by others.

More than all this, he came of the stock of Abraham, of the tribe of Judah, of the royal line, with genealogy recorded. He came "a minister of the circumcision for the truth of God to confirm the promises made unto the fathers" (Rom. xv. 8). That is, a minister of the Jews to confirm by its fulfillment the promise made to Abraham, Isaac and Jacob, "in thee and thy seed [Christ] shall all the families of the earth be blessed." Christ coming in this way, of the Jews to the Jews, was himself, in his own person, to fulfill the law, and the promises, and the covenants. His ministry was to be with the Jews. The new covenant was to be made with them. After it originated with this people, the Gentiles were to be added indeed, but the gospel of the risen Lord was to be preached first at Jerusalem. So it was done, and not till some time after, with the household of Cornelius, were the Gentiles introduced as fellow heirs; while Paul, the last apostle, was sent to them.

The Jewish origin and mission of Jesus, rendered it proper that he should respect the Jewish national law, just as, had he been a Roman, he would have respected the Roman law. The thirteenth chapter of Romans clearly teaches the duty of Christians to obey the powers that be, as exercising just authority over their subjects. Christ therefore was found a loyal citizen of his government, as it then was, whether in those matters which the Jews still directed, or those which the Roman sovereignty arrogated to itself. As he could not be led to refuse tribute money to Cæsar, so he was never found disregarding the law of his own people, even though, in so far as pertained to his mission, it was vanishing away. In this way he decided the case of the woman taken in adultery (John viii.), applying the law in all strictness, and yet so as to give significant intimation of the character of that rule which should obtain in the new order of things soon to appear.

In this way he answered the young man (Mark x. 17; Luke xviii. 18,) that came running to him saying, "Good Master, what shall I do to inherit eternal life?" He did not direct him to the requirements which were made of men after the crucifixion, and after the resurrection (see Acts), when the grand facts which Paul, in the fifteenth chapter of First Corinthians, declares to constitute the gospel had occurred, and the people were called upon to believe and obey it; but rather the law under which he then lived, namely the law of Moses. But of this law he selected such items, at least in the mention, as should of necessity be incorporated in the new. Neither Sabbath day nor any ceremonial observance was mentioned; and when the young man said that he had kept these from his youth, the Lord made one other demand which neither Moses nor any other earthly lawgiver had before required. "Go and sell all that thou hast, and give to the poor, and come and follow me."

In this instance Jesus took a case as it came before him,

under the Jewish law, and treated it accordingly, but both in the selection of the items and in this added requirement, there was, as before, a clear looking forward to the principles of the approaching kingdom, especially to that entire renunciation of self, which was to be exacted of all his disciples.

When (Luke x. 25) the lawyer stood up to put him to the test, asking him, " What shall I do to inherit eternal life?" the divine teacher again quotes a passage from the law (Deut. vi. 5; Lev. xix. 18) : " Thou shalt love the Lord thy God with all thy heart, and with all thy soul, and with all thy strength, and with all thy mind, and thy neighbor as thyself." These words are not taken from the decalogue. And yet the Saviour said, " This do and thou shalt live." Here then we have eternal life offered on the condition of doing what the ten commandments do not contain, and what the most expansive interpretation can not derive from them. He says again (Matt. xxii. 38–40), that this is not only " the great commandment of the law," but that upon it " hang all the law and the prophets." After all, " the great commandment " then is not in the decalogue; another portion of the Mosaic code is awarded the preëminence. As in the other cases so here, he recognizes the binding obligation of the law as such, but yet it must be noted that he especially, as before, refers to those principles which are to obtain in the coming kingdom.

If one should say, for instance, that all the commands of the father depend upon filial love, we should understand that in case the son were directed to bring an armful of wood, he would be led to obey from the regard which he entertained for his father. And so of any other order that might be given him. Thus a law may depend upon a principle, and without the latter the former would become a dead letter. The law and the prophets then hung upon the precept which Christ quoted, in the sense that the latter produced obedience to the former, not that the two were equivalent. The less "hangs" upon the greater, is contained in it, may be abolished without loss while that remains, may be substituted by other subordinate enactments, which in like manner will depend upon, be contained in, and derive their authority from the same great fundamental principle. The "law and the prophets" while they were the rule of life, were justly said to "hang" upon, just as any divine, or even any just human rule may at any time be said to depend upon this precept.

System builders, therefore, who have the ten commandments as separate from and superior to the rest of the Mosaic institution, who regard them as imposed upon man at creation and authoritative over all while time exists, who estimate them as the rule by which sin is marked and defined in this life, thereby fail to incorporate in their legal scheme what Christ declared the first and greatest of all. They should see in this teaching two things; first, that he does not persistently seek the ten commandments as the supreme authority on every subject; and second, that as between them and other parts of the law they are here decidedly in the back-ground.

A careful analysis of the four evangelists will reveal that Christ, when he declares himself "Lord of the Sabbath" (Mark ii. 28), does so in keeping with his claim over the entire law. His attitude toward it is well illustrated, at the very commencement of his active official career. Matthew records (iii. 13), "Then cometh Jesus from Galilee to Jordan unto John to be baptized of him. But John forbade him, saying, I have need to be baptized of thee, and comest thou to me? And Jesus answering, said unto him, suffer it to be so now ; for thus it becometh us to fulfillall righteousness." Here the narrative clearly teaches both the superiority of Jesus to the act to which he was submitting, and the recognition of that fact by John the administrator. Submission, and a manifestation of authority over that to which he submitted, ever with him went hand in hand. How else could the combination of human and divine find expression? As man, he would submit to baptism, to keep the sabbath, and obey the law; as God, appeared his superiority over baptism, lordship of the sabbath, and authoritative declaration as to the law.

The several instances in which Jesus came in contact with the narrow bigotry of the Jews, to which such treatment of the sabbath would naturally lead him, are few in number and easily understood. The disciples in passing through the fields of grain on a certain Sabbath day—seventh day of the week (Matt. xii. 1; Mark ii. 23; Luke vi. 1),—began to pluck the heads, and rub out and eat the grain. At which the Pharisees charged upon them acts unlawful upon that day. But Jesus assumed their defense, quoting the former action of David and the priests in the temple, showing thereby that merely satisfying the claims of hunger was not a sin under the precedent adduced, nor by his own high views of the sabbath itself, however their traditions might regard it. Mercy rather than sacrifice, expressed in his interpretation the real essence of all law. Had they understood the beneficent object of the institution itself, they would not have condemned the guiltless. "The priests in the temple under the law, profane the sabbath and are blameless." If this sabbath law were made subordinate to temple service, how much rather should it yield to the Son of Man. "But I say unto you, that in this place is one greater than the temple. For the Son of Man is Lord even of the sabbath day."

Immediately succeeding this narrative in the synoptic gospels, is another, a case of healing. "A man with a withered hand" was found in the synagogue which Jesus entered. And they asked him, for the purpose of finding pretext of accusation against him: "Is it lawful to heal on the Sabbath days?" His reply, as Matthew records it, expresses his authority, looks forward to the same divine benevolence which, in his teaching, overshadows and fulfills all law, and at the same time, in a characteristic way, involves his would-be accusers in such a dilemma, that, if his conduct was censurable theirs would be equally so with much less excuse. " What man among you having one sheep falling into a pit on the Sabbath day, will not lay hold on it and lift it out? How much, then, is a man better than a sheep? Wherefore it is lawful to do well on the Sabbath days." John records (ch. ix.) the giving of sight on the Sabbath day to one that was born blind. This seems to have awakened great interest from its striking character. The Pharisees, after inquiring very carefully into the case, as all heresy hunters and officious meddlers in other peoples' conduct, especially respecting religious non-essentials, are sure to do, declared: " This man is not of God because he keepeth not the Sabbath day." Others replied, forcibly enough, it would seem: " How can a man that is a sinner do such miracles?" Afterward, in conversation with the man, they seem to have discovered a way out of even that difficulty. " Give God the praise; we know that this man is a sinner." John does not state that, in this instance, Jesus attempted to instruct or confute the Pharisees in their stubborn reasonings. His mission to the physically and the spiritually blind, he, however, sharply characterized. " For judgment I am come into this world, that they which see not might see, and that they which see might be made blind."

In yet another case of healing, the Saviour incurred the enmity of the superzealous Pharisees (John v). An infirmity involving total helplessness for thirty-eight years, healed under the formula, " Rise, take up thy bed and walk," aroused not the astonishment, gratitude and veneration which any just view of it should inspire, but provoked, instead, the snappish, contemptible comment: " It is the Sabbath day ; it is not lawful for thee to carry thy bed." Towards Jesus himself it directed their active hatred. " Therefore did the Jews persecute Jesus, and sought to slay him, because he had done these things on the Sabbath day." But Jesus answered them, "My father worketh hitherto, and I work." "Therefore the Jews sought the more to kill him, because he not only had broken the Sabbath, but said also that God was his father, making himself equal with God." When the divine power was revealed in Jesus, the Mosaic law, at least as held by the Jews at that time, was placed in abeyance to that high philanthropy in which Christ presented his divine nature to the world.

In the course of their subsequent complaints Jesus gave his opposers another personal argument. (vii. 22): "Ye on the Sabbath day circumcise a man. If a man on the Sabbath day receive circumcision, that the law of Moses should not be broken, are ye angry at me, because I have made a man every whit whole on the Sabbath day?" Luke records (xiii. 11) another instance whereat the Jews were incensed as before, and for a similar reason. "There are," said the ruler of the synagogue, "six days in which men ought to work; in them, therefore, come and be healed, and not on the Sabbath day." "The Lord then answered him and said, Thou hypocrite, doth not each one of you, on the Sabbath, loose his ox or his ass from the stall and lead him away to watering? And ought not this woman, being a daughter of Abraham, whom Satan hath bound, lo these eighteen years, to be loosed from this bond on the Sabbath day?"

The case mentioned at the beginning of the fourteenth chapter of Luke, is similar, in all essential points, to the first case of healing in this enumeration. The question of the lawfulness of the act was answered by the same pertinent example of an ox falling into a pit.

But few other references to the Sabbath remain to be noted. We are informed (Mark vi. 2; Luke iv. 16; xiii. 10) that his custom was to go into the synagogue on the Sabbath day, to read and teach. This fact involved nothing more than that, on this particular day, he had a better opportunity, owing to their presence, and their custom of devoting the time to the study of the Scriptures, to teach the people upon the subjects involved in his own mission. Yet if any one chooses to suppose that Christ thereby meant to observe the day according to the law, this book will not object, since such keeping of the Sabbath is in entire harmony with the theory herein presented. So also is the fact that Christ's body lay in the tomb over the Sabbath, rising in the morning of the first day of the week. The anxiety of the Jews to get the bodies from the cross before the Sabbath began (John xix. 31), the resting of the women on the Sabbath day, "according to the commandment" (Luke xxiii. 56), after they had prepared spices and ointment for embalming his body, simply illustrate the uniform care with which the day was then observed.

In the twenty-fourth chapter of Matthew, the Saviour, predicting the destruction of Jerusalem, gives an intimation as to when his disciples in Judea should flee to the mountains to escape the impending destruction. For there should be " great tribulation, such as was not since the beginning of the world to this time, no, nor ever shall be." The haste of this flight should be extreme, and whatever should oppose it would be a grievous calamity. " Woe unto them that are with child, and to them that give suck in those days. But pray ye (ver. 20) that your flight be not in the winter, neither on the Sabbath day." One who has ever belonged to a defeated and retreating army, can realize, somewhat, the hardships which the unfavorable circumstances, mentioned in this Scripture, would necessarily imply to the unfortunate Christians of that time. A soldier, ill-fed and scantily clothed, who might have escaped, during our civil war, from an extreme southern or northern prison, striving to make his way to his own people, could imagine the condition depicted in one of these causes. A poor slave mother striving to gain the land of freedom, might experience something of another. But what are we to understand of the clause relating to the Sabbath? Does it imply hardship like the preceding, or is some different idea to be gathered from it on account of its sacred character?

So old and well-known a comment as that by Adam Clarke says: "That you may not raise the indignation of the Jews by traveling on that day, and so suffer that death out of the city, which you had endeavored to escape from within. Besides, on the Sabbath days, the Jews not only kept within doors, but the gates of all the cities and towns in every place were kept shut and barred, so that, if their flight should be on a Sabbath, they could not expect admission into any place of security in the land." A people who could not tolerate the healing, by a simple word, on the Sabbath day, of a life-time cripple, but would seek on account of it to slay the benefactor, were not likely to assist or forgive, but would surely put to death the hated Christian who should add, by his flight, to the sin of Sabbath-breaking the cowardice of fleeing from the enemy, when, too, they believed that the God of their fathers would rescue them from the threatened overthrow.

On the other hand, those tenacious believers in the validity of a seventh day Sabbath, who claim that this passage is an evidence of the recognition, by our Lord, of the authority of the fourth command at the time when this prediction was uttered, or at the later date, that of the flight itself, have mistaken the reason that lies at its foundation. The connection of the clause most strikingly indicates the hardship resulting, and not the sin, as the fundamental thought. Indeed, it would be quite inconsistent, if Christ, who distinctly practiced and commended healing and charitable deeds on the Sabbath, and even, by implication, approved the rescue of animals from a pit, should teach his disciples to pray that they might not on that day be called upon to escape the most terrible calamity the earth should ever see, because of the great sin which it would involve. According to the Saviour's teaching the flight would not be a sin at all. "If you had known what this means: 'I will have mercy and not sacrifice,' you would not have condemned the guiltless," were his words upon this subject. "Wherefore it is lawful to do well on the Sabbath day." "The Sabbath was made for man and not man for the Sabbath."

That the clause in question recognizes, prophetically, the fact that the Jews, at the destruction of Jerusalem, would still be rejecters of the Messiah, and consequently the same bigoted Sabbath observers and persecutors that they were when the prediction was uttered, can not be doubted. And so history has since revealed them.

Let the reader distinctly understand that this chapter would teach that the Jews as a nation were, during all this time and subsequently, Sabbath keepers; that Christ himself was, as a man, submissive to the Jewish law in regard to this day as in other things, as also were his disciples; that Christ, however, as Lord of the Sabbath day, was free to place, *by his own authority*, higher interpretations upon it, such as the law itself did not contain, nor the people recognize, as he had been, in the Sermon on the Mount, to add to the body of the law itself. All these perfect teachings which he placed, by his comments, upon the existing state of affairs, were designed to be glimpses of that which should more fully appear in the spiritual life of the Christian church.

Now, strange to say, Christ gave no instruction in regard to a correct observance of the Sabbath, as he must certainly have done, in view of its abuses, had it been an institution which he proposed to perpetuate for his followers. The prophets, as we have seen in chapter vi. of this work, were frequently warning the people upon this matter; but the Son of man, greater than all, self-styled "Lord of the Sabbath," gives no intimation whatever that he would have rebuked any man, had he been an open violator of the day. This course is entirely inconsistent with the view of its perpetual sacredness by his authority.

Regarding the relation of the sabbath to the Almighty, some have entertained the idea that God rested in some such sense as man rests; that is, as if it were in a measure a necessity of his being, from weariness which had ensued to him because of his labors. And indeed in one place (Ex. xxxi. 17), the Scriptures speak of his refreshment in rest. But this is more than likely one of those numerous instances in the most ancient Scriptures, in which language spoken of God is accommodated to man; that is, expressed as though God were such a being as man, in reference to the particular matter considered. Thus God is said to repent when a change in his course of action is such as would imply repentance had he been a man. That God rested and was refreshed means only that having finished creation he ceased creating. When man finishes an important work he is weary, needs rest, and by taking it, is refreshed. In an accommodated sense the same form of expression seems to be employed in reference to God.

Those err, therefore, who suppose that, first of all, God had a rest day of his own, that that day was twenty-four hours in length, and the seventh in the week, that proposing himself to keep that one day of the week for his own necessity, convenience, or comfort, it was and is, in that sense, the Sabbath of the Lord our God. Jesus sets that idea aside in the clearest terms, asserting (Mark ii. 27) that "the Sabbath was made for man and not man for the Sabbath." The institution was represented as belonging to God because he had established it. Moreover it was ever thereafter a day devoted to God; first, in the complete abstinence from man's labor in his own interest; and second, in the increased activity in whatever tended to the worship of God.

It was called the Sabbath of the Lord, but it was made for man, having as the passage clearly teaches, its beginning and end in the necessities or advantage of man. God had instituted it and surrounded it with all the sanctions of his authority that he might thereby benefit man. It had been adjusted to man, suited to his wants, not first instituted for God's own use and then man fitted to it. It was, then second in importance to man; not superior to him. It was not a trap to catch him in sin, a law to oppress him, an irksome observance without compensating benefit. Before this book is fully read, it is hoped it will appear as both temporally and spiritually a gift to man of greatest value.

First of all, man needed a day of rest. The Sabbath was made for him. Second, and more important, he needed to worship the supreme being for his own benefit; such worship was appointed on that day. Third, and chief, he needed faith in the future glorious freedom from the weariness and sin which were inseparable from his lot in this life, that he might be hopeful and zealous in striving to gain it. The Sabbath was in itself a pledge for that future which it foreshadowed, and its most fitting typical representative, besides by the training which it induced preparing him for the future enjoyment.

If the Sabbath was made for, it was subordinate to man; and when the Lord of the Sabbath saw fit, in the interest of man, to change or remove it, this might be done. In what sense could it be more appropriately said to be made for man, than in the view which this book presents, of a great type, a pictorial promise or prophecy of a coming rest to him, enthralled in sin, driven from his patrimony, deprived of his birthright, condemned by sin to weariness, woe and death, but promised through him in whom types had their fulfillment, the Lord of the Sabbath, a restoration to the lost estate, an eternal rest.

A singular attempt has been made to extract from this language, a meaning entirely foreign to it, by reference to the Greek original. We say singular, because it is not usual to find such complete ignorance thrust into the domain of criticism. No conscientious scholar of any creed would for one moment indorse it. It is a well-known fact, as laid down by all Greek grammars, that general terms, like abstract ones, take the article. In some cases the same occurs in English though not usually. Thus we say "the horse is a noble animal," using the article "the" before the noun "horse," "the horse" being in this use not definite but general. The horse species, not one particular horse, is, in the sentence quoted, meant to be designated as noble. When therefore the Greek text says: "The Sabbath was made for (the) man, and not (the) man for the Sabbath," it is correctly rendered general, by omitting the article, as in the English text, and should be so understood. No definite man is or could be referred to.

It is violence to the Greek language, therefore, either ignorant or dishonest, which makes "man" definite in the passage, because the Greek has the article, and selects Adam as the particular man referred to, because thus the Sabbath can be traced, as it can not be otherwise, to the head of the race for its origin, from whom, there might then be some show of reason to suppose, it had descended to all his posterity. How would it do to interpret the sentence: "the horse is a noble animal," as referring to the Adam horse, the first of the species. Unfortunately for these crafty interpreters, another class, having in view the similar passage, "It is appointed unto (the) man once to die and after that the judgment," have been wont to assume that "the" man in this instance was the Jewish high priest, who ceased officially, after which the judgment, or destruction of Jerusalem came. Both of these are special pleaders, tricksters, who contradict each other, while by a show of learning each strives to deceive the ignorant.

Finally, it should be noted that because the general form "man" is used, we are not required to understand that the Sabbath was instituted at the beginning and to be in force while the race should continue, or that even while in force its authority extended to every nation and individual. Rather the humanity of those to whom it did belong was in contemplation. The human being (in this case the Jew) was of vastly greater value than the institution which was given him for observance. And yet as a representative people, the Jews did stand for the race, and the Sabbath which they alone were required to keep, was in many important senses, to contribute to the welfare of all, because part of the preparatory work of that great scheme of redemption which had for its object the blessing of all.

CHAPTER X.

THE COUNCIL AT JERUSALEM.

The introduction of Christianity, in both its collective and individual aspects, was in many particulars gradual. It were not difficult to conceive of Christ's appearance in an abrupt way, with immediate commands for men to hear and obey him, followed by punishments sudden and terrible as ever came upon the transgressor at the giving of the Mosaic law. But such was not to be the manner of the new dispensation. There had been a development both in the times and the people. Besides, under the old covenant certain prejudices had been established, and such deeply seated habits of thought, and fixed peculiarities growing out of the old system, had fastened upon the Jews, that, retaining those and at the same time misapprehending and rejecting Christ, they became, towards the new development of the divine plan, the most stubborn opposers that the world has ever seen. This fatal misconception and blind bigotry, however unreasonable, it was not God's purpose ruthlessly to override. Leniency, persuasion, instruction, mercy, were to characterize the new order. To seek and save that which was lost, to lament over Jerusalem even when foretelling its inevitable downfall, to leave unquenched the smoking flax, to address harsh words to dishonest hypocrites alone, while befriending poor sinners, social outcasts, the helpless, and those upon whom had been imposed, by tyrannical leaders, "burdens grievous to be borne," to call the weary and heavy laden to rest in him; these are representative items of the work of Jesus.

These methods result from, as they indicate, the gradual, unarbitrary, voluntary introduction of Christianity. It has already been discovered that Christ did not deal summarily with the old Mosaic law. He gave evidence sufficient that a greater than the law, a qualified amender or abrogator of it, had appeared, "the Lord of the Sabbath," but he also conformed to its harmless rules, as the custom and law of his people, while he foreshadowed for his future spiritual kingdom a far higher rule of life. The necessity of repeating this thought with emphasis arises from the fact that two mistakes are common: one party persistently exaggerates his human obedience, another exalts his divine authority. Forget not, if you would rightly understand, that the dual nature of Christ, " God manifest in the flesh," reveals itself, as in everything else so in his relation to the Jewish law. Only the partisan of some unsound religious theory will studiously ignore either.

A second caution lies at the threshold of the present special subject of investigation. It refers to the difference between divine and human governments. The Mosaic law had included both. It was a theocracy. Its religious, ritualistic, ceremonial system, was embraced in and enforced by its national code. The new system, however, was to deal with men as individuals chiefly. The requirements as an organized church were to be very limited, and not to interfere with the outside relations which its individual members might sustain to associations and the governments of earth. A Christian might be a Jew, a Roman, a Russian or an American, and be in either case subject to his own national government. Unless you rightly understand Christ's relation as a Jew to both the Jewish and the Roman law, and can distinguish, in his teaching and example, what is properly attributable merely to that submission, from what, on the other hand, is the law of his own spiritual kingdom, you are again liable to become the prey of seductive false theories instead of resting on the rock of truth.

Once more it is necessary to observe that, as with the prophecies, so with the types that were fulfilled in Christ, they related to different parts of his mission. Thus sacrifice found its fulfillment on the cross, so far as the slaying of the victim was concerned. But there was, after that, much to do under the old type. Use was to be made of the blood, a formal offering of it by the high priest for the whole people. Now Christ, after suffering as the lamb of God, the slain victim, was himself to officiate also as priest. Hence, in part, his resurrection from the dead. Hence, also, after rising, mindful of the ceremonial cleanness required of the priest under the law, while in the performance of his official functions, he could firmly say to his loving friends, " Touch me not, for I have not yet ascended to my father, but go to my brethren and say unto them, I ascend unto my father and your father, and to my God and your God." And yet after a certain space he was prepared to address skeptical Thomas, " Reach hither thy finger and behold my hands; and reach hither thy hand and thrust it into my side; and be not faithless, but believing " (John xx.) When he had made this offering once for all, as in Hebrews it is declared (ix. 12,) " by his own blood he entered in once into the holy place, having obtained eternal redemption." And again (ver. 14) " How much more shall the blood of Christ, who through the eternal spirit, offered himself without spot to God, purge your conscience from *dead works*, [obedience to the law,] to serve the living God."

After this completion of the sacrificial offering of himself, it was necessary that by showing himself to his disciples again, they should be made competent witnesses of his resurrection; also that he should instruct them somewhat as to their future mission as his apostles, and that he should give them his formal charge or commission. All this he did, and with the command to tarry at Jerusalem until they should be endued with power from on high, he left them for the heavenly courts, while they waited "for the promise of the Spirit" which they were to receive after not many days.

Luke, the historian of the Acts of the Apostles (ch. ii.) records the wonders of that divine manifestation. As Christ had died on the passover, as the fulfillment of the paschal lamb in time and fact, so the Spirit was vouchsafed, wondrous in form, compass and effect, on the day of Pentecost, the first fruits of a rich harvest of spiritual life. Here was a striking fulfillment of the prophecy of Joel. Here too was fulfilled in part the declaration of the prophet Jeremiah as to the new covenant: "I will put my law in their inward parts and write it in their hearts." The law which these apostles had "in their inward parts," judging by their speech, was not the ten commandments. But such as it was, it was the law of the new covenant. God placed it there, and God gave them power and courage to reveal it to the people. This instruction of men in the new law of God has been in progress ever since, first by inspired teachers, then by the written word and uninspired teachers of that word. During the successive generations of men of every clime and every nation whither that law and the promises of God have been carried, its proclamation has been met on the part of some by both faith and willing obedience, and thus in these God's terms have been supplemented by man's acceptance, and the new covenant has been completed.

Now when God's formal presentation through the chosen apostles, after the completed sacrificial offering of Christ, of his terms under the new covenant, with the miraculous signs of the divine presence, on that memorable Pentecost, had been made, there was no longer any use whatever for the old law, since a new one had actually come to take its place. It would be well for the reader as a third caution to keep this fact in mind. For, although in one sense the obligation of the old law relaxed at John the Baptist (Luke xvi. 16), and the general principles of the new were announced by the Saviour, and although in another sense the old was abolished by the grand central fact of the gospel—the cross of Christ (Col. ii. 14), and although, if one during all this time had been acquainted with the "mysteries of the kingdom of heaven," he would probably not have recognized the authority of the old; yet it was not until that final occasion on the Pentecost after the resurrection, that any man fully comprehended or fully received the will of God according to the new order. Allowance may rightly be made for this fact.

We are ready for the real issue to be canvassed in this chapter, when the suggestion has been penned, that forbearance, instead of immediate compulsion or punishment, is to characterize the new administration. We are not to expect the same kind of treatment for clinging to the old or neglect to conform to the new, as a like negligence or disobedience would have incurred in primitive Jewish times.

In these initial activities of the new covenant, it may be well to observe that it was made "with the house of Israel and the house of Judah," according to the strict terms of Jeremiah's prophecy. Nor was it any limited affair. For there were "sojourning at Jerusalem," at that particular national occasion, "devout men" (that is, men earnest in the Jewish law) "out of every nation under heaven" (Acts ii. 5). With these, or with such of them as came together on the occasion and heard Peter "with the eleven" speaking in their several tongues, and hearing were convinced by his wonderful utterances, propounded the serious inquiry "What shall we do?" and willingly obeyed his answering command, the covenant was fully completed; and so, as a pledge of their acceptance, they received God's promises and the seal of his favor—the gift of the Holy Spirit.

Let us inquire somewhat, from our knowledge of human nature, illumined by such intimations as the record has left us. What, henceforth, was the conduct of those new converts towards the old law from which they were released? Would they, could they abandon it in a day? Imagine for a moment a people that during an existence of fifteen hundred years had been the most peculiarly separate of any on earth. They had abundant reason not only to acknowledge no superior, but even no equal. Under the special favor and care of God, subject to a law received from him, unlike any other in the world, with a history most remarkable, a treasured lineage, a magnificent temple in a world-renowned capital, the Jews were national egotists, regarding themselves the chosen of God and others as unworthy of respect as heathen dogs, with this individuality so impressed upon them during the period from Moses to Christ, that they have retained it to the present day though dispersed among all the nations of earth. Prophecy had prepared them for a still grander future under the expected Messiah. They were to be the nation of nations. The coming Son of David was to be greater than the former, and in all and through all, the law was to continue forever. Add to what they already thought themselves to be, what they expected to become, and it would seem that no persuasions could lead them to embrace anything which might seem opposed to this future glory.

Such bright hopes, such self-satisfaction, such confidence in their present righteousness, was not likely to surrender to the revolutionary demands of Christ. Judaism is not the only system which from being dependent on the divine dictation for its law and ritual grew to depend on itself. Doubtless many church organizations of our day have taken the bits fully into their own mouths, and with louder and louder claims to be Christian, and Christian too above their neighbors, of special grace, of infallible truth, of immaculate holiness, are really so far from God by this time, that neither Moses and the ancient prophets, nor Christ and the later ones, nor the clearest teachings of the divine volume when brought to their understanding would swerve them from their course. At least, thus it was with the Jews.

The old law had been abused in the name of God till all of God was well nigh out of it, and only stubborn man remained. The lusts, the ambition, the selfishness of man were its remaining inspiring principle. Indeed, it is not hard to detect the fact that Moses and Abraham were in the mouths of leading Jews with greater relish than God. True, of him they could prate with sanctity, they could divide hairs to carry out the divine law with absolute precision, when they were miles away from it. The love of God had given place to tenacity of forms, and not such merely as God had required, for that were well, but such as they had themselves devised. They had reached just that point when religion leaves the man, but he begins to think he has a monopoly of it, when the demon spirit of persecution enters him. Prayers and a ritual, self-righteousness, religious partisanship, the meanest bigotry, are the cloaks under which Satan comes into the hearts of men, when God has been forced out.

Did not Christ detect this spirit at once in the Jews? Did not subsequent events prove the accuracy of his estimate of them? Did they for once accept his gracious loving words, in themselves a manifestation of his divine nature? Did they acknowledge his works though they were clearly wrought in God? Did they not hate his goodness, and choose a murderer in preference to the sinless one? Was there ever a moment when, had they been able under cover of forms of piety and with the approval of the people, they would not have put him to death?

This spirit followed them afterwards, during the origin and early growth of the church. They persecuted the apostles and the early Christians. They incited Jewish Christians themselves against Gentile converts. The very fewest among men ever change as completely even in conversion as did Saul of Tarsus. A man is liable to show some of his former prejudices and evil habits after he enters the church. Many men do not seem to improve much in their lives when, to be consistent with their profession, they ought. We are even led to doubt whether they have been really converted or not, they behave so badly afterwards. And then some in a little time grow cold. They seem to forget their first love. They make good fault-finding, good persecuting Christians, (if the term be allowed,) but we feel not the ever out-flowing sympathies and affections of the renewed heart.

If human nature be true to itself in all nations many such there were among the Jewish converts. A show of religion they had, and yet but little that could be called "pure and undefiled." Paul calls them "false brethren" (Gal. ii. 4). In their own estimation they were quite competent to direct the religious conduct of their brethren. Were the Jews unlike others in this respect? We are inclined to think that the mischief-makers between Jew and Gentile Christians, these sowers of discord in the primitive churches, opposers of the apostle to the Gentiles, had a large element of wickedness in them. We can not feel sufficiently charitable, at the expense of our better judgment, to attribute their course to mistaken zeal. If they were not, some of them, hypocritical pretenders, urged on by other Jews, exercising the same crafty treachery which they displayed in watching the ways of Jesus, desiring to put him to death while they claimed to take great interest in him; then these Judaizers were belied by their conduct.

Why should they not have been content to accept the teachings of the apostles? Had they been good men, honest and humble, gladly would they have trusted Paul, Peter or James. Well they knew that these men spoke by inspiration of the Holy Spirit, and that not one selfish motive controlled them in their official conduct. Had these appointed and qualified guides received no revelation on the subject of the authority of the law upon Christians, then might each have been at liberty to judge and act for himself, while common fairness would accord the same privilege to others.

We do not suppose they had much knowledge. The church was in its beginning. Long years and centuries of experience might have given some ground for assumed confidence that they were right; or a completed canon of Scripture might have formed the basis of conclusions to which they would cling with tenacity. But they had heard only the oral instructions of apostles and religious teachers, most of whom had doubtless been chiefly occupied in rehearsing to the unbelieving multitudes, such primary facts of the gospel as would convince, and persuade, and make disciples. Whence then, if not from the depths of wicked hearts, arose the disposition to force their national rites, not only upon Christians of their own people, but upon Gentiles also, as necessary terms of salvation. "And certain men which came down from Judea, taught the brethren and said, except ye be circumcised after the manner of Moses, ye can not be saved" (Acts xv. 1). "When, therefore, Paul and Barnabas had no small dissension and disputation with them," they were, it seems, not yet quieted, and most thorough means had to be employed, to decide the question at issue once for all, that it might be no more a disturbing element among the brethren. Before following this question up to the great court of arbitrament, the council at Jerusalem, one or two preliminary suggestions should be made.

1. As to what extent such matters were already fully decided by revelation to the apostles and through them to the church. If the apostles were known to speak at all times, and on all subjects, by the Holy Spirit, then these teachers, differing from Paul, were uninspired, and it is difficult to understand how they could have made so strong a stand against him. It is more reasonable, probably, in view of many intimations in the epistles and history, which bear upon the point, to suppose that the apostles were guided by

known revelation only in the most important matters, while in others they were left to the use of their own wise discretion. This subject, at that time, was yet in the latter category, though the deliberations of the council itself may have been divinely guided, and certainly such statements upon the subject as have been handed down to us in the Scriptures are inspired oracles upon it. Although the subject of inspiration is a difficult one, such a view can not lead us far astray.

2. As to the relation which this bears to the Sabbath. The imposition of the Jewish national law upon Christians as a condition of salvation, was the point aimed at. " Except ye be circumcised after the manner of Moses ye can not be saved." Circumcision was the one distinct rite which marked the Jewish nation. It was the sign of their national covenant from Abraham down. It was distinctly and exclusively Jewish, not Christian. To require it " after the manner of Moses" as a condition of salvation, was to place a Jewish yoke upon the necks of all Christians, to make Christianity a sect of Judaism. On the mount of transfiguration Moses had already yielded to Christ; this would have been to subject Christ to Moses. The naturalization laws of the United States might with the same propriety be forced upon the church now, as those of the Jews then. That the latter had their origin with God gave them no preëminence over ours, since they were only naturalization laws after all. At least that was all they amounted to after the coming of Christ. Though circumcision was that, as being first in order and for various reasons, upon which the controversy turned, it involved the Sabbath likewise, since it, too, was a part of the law, and from being found in the decalogue while circumcision was not, many modern religionists believe it of more lasting obligation than the other. When we correctly estimate the status of the primitive Gentile Christians towards the Mosaic law, we rightly gauge our own relation to the Jewish seventh day Sabbath.

3. Paul undoubtedly rightly expressed the truth in the whole case as inspiration has brought it down to us (Gal. vi. 15) " For in Christ Jesus neither circumcision availeth anything, nor uncircumcision, but a new creature." That is to say, no nationality, no badge of any particular citizenship, shall advance you one iota in the Christian life. You shall not be more acceptable to God as a Jew than as a Gentile. For as Peter learned at the household of Cornelius, " God is no respecter of persons, but in every nation he that feareth him, and worketh righteousness, is accepted of him." By circumcision was meant the whole law, as by faith is implied the whole gospel. " Circumcise them and command them to keep the law of Moses," said the Pharisees at the council (Acts xv. 5). If Sabbatarians of the present day would begin where these men did they might be more consistent; but to command to keep the law before you get into that association to which the law belongs, is like proceeding with the ordinances of the church of Christ without the essential antecedent faith.

But if circumcision was of no value whatever to a man as a Christian, neither was uncircumcision. There was no reason why a Jew should refuse, as a Jew simply and only, to continue this rite as his national badge. There was no sin in it, no merit in refusing such use of it. If the national law retained it he might obey that law. The Jewish nation, like every other, must have its customs and its laws. This was not a matter with which Christianity had directly to do. God no longer had an elect nation under his especial care. The new and spiritual Israel was chosen on the principle of faith, from all nations by individuals. It would be as manifestly improper to subject Christians to the law of Moses as such, as to that of Lycurgus. Neither was it the province or purpose of Christianity to abolish, as a mere worldly code, the law of Moses any more than that of Lycurgus. Doubtless had the Jews mainly become Christians, and independent of foreign rule, many things in their law would have been voluntarily abrogated.

They might or might not have thought circumcision of national utility. They might have retained some sort of Sabbath laws, transferred them to the first day of the week, or abolished them altogether. A rest year to the land, a year of jubilee, and numerous others, all others indeed, were subject to their own revision. They might have abolished the ten commandments. What was to hinder them from adopting, for example, just such a code as we have in the state of Indiana? Christians could be such and live subject to the rule of Rome, Russia or England. Rarely have human governments directly antagonized the law of Christ, and in such cases to "dare to be a Daniel" was to bring the difficulty to a speedy solution.

These preliminary observations may be concluded by the summary statement that it was not the Mosaic code as a Jewish but as a divine law, that was abolished. As such it was fulfilled, accomplished and removed, and a better one, adapted to a better covenant, instituted. At the same time Jews kept it as Jews, not as Christians. The controversy to be settled by the council was whether it should be made a Christian law likewise. The Judaizing teachers so desired, but Paul stood opposed.

The very silence of the Holy Spirit upon this subject heretofore is significant. Christianity did not assume to meddle with the governments of earth. It said nothing of emperors, kings or presidents. It left these to come and go, change by the vicissitudes of revolution and the veerings of the popular will. Had not these officious Jews attempted to force their law upon the church, and provoked the dissension upon that subject, it may be doubted whether much that is in the epistle to the Galatians, for example, would ever have found place in the sacred oracles. The Jewish law, including circumcision and the Sabbath, not being commanded by the Spirit to the churches, would have passed

THE COUNCIL AT JERUSALEM.

in silence, the especial property of the nation. They had been "shadows of good things" which had now come, "the body was of Christ," they were now perfected, fulfilled, accomplished, they had grown old, vanished away, been nailed to the cross, abolished. So far as Christianity was concerned, they were a dead letter. The Holy Spirit, in revealing through the apostles the terms of the gospel, the law of induction into the church, and of Christian or religious life within it, ignored it altogether because it was dead.

Recurring again to the fifteenth chapter of Acts, which begins with Paul and Barnabas at Antioch, where they are involved in heated controversy with the Judaizing teachers from Jerusalem, it is determined that both of them "shall go up to Jerusalem to the apostles and elders about this question." Paul elsewhere (Gal. ii. 2) declares that he went up "by revelation." We know from various indications that the different apostles and prominent teachers, each had his special friends and followers, a council of all of them, then, would have more influence, if its decision was harmonious, than could the authority of either of them alone. Especially Paul, having been engaged in an extensive work among the Gentiles, had not the sympathy or confidence of the Jewish brethren on this question.

But at Jerusalem was stationed James, one of the chief apostles. The importance of the post seems to have been fully recognized, and the man selected best suited to fill it. Surnamed the Just, his decision would doubtless have great weight. Here Paul also met Peter and John, and these three, he writes to the Galatians, "seemed to be pillars," and they gave to him, at the conclusion of their conference, "the right hand of fellowship" in his mission to the Gentiles. Now while there are indications in the chapter that the Jews, especially some of the Pharisees, urged the necessity of circumcision and keeping the law, such was not the case with Peter or James. Their words were directly in harmony with Paul's own view. Peter referred to the well-known fact that he had been made the instrument in the conversion of the first Gentile Christians, those of the household of Cornelius, and that God himself had directed and attested his course, giving to them the Holy Spirit as to the apostles at the beginning. Since God had placed no difference between them, why should they put a yoke upon them. When Paul and Barnabas proceeded to recount the history of their work among the Gentiles, "all the multitude" kept silence, for it was a remarkable narrative of "miracles and wonders which God had wrought by them."

With such clear evidence of God's first instigating and then acknowledging with most emphatic blessings this work among the Gentiles, it must have been apparent to the assembly that it was impossible either to question the validity of what was done, or to amend it in any way. There can be no doubt that had the apostles or Jewish Christians been left to pursue their own course, they would first have made Jews of the Gentiles and then Christians. But this was clearly overruled from the first, God himself teaching them that a Gentile to become a Christian required no other acts of obedience than did a Jew.

James, in summing up the case, referred to the facts recounted by his fellow-apostles, and then added the statement that prophecy had foretold these very things. The true solution of their difficulties, it was, therefore, quite easy for him to suggest, namely, that they should not trouble these Gentile brethren further about these matters. What he did require, "that they abstain from pollutions of idols, and from fornication, and from things strangled and from blood," were in themselves, growing out of the idolatrous state of the times, the special significance which was attached to blood in the remedial scheme, and the former habits which these people must have practiced as heathen, very necessary both to their good name and to consistency and propriety of conduct. Further than that, on every Sabbath day, throughout all the cities of the various countries, in the synagogues everywhere, the law of Moses was read and expounded. If, therefore, there was any wholesome or restraining effect besides, to be gathered by Jew or Gentile from the precepts of Moses, it might safely be left for the event to determine. Certain it is that no Jewish law was imposed upon Gentile Christians, and Peter's words accord with that elsewhere expressed in the Scriptures. " It was a yoke which neither we nor our fathers were able to bear. But we believe that through the grace of the Lord Jesus Christ we shall be saved."

There are three incidents related in the Acts, bearing, each in a peculiar way, upon this subject thus happily settled. First, the case of Titus. From the second chapter of Galatians we learn that he was a Greek, that is a Gentile, also that he went up to Jerusalem with Paul and Barnabas to the council, and lastly, that as the result of the council he was not required to be circumcised. A clear case coming directly under the rulings of the council, and decided in favor of the full liberty accorded by that body to the Gentiles, it needs no further comment at our hands.

Second, Timothy. The next chapter in Acts, and certain passages in the letters of Paul addressed to him, show that he was of Jewish origin and education, except that his father was a Greek. But in his faith and knowledge of the Scriptures he had followed his mother, Eunice, and his grandmother, Lois, so that to all intents and purposes he was a Jew. That he should have been circumcised by Paul, then, when he started forth with him on a missionary journey, meant nothing more than that as he was about to go into the midst of communities more or less Jewish, he exercised the freedom which he had, being a Jew, of conforming to their national law. Not that the rite had longer any religious significance, which to impose it upon Gentiles would have shown, but that it were better for a Jew to conform to the rites of his nation, that he might be favorably received by them.

Third. In a somewhat similar way may be explained Paul's subsequent conduct in Jerusalem (Acts xxi.) He had returned to that city after long and successful labors among the Gentiles. He had come again into the presence of "James and all the elders." His action, therefore, founded on the advice of the same parties that had participated in the famous council, must be understood to be entirely consistent with the former decisions of that tribunal. They say to him (ver. 20, etc.): "Thou seest, brother, how many thousands of Jews there are which believe; and they are all zealous of the law. And they are informed of thee that thou teachest all the Jews, which are among the Gentiles, to forsake Moses, saying that they ought not to circumcise their children, neither to walk after the customs. What is it, therefore? The multitude must needs come together, for they will hear that thou art come. Do, therefore, this that we say to thee: We have four men which have a vow on them. Them take and purify thyself with them, and be at charges with them that they may shave their heads: and all may know that those things, whereof they were informed concerning thee, are nothing; but that thou thyself also walkest orderly and keepest the law. As touching the Gentiles which believe, we have written and concluded that they observe no such thing, save only that they keep themselves from things offered to idols, and from blood and from things strangled, and from fornication." This course Paul endeavored to carry out, and yet great uproar arose against him in the city. He was rescued and removed from danger with the greatest difficulty.

It will be observed that in all these instances questions arose in the Jewish law outside of the decalogue. All parties admit that circumcision never was a necessary rite in the Christian church, nor does this last case of purification in connection with the Nazarite vow pertain to anything in the decalogue. It, therefore, is evident that the Jewish Christians in a body, especially those at Jerusalem, did not surrender their attachment to Moses when they embraced Christ. They still clung with jealous patriotism to the law of their fathers. Nor, as we have already suggested, were they opposed in this, so far as we have any information. Such a change should come about gradually, if at all, and after the destruction of their city and state. But as to binding any of these regulations upon others, as necessary to salvation, this we have found the apostles positively forbid.

Yet it can not be denied that the zeal of these people for their law, now useless in many of its provisions even for a worldly code, was misguided and even wicked. These Judaizers were a pestilent set of schismatics, and are well characterized by Paul to Titus: "For there are many unruly and vain talkers and deceivers, specially they of the circumcision, whose mouths must be stopped" (i. 10). The difference in Paul's dealings with these, in distant provinces, and that of James and Peter, may be accounted for, or should be, by the varying circumstances under which they were placed; for it is impossible to deal with sin even in all places alike, and moreover in Jerusalem among themselves, these peculiar views, when unprovoked by the advent of some conspicuous opposer like Paul, would do little harm, and might be left to time and the growth of a more positive Christian spirit to gradually extinguish; whereas, out among foreign converts, they were absolutely hurtful, and if allowed to be urged, would both check the growth of the church and plunge it into irremediable contentions.

The whole question of the law was involved in these controversies. The sabbath clearly goes with the rest; first, because there is no distinction drawn between particulars, and, second, because " circumcision and keeping the law " is mentioned as the distracting question. To infer, because it might suit one's purpose, that the ceremonial law, in the absence of any scriptural distinction, was that only which was involved, while in other cases, when "the law" is referred to, it is applied to the decalogue alone, is complete self-stultification. The entire unanimity upon the part of all the apostolic fraternity and of the elders, in sustaining the course of Paul, gives a united verdict against the authority of any part of the Hebrew law over Christians.

If, finally, it should be thought that Paul did dissuade his Hebrew brethren in the remote provinces from clinging to the law, it was as a worldly code; and if as such it stood in the way of Christianity, or was an inconvenience to them in any point of view, he might properly advise its abandonment. In Jerusalem the case would be far different.

CHAPTER XI.

THE LORDIAN DAY.

A subject opens before us of surpassing interest. The wonders of past ages, through which we have thus far traced our course, have given way to others vastly greater. So the moon vanishes from sight when rises the king of day. The desire of the ages has come. "The glory as of the only begotten of the father" shines about his head. All other luminaries in the spiritual world pale in his presence. Moses, eminent in his day, is overshadowed. David, the prince, is no longer chief of the royal line. Solomon's wisdom does not now attract attention. "Behold a greater than Solomon is here." His temple, though its magnificence made it one of the wonders of the world, was but a faint type, a feeble picture and illustration, of that which has since appeared. Burn all the gorgeous man-made temples. Overthrow the nations whose history is most illustrious. Away with the vaunted philosophic systems of the past. Let the science, the literature, the refinement of the centuries gone be forgotten. Let heathen hordes overwhelm the mighty universal empire wherein are treasured all that remains of ancient thought, and learning, and success. It is but rubbish.

Behold the little leaven has been cast into the meal. The little seed has sunk beneath the soil, from which shall grow the greatest of trees. Its leaves shall be for the healing of the nations. Under its spreading branches shall gather innumerable multitudes from all the tribes and climes of earth, and find shelter. Though all that the people have been wont to prize shall be forever buried from sight, greater and better shall come to us in the new order of things. Not a thing across the line of time that is marked by the Christian era need be sighed for if lost. The history beyond may be instructive, it may interest, it may even edify, but it is not indispensable. The institutions of the ante-Christian world may have served a temporary purpose, prefigured the better to come, prepared the world for them; they may have appeased but they never satisfied the longings of human nature. The sacrifices may have kept up a remembrance of sin from year to year; they never washed it away. The Jewish Sabbath may have pointed to a rest; it was never enjoyed as that rest. It was a promise, not a realization.

As the nineteenth century is growing old, we hear much of a "Christian Sabbath." In many circles this is the favorite expression to designate the day now generally observed by religious people. There are other terms employed. But "Sabbath" and "Sabbath-school" and the like, seem to fall most smoothly from the tongue. They are the height of the fashion, to say the least. Not that we would be so uncharitable as to suppose that they are used for mere fashion's sake. But many proper and precise and conscientious people, those accredited orthodox, whom the general public regard as models in religious forms and speech, have adopted this style, and from them it has grown popular. It must have arisen from the combination of two ideas: first, that the fourth commandment is the authority for the observance, hence a Sabbath; and second, that the day has been changed, though still under the same law, to another day of the week, hence the term Christian to distinguish it from the former. The reader has already been instructed in these pages that the fourth commandment is no longer a rule of religious life for any one. He will expect of us a clear and satisfactory elucidation of the principles upon which the present Sunday observance rests, and as the result of a correct understanding of the institution itself the proper name by which to designate it will appear.

Had the name Christian Sabbath, or even Sabbath, been

THE LORDIAN DAY. 173

found in the New Testament, according to the modern usage, it would have sanctioned that usage and made it imperative. Being wanting, we are left to reason the matter out in the light of unquestioned principles, of which some have already been developed and others will be found in place. It will be an interesting and profitable study for us to ascertain the precise character of the worship day under the Christian system; in what respects it coincides with the old, in what it differs from it. We shall come out of the investigation at last, it is to be hoped, with ideas so definite, and distinctions so clearly drawn, the need and purpose of the day so apparent, with so many manifestations of God's grace coming to us in it, that ever after its faithful observance will be to us the delight of the soul.

The words standing at the head of this chapter are the proper substitute for the expression "the Christian Sabbath." That they are not in current use at the present time throws the burden of proof upon us in attempting to introduce them. They may strike the ear unpleasantly at first. But utter them aloud a hundred times till the novelty wears off. It would be well also to bestow some thought upon the question what such a phraseology would mean. Familiarity in this instance will breed respect. Investigation will reveal a reasonable basis and sufficient justification for the innovation.

The first step in the exposition now beginning, is an inquiry in regard to the official titles of the Saviour. These are two—Christ and Lord. It will not be denied that there are others. But these are in every sense chief. Especially are they the only ones that could enter into this consideration. United with the human name, they make up the frequent designation Lord Jesus Christ. This by virtue of its completeness has ever been a favorite combination with all Christians. Messiah, the equivalent of Christ, and Saviour, the definition of Jesus, as well as almost, if not all, other descriptive appellations, are found expressed in it. Peter declares in the first sermon after the divine offering (Acts ii. 36), "Let all the house of Israel know assuredly that God hath made that same Jesus, whom ye have crucified, both Lord and Christ."

The term Christ is applied to Jesus alone in the Scriptures, a fact universally recognized. Not so, however, with Lord. A much more limited statement must be made. In a strict official sense only, it may be said that in and of the Christian dispensation, Jesus alone is spoken of as Lord. Jehovah himself was Lord in creation. He is Lord over us now, properly speaking, when we are considered as human beings, in all that view which precedes and is outside of the scheme of redemption. He is Lord of all created beings, Lord of heaven and earth, the Lord God omnipotent. Jehovah himself was also Lord, during all the progress of the old covenant, in a religious sense. Thus the Mosaic institution regarded him. Thus the prophets, proverbs and psalms accounted him, except, of course, when they glanced forward to the Christian age. A striking example of the use of both occurs in the passage "The Lord [Jehovah] said unto my Lord [Jesus], sit thou on my right hand till I make thine enemies thy footstool."

Of the whole scheme of redemption, and its work from the resurrection onward, Christ is alone designated Lord. Peter's declaration above is the first positive proof adduced. It stands at the beginning and is the first definite announcement of the accomplished fact. Jesus was crucified "by wicked hands," but him had "God raised up," and "made both Lord and Christ." As here used, this is no indefinite or vagrant appellation. Of such inferior uses of the word there are numerous instances in the Scripture. Thus the husband was lord of the wife, as in the case of Abraham and Sarah, the master lord over his servants and property.

The Lordship of Jesus, within the limits named, is not only a fact, but it is one of which God will require every human being to make acknowledgment. A brief explanation will show that this is precisely what the prophet means when he says (Isa. xlv. 23): "I have sworn by myself, the word is gone out of my mouth in righteousness, and shall not return, that unto me every knee shall bow, every tongue shall swear." Paul quotes this last clause (Rom. xiv. 11), using the word "confess" instead of "swear." He applies it to the judgment, "So then every one of us shall give account of himself to God." In the context preceding, this is ascribed directly to Christ: "For we shall all stand before the judgment seat of Christ." And how emphatically and universally this lordship is asserted: "For to this end Christ both died and rose, and revived, that he might be Lord, both of the dead and living." Take with you the four expressions found in these quotations, "Lord," "confess," "dead and living" and "judgment," and turn to that graphic description of the final day found in Matthew at the conclusion of the twenty-fifth chapter. Here the Son of Man is represented as coming in his glory, in company with all the holy angels, sitting upon the throne of his glory, the nations as gathering before him and divided by him as individuals into two great classes, as distinct, as emphatic, as reasonable a division as that made by a herdsman when he separates his sheep from his goats. But mark when the sentence is pronounced by the Son of man—Christ—the King—of blessing or of cursing upon the two parties, for specific reason given, they each make the same inquiry, "Lord, when saw we thee, hungry, thirsty, a stranger, naked, sick or in prison?" Each distinctly admits his lordship, his rightful authority over them. Whether before they had acknowledged or rejected him in the character either of loving Saviour or of rightful ruler, now at least they all confess him Lord. Paul, in Philippians (ii. 10), applies the prophecy in the following language: "That at the name of Jesus every knee shall bow, of things in heaven, and things in earth, and things under the earth; and that every tongue should confess that Jesus Christ is

Lord to the glory of God the Father." The fulfillment, then, of the declared submission to God, will be found in the complete acknowledgment by all intelligences that Jesus is Lord of the Christian age. Those who will not assent to this by voluntary submission to him in this life shall certainly do so in the end, when standing before him in judgment.

This, then, in this dispensation of God's grace, is what constitutes submission to God himself. In the Christian age there is but one way to reach God, that is, through Christ; but one way to acknowledge God and conciliate his favor, that is, to recognize his son as Lord. Jesus is Lord in the full acceptation of the term, and it is unbiblical to apply it to any one else, divine or human. More than this may be affirmed. The acknowledgment of that Lordship is the consummation foretold by prophet and sought in the present dispensation. When that end is reached, another change occurs (I. Cor. xv. 24): "Then cometh the end, when he shall have delivered up the kingdom to God, even the Father; when he shall have put down all rule, and all authority and all power. For he must reign, till he hath put all enemies under his feet. The last enemy that shall be destroyed is death. . . . And when all things shall be subdued unto him, then shall the Son also himself be subject unto him that put all things under him, that God may be all in all."

The uniform New Testament usage accords with the declarations of the Bible, that Jesus Christ is in this age officially Lord, and he only. In this light we must approach the study of the expressions "Lord's supper" (I. Cor. xi. 20) and "Lord's day" (Rev. i. 10). We are to understand them as Christ's supper and Christ's day. We know that such is the reference in the former case, for the institution of it by Jesus himself is recorded in the gospels. But the latter passage, wherein John, the Revelator, opens his apocalyptic vision by declaring, "I was in the spirit on the Lord's day," is that upon which this part of the investigation turns.

Accepting the principles just established as our guide, since the period of their application comprehends the time of John's vision and the writing of his book, the "Lord's day," as he used the term, could not have been the Sabbath or seventh day of the week. For that day was founded on the creation of God, its observance commanded on his authority previous to the time in which Jesus became Lord, or at least was officially exclusively designated as such; and it was, moreover, called his holy day. While then the Sabbath was God's day, as anciently instituted by him, this was Christ's day. In our view it would not be possible to suppose them the same, unless there were no clue whatever to any other reasonable conjecture. We can not think it probable that the expression would have been employed had it referred to the Sabbath. Surely it can not be that the same day, which in ages past, had been called God's holy Sabbath, and which was founded upon his cessation from creation, should now be called Christ's day, unless some important reason could be assigned for the change in designation.

Postponing for the present the question of the particular day of the week, until we inquire more narrowly into the meaning of the phrase, the two official titles Lord and Christ come into view. Let us trace the latter, if perchance it may assist our inquiry as to the former. Inspiration or providence no doubt directed its use. This is evident from prophecy. "Where I record my name" was a favorite expression of Jehovah, to indicate sacred places. Isaiah, speaking of Zion, (lxii. 2,) declares "the Gentiles shall see thy righteousness, and all kings thy glory; and thou shalt be called by a new name, which the mouth of the Lord shall name." Again, condemning his ancient people and at the same time referring to his chosen under the coming new dispensation, (lxv. 13,) he utters words of unmistakable meaning, "Behold, my servants shall eat, but ye shall be hungry; behold my servants shall drink, but ye shall be thirsty; behold my servants shall rejoice, but ye shall be ashamed; behold my servants shall sing for joy, but ye shall cry for sorrow of heart, and shall howl for vexation of spirit. And ye shall have your name for a curse unto my chosen; for the Lord God shall slay thee, and call his servants by another name."

God in ancient times was said to have set or recorded his name in various places appointed for his worship. In exact typical keeping with that fact, Christ's name is employed in the church in which his worship is now held. "In the name of Christ," and kindred phrases, will occur to the reader of the new Testament, as of very frequent and significant use. James, in the great council at Jerusalem (Acts xv. 17), quotes from the prophecy in regard to the Gentiles, upon whom the name of the Lord is called, meaning such as became Christians. Has the reader forgotten the importance attached to names throughout the Scriptures, the changes of those of Abraham and Jacob for a particular purpose, the requirement made of the prophet that he should name his children, so that the import thereof should be a standing witness to the people, the meaning of Joshua and Jesus, each a Saviour of his people, and others far too numerous to mention?

We are prepared then to find the followers of Christ receiving a name by authority, as the prophetic declarations given indicate. The introduction of that name is recorded in the simplest manner by the historian: "The disciples were called Christians first at Antioch" (Acts xi. 26). That is, the official title Christ was formed into an adjective, which also was used as a noun when occasion required. Though the appellation were given as a term of reproach, or assumed by them, or given directly by the apostles, or however it came about, a question which it would be a digression to discuss here, there can at least be no doubt of this that it was in accordance with the divine purpose.

Why was not the title Lord, of the two, chosen from which to constitute the name and thus the followers of Jesus forever afterwards called Lordians. To think a moment, is to find the answer. Lord indicates authority, Christ indicates chosen, appointed, anointed, consecrated. The latter terms are applicable to the disciples of Christ here, not so the former. In the use of this name, then, Christians bear one which not only is suitable and exceedingly significant, but, at the same time, by embodying an official title of their Lord, honors him both in himself and in respect to his great mission. No other so appropriate name could have been selected.

When we recur to the other official title, Lord, it is discovered that this, too, takes on the adjective form and is thus exactly expressed, in the two cases of its application, Lordian supper, (Lord's supper, I. Cor. xi. 20,) and Lordian day (Lord's day, Rev. i. 10). We shall not be diverted from a correct analysis of this subject because the accepted versions give "Lord's day" instead of a rendering which is absolutely correct, like the one we have chosen. Are they equivalent expressions? By no means. As well say that the Washingtonian Society was Washington's society, which it was not. It was named in honor of Washington, but it was not his. As well say that a lyceum organized in these days by a band of literary young men and styled the Ciceronian Society was Cicero's society. It is seldom, if ever, that a purely adjective form expresses the exact idea of the possessive case of a noun.

Since the Greek text of the New Testament employs the adjective, and no translation by a noun is adequate, and a suitable word must be formed, we prefer, immeasurably, Lordian, since it is similar in its termination to Christian, besides being best in other respects. Hereafter this word will be employed in all its adjective connections. The view of our Saviour is an official one, which regards the efficacy of his body and blood in the great sacrifice to procure our salvation. At the same time it is better perhaps in such connection to think of him as Lord than as Christ. At any rate the apostle makes use of the former term rather than the other, when referring to that commemorative use of the bread and wine " to show forth his death till he come," speaking in one of his epistles (I. Cor. xi. 20) of certain discordant proceedings in connection with that solemn festival of the church, in the words " This is not to eat the Lordian supper."

With the facts thus sketched and illustrated, we are prepared again to refer to Revelations (i. 10) in which John informs us that he was "in the spirit on the Lordian day." This day, whatever it was, had direct reference to the official character of the Saviour of men. And from the word employed it seemed to have a nearer relation to him as Lord than as Christ, a closer connection to his authority than to his anointing. Whoever keeps the Lordian day, in so doing directly recognizes the authority of Christ. He who was "in the spirit on the Lordian day," was doubtless impressed by that same authority, and most wonderfully was it manifested in the revelations of the vision then received.

Some have stoutly maintained that the time referred to by the term under consideration, is the end of the world, or the future day of judgment, to which the apostle was in vision carried. Other passages may be quoted to assist us in the determination of that question. "That great and notable day of the Lord" (Acts ii. 20); "That the spirit may be saved in the day of the Lord Jesus" (I. Cor. v. 5); "Ye also are ours in the day of the Lord Jesus" (II. Cor. i. 14); "The day of the Lord so cometh as a thief in the night" (I. Thess. v. 2); "But the day of the Lord will come as a thief in the night" (II. Pet. iii. 10). A reference to the original Greek will disclose the fact that in these instances the translation is accurate. "Day of the Lord" in every case is the exact utterance of the inspired author and not Lordian day, as in the passage we have heretofore been considering. What, then, is the difference in meaning? Or shall we understand the thing signified to be the same, while the change in name is a mere casual variation? A "Day of the Lord" would naturally be his own; a Lordian day might belong to some one else and only named or kept in honor of the Lord. "Day of the Lord" would imply one in which the marked features would be a display of his mighty power; Lordian day might be one in which no such display should occur, but which his loving friends, without reference to what he might do or be doing, should keep in recognition of his authority over them. If there were nothing but this difference in name, we should not only be inclined to suppose the days not the same, but essentially unlike in character. Since human history began there have been few times so marked by supernatural agencies as that there should be any special propriety in calling them days of God. But it might well be called the day of the Lord, " in the which the heavens shall pass away with a great noise, and the elements shall melt with fervent heat, the earth also and the works that are therein shall be burned up." Such would not be appropriately called the Lordian. That would rather be a day of cessation from toil and of religious occupations, according to the will of the Lord and in the honor and worship of his holy name for whom it was called.

Day of the Lord and Lord's day are equivalent terms. The first day of the week, as it is now observed by Christian people, exactly accords with the expression, Lordian day. The great judgment day of the future, as it is pictured by Christ and the inspired writers in the New Testament, is clearly the "day of the Lord," or Lord's day.

While the Spirit is ever present with the Christian, it is especially the Lordian day, devoted to worship, and meditation, and religious instruction, that brings to us the clearest consciousness of his presence. It is impossible to think of John as the record acquaints us with him, and the Lordian day devoted to the memory and worship of his Master, and Patmos as the place where the veteran disciple was still lingering in mingled contemplation of the past and joyous expectation of the future, without regarding it as the most probable occasion for such a wondrous divine visitation as that of which he has given us account.

Assuredly, it was not on a "great and notable day of the Lord," it was not on a day of God's wrath, of punishment of the intractable and vile, of destruction of the physical universe, or even of the ushering out, in the midst of remarkable displays of his power, one age or dispensation and the introduction of the new; but rather on a far more peaceful and quiet occasion, that the beloved disciple John, last of the apostles remaining on earth, in the seclusion of the rocky isle, received a revelation from his Master of what was to be, in the fortunes of that church of which one was a pillar and the other the head. What more probable than that the Lord, on a day of the week devoted to solemn communion with himself, through revelation of the Spirit, gave him this gracious view of the future, which, ere his departure, he was to convey in written form to the church, a legacy for all future time.

As the word "Christian" designates a person who has publicly espoused the cause of Christ, devoting himself to his service and consecrated to the honor of his name; as the Lordian supper denotes a feast commemorative of the Lord, its bread and wine representing his body and blood, to be partaken of only by those who are his acknowledged disciples, as it is a distinct recognition of the Lord Christ himself, requiring faith in him as an efficient sacrifice whose death it shows forth, appointed by him, so called in his honor, and utterly without meaning as referred to any other divine personage, so the Lordian day is without doubt a day of the week, devoted to religious worship, called Lordian because distinctly set apart to him as Lord, having no reference to the Holy Spirit or the Father as such—a day, too, that was chosen to mark one of the three great gospel facts (I. Cor. xv.), the death, burial and resurrection of Christ. Such a day would most properly be called the Christian or Lordian day, and of the two, the latter in preference, for various reasons.

A day in which God finished the creation of the physical universe, and which, by his command, had been celebrated as referring to that event, could not be made distinctively Lordian, so that the thoughts that it should awaken, and the incidents to which it should refer, would exclusively pertain to Christ. Nor since, on that same day, the Mosaic sabbath, Jesus, the world's Redeemer, lay under the power of death in the tomb, would it be a fitting day to celebrate in recognition of his Lordship. Rather would it be the day, if any, that heathen, infidel and the wicked of the world might choose for the darkest orgies in exultation upon their temporary triumph over him.

With the first day of the week the case stands very differently. Instead of marking the finished work of God at creation, it celebrates the accomplishment of Christ's great work for human redemption. On it he rose from the grave and was first made Lord. Grand triumph! An effectual sacrifice has at last been made for man. The High Priest lives who shall enter for him into the holiest of all. Immortality has been brought to light. One clothed in mortal frame has brought it forth from the abodes of death. This mortal shall hereafter put on immortality. He has risen "who shall change our vile body, that it may be fashioned like unto his glorious body." The last fact of the gospel is accomplished. There is now good news for all the people. Without the resurrection there was nothing; with it, everything. If there is to be a day called Lordian, let it be the first day of the week. This is the proper day for

Christians to rejoice in his name, to sing his praises, to worship before him. We worship only one whom we call Lord.

As typical institutions are a prominent feature of the old covenant, so commemorative ones belong to the new. This conforms to our view of the whole Bible as setting forth, simply and only, a scheme of redemption. As Christ is the grand center of all this, what is before points forward to him. Hence, types and prophecies. They testified that he should come, what he should be, do and give. The sabbath was kept an ever present promise and prophecy of rest in Christ, founded in symbol and form, authority and pledge, on God's law and creation. As sure as he was God, beside whom there was none other, the Creator of all things, the one who gave the select people the Sabbath, modeled after his own rest at creation, the promised rest in Christ should come. As his chosen people received and kept the Sabbath, so should his elect people enjoy the prefigured blessing in Christ. And so with all the leading features of the old; sacrifice or tabernacle, priest or victim, passover or pentecost, manna or shew bread, candlestick or altar of incense, Red Sea or Jordan, Moses or Aaron, all alike pointed on. The desire of all nations shall come. The anointed of God shall bring to his people greater blessings than the shadowy forms can picture or it hath entered into the heart of man to conceive.

Pass the resurrection morn, the first Lordian day whose beams ever shone upon the glad world. Hope has changed to fruition, prophecy to fulfillment, type to antitype. It is no longer "we trusted that it had been he that should have redeemed Israel." It is now "the grace of God that bringeth salvation hath appeared unto all men." Faith with the child of God is mainly applied to things of the past, that Jesus is the Christ the Son of God, that he died for our sins according to the Scriptures, that he was buried and that he rose again the third day according to the Scriptures. The institutions of the church point back to those events: baptism to his burial and resurrection; the Lordian supper to his body and blood, which were offered for us; the Lordian day to his resurrection; the Christian himself to the fact that he was the Christ, the appointed Saviour of the world. Our Christian enjoyment in this life, and our confident anticipations for that to come, are all founded and grounded on belief of these events of the past, together with a personal reliance upon Christ our Saviour and Redeemer.

If the old seventh day sabbath is done away in the Jewish law as an observance, by divine command; if, as a type, it is accomplished, where do we find a requirement for the rest which is practiced upon the first day of the. week? Surely not from the law. Sinai is not an authority now, "for out of Zion shall go forth the law and the word of the Lord from Jerusalem" (Isa. ii. 3). This passage refers to Messianic times, and the law must therefore be that uttered by Christ and his apostles. Whatever of authority we have for rest from labor on the Lordian day, will be derived according to just and proper principles of interpretation from these sources. This will be left mainly for another chapter.

The day which the original text calls Lordian, as before intimated, is not so much the Lord's as ours, in an important sense. It is our day, because given to us and employed by us for a certain purpose. We call it Lordian, in part because the work to which we devote it pertains to him. We have certain Christian duties and privileges which require time to fulfill and enjoy. The day is given us for that purpose. We fill its hours with these employments which pertain to the worship and service of the Lord, and hence, devoting it to him, it is called by his name. It is not the Lord's day in the sense that the Lord directly appointed it for the particular purpose to which it is devoted. We say, directly appointed it. It is the Lord's day in the same sense, for example, as the Forefathers' day is theirs, or in the same sense as Decoration day belongs to the soldiers whose death for the country we affectionately remember while we formally do honor to their memories. All these may properly be designated by descriptive adjectives embodying the names of those honored. For these reasons it is better to say Lordian than Lord's day, especially since the Scriptures so give it.

In concluding this chapter, we are moved to say that it is high time the term herein used had found its way into our common speech. It is even discreditable to the scholarship of the age, that two distinct Greek forms referring to separate and very unlike ideas, should have renderings different, indeed, yet substantially equivalent, and either of which would very properly represent the thought of one of the original terms only, while the other is not at all adequately expressed. Surely, a distinction found in the Bible and strictly preserved by the Greek fathers, and which marks the important difference between the peaceful weekly day of rest and the final judgment, is worthy to be carefully followed in the English versions, and in every-day language. Let all the readers of this book, at least such as approve its course of reasoning, adopt the term "Lordian day," and use it exclusively as the religious name for the first day of the week.

CHAPTER XII.

APOSTOLIC PRECEDENT.

Some points under the last topic were purposely left incomplete because it was expected that this would supply what was lacking. For example, when it was stated that our Lord did not himself directly appoint the day now religiously observed in his honor, it was understood that it could here be shown, that by his authorized representatives, the apostles who executed his will under the guidance of the Holy Spirit, the day came to be thus set apart and employed in just such a manner as was appropriate under the circumstances. Let no one complain of the language here used as timid or halting. There is a great demand by many who seem to have very inadequate conceptions of what such a day should be, or how it should come into existence, for a positive command on the subject. These either ask you with an air of triumph, where is the command for the observance of the first day of the week, or they refer you, with equal assurance, to the fourth commandment as the basis for it. Let us entreat the patient attention of such until we show a more excellent way.

Jesus was not egotistical. Human nature brought into combination with the divine all its native modesty. He was prone to assert no more than had actually been proven. After his introduction to men at the waters of baptism by his Father's voice from heaven, it would seem that he might properly assume and assert all the most radical facts in regard to his own being and authority. But did the Pharisees object, "Thou bearest record of thyself, thy record is not true," while he hesitated not to say: "Though

I bear record of myself yet my record is true," he also declared "The Father that sent me beareth witness of me," and "The works that I do bear witness of me." Frequently he charged those that were healed by him not to report it abroad, and we have already seen that the important event of the transfiguration was not to be made known till after the resurrection. Everything of this kind was subject to the success of his mission, and we have the right to believe that the proprieties as well as the necessities of the case were consulted.

The Lordian supper was instituted by the Saviour, whereas the Lordian day was not; and to consider the reasons for this difference will facilitate our argument. These are two. First, the supper is a communion (I. Cor. x. 16). Jesus and his disciples sit together. He gives them, with his blessing, both the bread and the wine, as his body and blood. It is that which man may not take except Jesus himself shall give. While it is a commemorative ordinance in the church, it is more than that; it is the dispensing of blessings, on the one hand, by the Saviour who sits at the table with us; on the other hand, it is a partaking of those blessings by us. This active and actual participation of Christ, on the occasion of its first institution, must be regarded as attending it at all times. It was established formally and directly by him, and he still continues, representatively at least, one of the parties in its observance. The lesson would never have been as complete had only the apostles, even by inspiration, given it to us. Christ must ever be regarded as present at the feast, presiding and freely giving the bread of life. And yet therein the disciple shows forth his Lord's death, recognizes and represents him as Lord and honors him; hence it is Lordian.

In the second place we are brought nearer in fact and feeling to the death of Christ itself. It is as if he had taken each of us, which he did representatively in the person of the first disciples, all unconscious as they were, down with him to the very gates of death, and made us partakers of his sufferings, not of his agonies and the gloom which just then were weighing heavily upon him, but of the glad fruits. How sweet to remember that our Saviour thought of us in the darkest hour, not as of those that could help or cheer him, but as of those with whom even then he could hold fellowship, whom he could bless, for whom indeed he was willing to die. I would not forget that precious fact. If he could think of me then, surely when I come to die he will be with me too. In fever and pain, in the sundering of all earthly ties, he will be there to commune with my soul. Even so at his death were we present, and because unconscious, helpless, and lost, the more encouraging was it (may we venture to say,) to him to give himself for our redemption. Had the supper been established after the resurrection, the memory of that event would have been uppermost in the mind. Had the apostles appointed it, the personality of Christ and his death would have been still more remote from our thoughts.

The Lordian day differs in this. It commemorates the resurrection. The date of its origin must be after that event. There are reasons, too, why Christ should not in person have established it, but that action should have been left to the apostles. An illustration occurs, extravagant perhaps, but suggestive of the correct principle. In recent times birth-day parties, golden and silver weddings, are of frequent occurrence. It has even been known that a person, judging himself a fit subject for such an honor, and mindful of the rich presents that come with the occasion, has suggested, in a confidential way, to some friend to organize one of the "spontaneous" gatherings for him, which, when it came to pass, was made to appear as entirely unexpected on his part. For a person to know of such an event beforehand, and, especially, to participate in originating one for himself, even though carefully concealing his own part in it, is regarded as discreditable to him.

While it could not be supposed that such an impropriety would appear, in case of the institution of the commemorative day, by the one who was himself to be honored or remembered by it, yet to pursue the different course was a most beautiful exemplification of a positive grace of the opposite nature. The worth and modesty which were inherent in the Saviour of men, would leave such occasions of honor to be originated by others, as in every way more suitable and impressive. The apostles, with that remarkable wisdom which characterized their course in organizing the church, and full of faith and the Holy Spirit, could certainly be trusted to fix upon such days as would suitably perpetuate, so far as any memorials could, the memory of Christ together with leading facts of his mission. Nor in saying this, as from rather a human point of view, do we wish to imply that the appointment was not official, authoritative, and even inspired. Let it be distinctly understood that every act which the apostles did for the organization of the church and its government, was guided by the divine Spirit, and is as binding upon ourselves as though Christ himself had commanded it. And yet there was vastly greater propriety that institutions solely designed for man to honor Christ, should originate with man himself. We firmly believe that such thoughts as these in regard to the fitness of things are not foreign to the divine mind, nor ever ignored by him especially in view of their human application.

It was never the custom of Jesus to chant his own praises, however justly he might have done so. On the contrary, the Spirit and the divine Father, while of the same Godhead, were also in such sense distinct from him that their chief expression is in his praise. To the Spirit, then, would properly be left the institution of the first day of the week as a day of worship for the church, commemorating also, for all time, the resurrection of our Lord from the grave.

The more gradually such a day should have come into use, the more voluntary and spontaneous it should be, the better would it fulfil the purpose designed. We are not of those who think that either the value or authority of the day depends upon divine command. There are some things that come to the human soul with greater force than law. Faith, confidence, and love spring up of themselves. Their promptings ought to be heeded. He who gives no voluntary expressions to these, may obey law all his life and be a sordid soul, unworthy of the fellowship of the good. If the Christian Church has any occasion which it has set apart of its own free will, and kept with singleness of purpose in honor of the Lord, an outgrowth of its faith and love, no doubt it is quite as acceptable to him as any other. Such a privilege might be abused, as everything is liable to be, when dependent merely upon human direction, but this is no argument against a proper use. So far then as the Lordian day could be left, in its origin, to the church itself, would its value be enhanced rather than impaired. In precisely that way does it appear in the Acts of Apostles; a voluntary, spontaneous offering of the church to the memory of Christ. Its divine authority, which we shall hereafter attempt to prove, is kept properly in the back-ground.

Of church days since instituted, not by authority, there have been by far too many, and human ostentation, priestly pride, and papal superstition have presided at their origin. In such case they may be imposed upon men by ecclesiastical tyranny, and be neither beneficial to man nor honoring to Christ. But suppose there had been no such days, and without any of these great anniversary occasions coming down to us, we of this century, had in the true Christian spirit, instituted a Christmas festival, for example, in honor of our Lord, would it not be a commendable act acceptable to him? Had there been no Lordian day set apart by inspired apostles, and growing into general use by the custom of the primitive church, it would even now be a commendable thing for the church to institute and keep it. In that case, however, it would not be right to enforce it as law, (Matt. xv. 9) "In vain do they worship me, teaching for doctrines the commandments of men;" but it would have great authority over the individual conscience, since respect to the church itself, and the innate obligation of affection and honor to Christ, would force it upon every heart as a voluntary tribute of love.

The voluntary and spontaneous is a large element in religion. "Whosoever will let him come." "Thy people shall be willing in the day of thy power." The Christian soldier is a volunteer, not a conscript. He is invited into the field. He delights in the service. He rejoices in his captain. For him he esteems it a privilege to deny himself and take up his cross. For him he delights to attack sin in the citadel of his own heart. He "rejoices in his dear name." He holds the Christian banner high and marches under it to victory or death, with the same serene composure, the same exultation of soul. The service of Christ is not a heartless service. "This people draweth nigh unto me with their mouth, and honoreth me with their lips; but their heart is far from me," was written of self-righteous Jews, not of pious Christians. Such soldiers obey with alacrity every order. It is no infringement upon their liberty to serve in a cause to which they have given their hearts. Their commander's word is their supreme law. But beyond and outside of it, there are innumerable voluntary expressions of their interest in the cause, and their love for him whom they follow.

We have called attention thus at length to this phase of the Christian service because it is of much value, and, besides, bears directly upon a right view of the general question before us. He who never forced a human being to be his disciple, who never violated the principles which in human conduct constitute propriety, in regard to imposing institutions in his own honor upon men, saw fit to introduce, not by himself but by his apostles, and in a way perfectly consistent with their own free and spontaneous action, for the observance of Christians of all ages, the Lordian day, a time of solemn worship, of glad exultation and joyous praise. He who comes in company with his brethren, upon that day, into the courts of the Most High, and draws near to him through the mediation of the blessed Christ, with a pure heart and consecrated lips, is ever an acceptable worshiper. And no more delightful service can be imagined. It is a gratification, too, to know that into whatever clime you go, if Christians are found, they are worshiping God on the same day. This fraternity in such a service which places us side by side with primitive Christians, and with those of most distant lands, which associates us with martyrs who have died for him even as he has died for us, and which brings all ranks and conditions of men into one common fellowship of love in Christ, is the dearest thing among men.

Such observations as these prepare us for a right understanding of the Scriptures, as they relate to the day, both in respect to the evidences of its existence, and also, as to its authority and the manner of its observance. It will not be expected that more than scanty reference will be made to it, or that it will be brought to our view in the rigid form of dry and barren enactment. It will have rather the appearance of a free-will offering by the disciples themselves. Still, it will come, if at all, with all the force of apostolic sanction, and consequently with the authority of Christ himself.

On the question of the weight of apostolic usage, in determining obligation to Christians of later times, there is a wide divergence of opinion. Some search for the slightest traces of apostolic procedure in all matters of which there are intimations, or supposed intimations, derivable from logical investigations, and insist that these should be made the basis of rigid authority, even going so far as to question the early fathers of the church, and relying largely upon their testimony in fixing the eagerly sought precedent. Others confine themselves to strict Scriptural command, being of opinion that whatever is not so definitely set forth in the record as to be clearly imposed upon the church for all ages, is merely to be classed among the expediencies of the time and place. Besides, there is a third class placing very great stress upon all the forms and usages of the apostles, but claiming legitimate successors to these, vicegerents of Christ now existing, whose authority consequently is supreme, either in the abrogation of apostolic precedents or the imposition of new rules equally binding.

Judicial fairness would suggest to him who rejects the dogma of apostolic succession that there is some foundation for the authority of apostolic precedent, and that neither extreme view can be correct. There surely were many things done by the apostles and said by them which were merely local and temporal. There were in connection with the churches which they organized and guided, circumstances requiring definite instructions from the highest sources, the like of which do not now and may never again exist. On these points the value of the record is mainly historical. Again, there are other cases such as always occur. The management of these and the instructions given in reference to them, may well be our guide in like exigencies. Thus it appears that the first indication of an apostolic precedent is the universal applicability of it. Yet it may be conceded that this, while sometimes decisive, is not always so. Other considerations are needful to a correct estimate.

A second criterion is found in the essential importance of that which constitutes the precedent. That which related to the actual organization or government of the church would for this reason be material, and should be settled according to the primitive inspired usage. Quite different would be the case as to the hour of the day or evening in which Christians assembled at their regular seasons of worship. In this case, if no other consideration was found to have a bearing, the precedent should be rejected as too trivial to be regarded as law.

The third quality of an approved precedent is that it is significant in and of itself, so being in entire harmony with all parts of the Christian system. If a lesson be conveyed in it fundamental to the gospel, and which inspired teachers have used every possible means to impress upon the minds of the people, it may naturally be supposed that this is another means adopted and intended to aid in enforcing that lesson. Thus suppose it evident that the apostles always knelt in prayer, thus enforcing the lesson of humility, and recognizing the Lordship of him before whom we bow, or suppose a distinction between petition and thanksgiving were to be uniformly observed, the former indicated by an invariable kneeling and the latter by the standing position, each suggestive of an appropriate religious idea, such a precedent would be very influential with any thoughtful Christian.

As a fourth criterion may be mentioned the adaptation to benefit those who should follow the precedent. Surely nothing which practiced could be physically, mentally or morally injurious to any human being will be found to be an authoritative apostolic precedent. For instance, in regard to the greatly abused question pertaining to the so-called "mode of baptism," when the import of the original word itself has been sufficiently discussed, it is usual to attempt to adduce the apostolic usage on the one side or the other. It has sometimes been clamorously asserted that immersion is both dangerous and indecent. If such statements could be substantiated in the face of the long and extensive Baptist practice of that " mode," then the improbability of such precedent would be manifest. For surely this or any other ordinance can not be followed in a matter of " mode" merely to such disastrous consequences when a mere precedent, itself doubtful, and no explicit demand requires it.

Presuming that a more exhaustive analysis, such as we might attempt were this distinction a leading one in this book, would reveal other criteria of the authority of apostolic precedents, these will at least be sufficient for a crucial test in the case before us. Whether apostolic sanction carries with it the authority of Christ (as was remarked above in reference to the day) through all the ages of the church, may justly, perhaps, in view of distinctions just drawn, be said to depend upon the nature of that to which it refers. And here a wide field is open for difference of opinion among those who would be right, and unending controversy among others who adhere to form rather than spirit, to whom mint, anise and cumin are themselves the weightier matters of the law. But fear of controversy should not deter us from approaching any subject fearlessly, and declaring our calm and candid convictions upon it.

Suppose, for example, an apostle had written to the brethren at Philippi, telling them to build a brick house. It would hardly appear incumbent upon churches of all ages to build such houses. It might be in many cases impossible, in many more much more expensive. Such a matter would not appear fundamental or in any sense important. And yet, under the Jewish economy, the tabernacle was exact in materials, form and workmanship. "See that thou make it according to the pattern shown thee in the mount," was an explicit command of God. But this was a representative building, setting forth in these particulars " good things to come," and as such must be exact. Besides, God's definite commands are to be obeyed implicitly. The apostles, however, had many things to supervise which were necessarily temporal and local. We must exercise our best judgment in distinguishing between such and those which are in their nature lasting, universal and fundamental.

Tried by the principles adduced above, the Lordian day must be conceded to have greater weight of authority from apostolic precedent than any other institution, form or custom mentioned in the New Testament. First, it is applicable to all people and all times. There is no inherent reason why it should not be generally observed. Once let its authority be recognized, and all people brought to wish so to do, and there will appear no obstacle to prevent all from keeping it according to Christian usage. In the second place, it is important, essential, indeed, to Christian life and growth. Prayer, praise, exhortation, instruction in righteousness, assemblies of Christians for that purpose, the observance of the Lordian supper in common, and many good works, require stated and regular times for meeting together, as well as for special private study and devotions, and social religious intercourse with others. It is a matter of the utmost importance, one of vital necessity to the maintenance of the Christian religion. Had not the first day of the week been appropriated to this purpose, some other must necessarily have been chosen for it.

Under the third principle, not only is a day of the week, but more definitely the first day of the week, shown to possess the characteristics constituting it an institution, to which apostolic precedent would give the utmost authority. For the idea which it perpetuates, the lesson which it ever inculcates, the fact of which it is an everlasting memorial, is the greatest in all the Bible. The first day marking the resurrection of Christ, and selected to be religiously observed because it marks that event, becomes the most instructive of all outward observances. No other, setting forth any other fact even of the gospel, could hardly be regarded so important. The resurrection of Christ is given as the great test, the perfect proof of the divine purpose and power. When that is thrown upon the observation of the world, nothing else pertaining to the mission of Christ can be denied. But "if Christ be not raised," "your faith is vain," "ye are yet in your sins," "in this life only you have hope," "you are of all men most miserable." When, therefore, apostolic precedent fixes upon a day commemorating such an event, teaching to Christians and all others who notice its observance the chief fact of all the gospel, no greater authority could be desired. The footsteps of the apostles in regard to the day will be faithfully followed by all right-minded people, just the same as though a positive command had been left us. And when the reasons, as heretofore shown, for the use of precedent rather than command, appear with all their irresistible force, where shall there be found a professing Christian indifferent to the obligation of the day? Under this head it should be noted, in the nature of a climax, that nothing else marks the resurrection of our Lord as perfectly as does the Lordian day. The emblematic supper shows forth his death, baptism represents his resurrection together with the burial, but this is but one act of a lifetime. The Lordian day presents the resurrection to the thought of all people where it is observed, constantly, perpetually. When divorced from the ideas which inhered in the old Jewish Sabbath, and recognized as founded only on, and testifying to, the resurrection, and pledging the faith of the people in that event, it has no superior in importance among all the forms and ordinances of the church in instructing the people. Let him beware who trifles with the day.

We are called in the fourth place to notice the value of the institution in and of itself. Certainly here is no need of argument. In all that pertains to health, comfort, rest, social enjoyment and religious worship, the day which the Christian observes and the law protects, which common custom has made a rest day, is, as such, one of the greatest blessings known to civilized man. Without stopping to enlarge upon a thought both interesting and profitable, we are led to consider that no slight share of its utility is due to the uniformity. This is more and more apparent as we bestow thought upon it. Imagine in this country, for instance, among the various sects, as great diversity upon the day of the week observed as upon some other points. Suppose Presbyterians met for worship and transacted no secular business on Monday, Baptists in like manner on Tuesday,

Methodists on Wednesday, Episcopalians on Thursday, Dunkards on Friday, United Brethren on Saturday, Catholics on Sunday. Or worse still: suppose separate congregations, belonging to the same body, had each its own special day which it kept with punctilious strictness, it is evident that both worship and business would be inconceivably disturbed. Even if there had been only changes from one period of time to another, there would vast annoyance arise in tracing history, in establishing the validity of various documents and in a thousand ways not thought of beforehand.

If, then, the apostles established a day, even were it by uninspired action, the necessities of the case make it binding for all time, and any "religious reformer" who attempts to restore the old Jewish Sabbath does it at the peril of religious worship, business interests, and attempts to thwart the providence, if not to disobey the commands, of Almighty God.

Persons who advocate the Sabbath as an institution remaining in force since the establishment of the church, are wont to magnify the use which the apostles made of that day in proselyting among the Jews, while they correspondingly depreciate all references to the first day of the week. Now if there were five hundred instances of the Sabbath thus used, it would not support their view of the question in the least. For it is not denied that there were synagogues in all the cities of the land. In these, the Jewish law, still in force in that nationality, and, moreover, as already explained, strongly entrenched in the prejudices of even the converts from that people, was read as of old on these days, and words of comment and exhortation offered by such competent Jews as happened to be present. Not only therefore were all the apostles, but even Timothy, authorized to appear in these synagogues, on the various Sabbath days, when the people assembled according to time-honored custom. And they were free to speak, and improved such opportunities, by far the best they could possibly obtain, to reach the ears of the people. Now, to make this appear an argument for the religious obligation of the Sabbath, it would be necessary to prove, first, that this procedure on their part would be improper on any other but the religious day of the week; or, second, that such rites, if any, as were peculiar to the Christian system were practiced on the Sabbath and in the synagogues.

It so happens that neither of these is true. There was no time when apostles or any zealous Christians did not endeavor to convince all the people within their reach of the truth of the gospel and lead them to obedience. From house to house, on every day of the week, by every public and private means of persuasion, they carried on the good work. But who does not see that this was quite a different thing from the celebration of those religious forms which pertained to the church alone? The Lordian supper was never assigned to the Jewish Sabbath. It belonged exclusively to the resurrection day, to the worship day of the church. There is no intimation anywhere that it was ever celebrated on the Sabbath day, or in the synagogues of the Jews on those occasions to which Sabbatarians are so fond of referring. Consider the three names to which preëminence has been given by their formation from the official titles of the great Head of the church. They come together on the first day of the week and indisputably mark it as by apostolic precedent the religious day of the church for all time. The Christians partake of the Lordian supper on the Lordian day. The Lord himself is with them in solemn and blessed communion. He might lie in the tomb through the hours of the Jewish Sabbath, but he would dispense the blessing of the new covenant to his disciples, on a brighter and better day, that which was ushered in by the resurrection morn. It is the day of all days, immensely, immeasurably, infinitely superior to the Sabbath in every lesson which it teaches.

Now, strange to say, Sabbatarians illustrate in the most forcible manner the very principles to which we are alluding. They, too, recognize the difference between their special religious meetings for worship, and gatherings for proselyting. The former they hold exclusively on the seventh day according to their faith. The latter they hold just whenever they can get the people together. More especially do they employ the first day in this way since it is the custom of the people at that time in preference to any other to assemble for religious purposes. These great meetings of theirs for preaching their doctrines to the world, of which we have often observed them to hold two or three on Sunday, while on other days they held but one, and their exclusive worship service only on Saturday, render sufficiently plain their purpose; and, when you have reversed the days, show why the apostles used the old Sabbath and the Jewish synagogues for preaching the gospel to the people at large, while with more or less privacy they gathered by themselves together on the Lordian day, for the special worship of the church, and, most notably of all, the celebration of the Lordian supper.

The reader who desires to test these distinctions by references to the Scripture, will find (Acts xv. 21) that the Jews met in all the cities every Sabbath day to hear Moses read and preached in the synagogue. The thirteenth chapter of Acts informs us how Paul discoursed to them, of the new faith, on such occasions. The sixteenth chapter describes a gathering by the river side, at which Paul convinced Lydia and her household, while the eighteenth (4) expresses the fact that "he reasoned in the synagogue every Sabbath and persuaded the Jews and the Greeks."

Leaving these meetings in which Paul "testified to the Jews that Jesus was Christ," (xviii. 5), let us endeavor to find the worshiping assemblies of the saints themselves. The references to the particular day of such meetings are few. The allusions are incidental, as was to be expected, but all the more weighty in establishing the fact. They point clearly in one direction and indisputably prove that under the usage in apostolic times, the first day of the week was not only a Lordian day in all that is implied in the term, but also the only one. Preparation for the institution of the Lordian day may be traced in the appearing of Christ to his disciples on several occasions after the resurrection, on the first day of the week, also in the resurrection itself, when, for the first time, hope was fixed upon the living Christ, and the fact that Pentecost came on that day (fifty days after the high day of the Passover, when he lay in the grave), upon which the first fruits of the gospel were dispensed to the believing Jews at Jerusalem.

But we pass on for the positive evidence, to an allusion recorded in Acts (xx. 7), which can not but be regarded as conclusive. "And upon the first day of the week, when the disciples came together to break bread, Paul preached unto them ready to depart on the morrow." Now why is the first day of the week mentioned? Because it was a special day. To whom? To the disciples. It was such, too, by regular, preconcerted arrangement. It had been fixed upon for a definite purpose, which could not be accomplished until the day came. The distinguished visitors had remained at Troas a whole week. All the days were represented in their stay. But the first day of the week was the only one on which the disciples came together, for had they assembled at any other it would have been an appropriate time for the preaching of Paul. There was nothing in preaching which ever confined it to the Lordian day. At Troas, then, there was one day only, namely, the first day of the week, devoted to these assemblies.

But what is implied in the expression "to break bread"? It is strikingly similar to that used in the description of the institution of the supper by our Lord himself, "And he took bread and blessed and brake." If it was not this religious festival in honor of the Lord, what was it, and why mentioned at all, and why with both the day and the feast, were the Christians thus associated without any foreign admixture? "The disciples" alone met, not the people without distinction, nor any connection of them by blood relation, such as might be expected to come together to a worldly feast. It is clear that we have here the Lordian day and on it the assembly of Christians to celebrate the Lordian supper. Such a day we have now, which must have originated at some time, which is first mentioned by the Apostle John (Rev. i. 10), and which is indicated by this and other passages as existing in apostolic times. Such assemblies of the church are clearly enjoined by the apostle (Heb. x. 25).

On a certain occasion Paul wrote to the church at Corinth (I. Cor. xvi. 1), "Now concerning the collection for the saints, as I have given order to the churches of Galatia, even so do ye. Upon the first day of the week let every one of you lay by him in store, as God hath prospered him, that there be no gatherings when I come." Whatever is indicated by this passage in regard to the first day of the week has the same relation to all the churches in Galatia that it has to Corinth, so that if it may be supposed to allude to a day of assembly for religious purposes, we now have these added to that at Troas, and combined with Revelations (i. 10) it is only fair to conclude that a general custom existed among all Christians.

But what is the bearing of this passage upon the subject? It must be conceded as before that the day would not have been mentioned at all instead of any other, were it not that it was in some sense a marked day with the Christians. There may have been a convenience in laying by these contributions on this particular day. But as a supply for the necessities of the poor saints at Jerusalem, it was more,—it was a religious act (Matt. x. 42; xxv. 40). As such, participated in by the Christians of a vast scope of country, and the most universal and extensive, comparatively speaking, of any similar enterprise ever undertaken, it was fitting that by apostolic direction it should be especially assigned to the day, then taking character for all time, under the practice of the new-born church, and the warm and generous impulses of their new-born faith. Are we not taught to bestow our ministrations to the saints as an act of fealty if not of worship to the Lord himself, and is not the Lordian day the most appropriate for such an act?

Besides, if it were a set religious day, it was that on which the disciples, separated from their ordinary labors, gave attention to religious affairs, and may be reasonably supposed to have their business arrangements so adjusted as to be able to attend to special matters of this kind. And yet more, at the end of six days steady labor, they knew what they had acquired, how "God had prospered" them, and it was a suitable day to divide proceeds with him in this Christian service.

We shall not attempt to press these allusions of Scripture further. The simplest ideas which they convey on the surface, according to natural modes of interpretation, are all that we have sought, and they have been all that was necessary to make our argument symmetrical and complete.

CHAPTER XIII.

THE FATHERS.

Upon no other subject is the testimony of the Fathers of the Christian church more decisive than upon the validity of the Lordian day. Upon many others has it been evoked, and the writings of the first few centuries ransacked with partisan zeal, and contended over with anything but disinterested purpose. Such subjects as baptism, confirmation, papal authority, find here ground for much wordy warfare to very unimportant results.

The paucity of reliable conclusions from this field of research, compared with the expectations of those who explore it, is indeed marvelous. The anticipations of the reader are seldom realized in following a confident author here. And, in general, what is brought to light is not entitled to the weight which the learned investigator imagines. Why should we search a cornfield for potatoes or a vineyard for apples, when we have but to open our natural eyes to see what each contains? Why should we propound questions to the fathers which in all reason we should know they can not answer? Why should we ask their testimony on points where it would be valueless?

To one who honestly searches here for light, a very few guiding principles are necessary. If no distinctions are made, error rather than truth will be obtained. We shall not in this chapter call upon our witness until we have shown in what his intelligence, opportunities and credibility are such as to entitle him to be regarded. And when we have satisfied our readers upon this point, we shall allow him to give his testimony in his own way. Though little be taken, it shall be fairly done. There shall be no garbling, no selection of the favorable alone, no distortion, whereby the trivial shall be magnified and the important belittled. We have long thought that absolute dishonesty has often characterized religious disputants in dealing with the writings of the early church. Knowing that but one in a thousand can ever put them to the test, they have made white appear black, and black white, without scruple. They have found all sorts of testimony upon every subject, and have loudly clamored for the authority of patristic opinions which, in the nature of the case, were more likely to be worthless than those of an Illinois farmer on ocean sailing.

But what are the distinctions that should be made? Mainly should be noted the difference between fact and opinion. Upon the former, uneducated and very humble people are often the best of witnesses. At the same time, their personal opinions, if for no other reason than lack of opportunity to observe or study the data from which they could be formed or corrected, may be very crude. One can not read largely from the fathers without the conviction that this is exactly true of them. They were both ignorant and without experience. And yet they are quoted as if semi-apostles. That they were beginners in the Christian system, as well as mystified by innumerable whims and notions pertaining to the age in which they lived, is evident. We found many perverse and misguided brethren in the apostolic age. Notwithstanding the clear instructions of inspired teachers, when these had passed away the church resembled a ship on stormy seas with but theoretical sailors in charge. Only because it was a staunch craft, made by a wise master builder, was it saved from going to pieces. What a reckless assumption that it was manned by experienced seamen, able to give us instruction in navigation to-day!

For sensible views on any ordinary religious subject, a common, fair-minded Christian now is immeasurably superior to the aptest scholars and most eminent theologians of the early centuries. This is perhaps the most striking impression one derives from reading the religious history and writings of the time. The reason is, that while thought was not crystallized by long and extensive examination of the system itself, together with its related subjects, there was, at the same time, less of stability, more of credulity and wayward fancy in the minds of the people. Each individual was in a far greater degree alone and self-dependent in such views than now. At the present day all possible phases of religious questions have seemingly been canvassed by impartial and able criticism, so that anything imperfect and fanciful is met at first by well defined and established and well known ideas which throw it out of consideration at once, and expose its author, if he persists in it, to just contempt.

Nor does the fact that these men lived very near to the time of the apostles make their opinions more worthy of confidence. We live as near to Jefferson and Hamilton, with immensely better facilities for becoming acquainted with the views of the founders of our republic, than they had of the apostles, yet every year clearer and more correct estimates are given of our political fathers than ever before. So undoubtedly we can judge better from apostolic data than could the fathers of the church. The New Testament informs us of divisions, false doctrines and heresies while yet the apostles lived. Individual opinions upon religious subjects even then clashed and led their authors after fables and commandments of men and away from the doctrines of Christ.

As to facts, this was quite different. Notions might be vague and foolish, but if there was any such thing as baptism practiced, the Lord's supper observed, or the first day of the week kept, the testimony of the fathers must be taken as conclusive. Their ideas upon these subjects might be unreasonable, but their record as to the facts irresistible.

Whatever they may have thought of the significance of the Lordian day, or of the Sabbath, may not influence our minds, but their statement that Christians kept such a day, and the manner thereof, must be conclusive as to the fact.

The Christian church has an existence to-day essentially different from the Jewish theocracy. The testimony of the church fathers, together with the New Testament itself, places its origin with the apostles, its exact beginning the first Pentecost after the crucifixion. Baptism is traced the same way. So is the Lordian supper, and the Lordian day, each to its origin in proper place in connection with the Christian church. Now, while we may undervalue the opinions of the fathers upon many of these matters, as to the facts of their existence and origin, their evidence is complete.

We wish in this chapter to introduce their testimony in this field of actual occurrence, to tell us what really transpired among them relative to both the Sabbath and the Lordian day. Upon the theory of the relation of these days to the divine economy in general, we believe ourselves better competent to affirm than they. The long experience and patient study of centuries has given us better opportunities to understand than they.

We shall inquire of these fathers and early writers:

1. Whether the sabbath was still observed among Christians.
2. Whether the first day was also observed.
3. Whether this latter was called the Lordian day.
4. Why and how the first day was observed, if at all?

Extracts will be quoted from various writers, which, if their authority is to be received, like a good bank bill, at par, will be found in all cases to agree, and finally to give positive answers to every question in the list. Is not every inquiry one pertaining to their own times and within their own observation? If twenty centuries hence one shall examine such writers of the present as may then be known, as to whether from 1850 to 1900 the telegraph was in existence, he will surely get a correct answer, if anything like a considerable amount of our literature shall remain. So while there are many Christian and secular writers mentioning religious facts of the early church, we may expect to find correct testimony from several of them upon the inquiries propounded, for they are all leading ones, and must have been within the observation of all, and no motive existed for concealing them.

We have thought it desirable in this to disarm at first, if possible, all suspicion that we might be partial, selecting such passages as would tend to support our own theory and passing others by. As such quotations are a mere matter of compilation, to facilitate the examinations of any who may wish to test our fairness, we do not refer the reader for verification of the statements made to numerous obscure writers whom he may be unable to reach or to translate into English or understand, but refer him to a book the most likely of any known to us to be within his reach. If he will, therefore, consult the article, "Lord's-day," in Smith's Bible Dictionary (unabridged form), he will find what we shall take the liberty to use as citations from the early church fathers and much more to the same effect. He will find the quotations nowhere called in question or contradicted. A very few will therefore be sufficient to establish facts.

The letter of Pliny to Trajan is an official pagan document, and shows that "a stated day"—certainly not the Jewish sabbath, or it would have been mentioned—was observed. "The Christians affirm the whole of their guilt or error to be, that they were accustomed to meet together on a stated day, before it was light, and to sing hymns to Christ as a god, and to bind themselves by a sacrament, not for any wicked purpose, but never to commit fraud, theft or adultery; never to break their word, or to refuse, when called upon, to deliver up any trust; after which it was their custom to separate and to assemble again to take a meal, but a general one, and without guilty purpose."

Epistle of Barnabas.—" We celebrate the eighth day with joy, on which, too, Jesus rose from the dead."

Justin Martyr.—Space will not allow the direct quotation of his important testimony. An immediate successor of the apostles, he declares of Christians their custom to assemble on Sunday to read the writings of apostles, to offer prayer, celebrate the Lordian supper, and collect alms. The resurrection of the Lord on that day is assigned as a reason for its observance. Many points of interest in this author tend in the same direction, and also show clearly that to keep sabbath according to Jewish custom was understood to be quite a different thing from Christian worship on the Lordian day.

Ignatius also makes a distinction similar to this last.

Bardesanus states it to be the custom of Christians to assemble on the first day of the week.

Irenæus asserts the abolition of the sabbath, and the first day of the week as the proper day to celebrate the Lord's resurrection.

Clement of Alexandria mentions the Lordian day as a customary religious festival.

Tertullian uses Lordian day, Sunday, and first day of the week synonymously as to the time indicated. It was a day of joy, hence the kneeling posture in prayer on that day, in his judgment, is inappropriate. The distraction of the mind by business pursuits should be guarded against.

Origen regarded it as one of the marks of the perfect Christian to keep the Lordian day.

Cyprian (and his colleagues), following Justin Martyr, points to circumcision on the eighth day under the Jewish law, tracing its significance and reference to the resurrection of Christ, and to the Lordian day, which is at once the eighth and the first.

Commodian mentions the Lordian day.

Victorinus contrasts it with the sabbath.

Peter, bishop of Alexandria, says of it: "We keep the Lordian day as a day of joy, because of him who rose thereon."

The author of the article from which these citations are made, as Bampton Lecturer for 1860, treated of the same subject most thoroughly on that occasion, to which and to the article referred to, the reader is directed for much more extended evidence than we have thought it best to offer here. It is but just to all parties that we should append a summary of his conclusions:

"The results of our examination of the principal writers of the two centuries after the death of St. John, are as follows: The Lord's day (a name which has now come out more prominently, and is connected more explicitly with our Lord's resurrection than before), existed during these two centuries as a part and parcel of apostolical, and so of scriptural Christianity. It was never defended, for it was never impugned, or at least only impugned as other things received from the apostles were. It was never confounded with the sabbath, but carefully distinguished from it, (though we have not quoted nearly all the passages by which this point might be proved). It was not an institution of severe sabbatical character, but a day of joy and cheerfulness, rather encouraging than forbidding relaxation. Religiously regarded, it was a day of solemn meeting for the Holy Eucharist, for united prayer, for instruction, for alms-giving; and though, being an institution under the law of liberty, work does not appear to have been formally interdicted, or rest formally enjoined. Tertullian seems to indicate that the character of the day was opposed to worldly business. Finally, whatever analogy may be supposed to exist between the Lord's day and the sabbath, in no passage that has come down to us is the fourth commandment appealed to as the ground of the obligation to observe the Lord's day. Ecclesiastical writers reiterate again and again, in the strictest sense of the words, 'Let no man therefore judge you in respect of an holiday, or of the new moon, or of the sabbath days.' Nor, again, is it referred to any sabbatical foundation anterior to the promulgation of the Mosaic economy. On the contrary, those before the Mosaic era are constantly assumed to have had neither knowledge nor observance of the sabbath. And as little is it anywhere asserted that the Lord's day is merely an ecclesiastical institution, dependent on the post-apostolic church for its origin, and by consequence capable of being done away, should a time ever arrive when it appears to be no longer needed.

"Our design does not necessarily lead us to do more than state facts; but if the facts be allowed to speak for themselves, they indicate that the Lord's day is a purely Christian institution, sanctioned by apostolic practice, mentioned in apostolic writings, and so possessed of whatever divine authority all apostolic ordinances and doctrines (which were not obviously temporary, or were not abrogated by the apostles themselves) can be supposed to possess."

One quotation from an author, whether Christian or pagan, known to belong to a date immediately succeeding the apostles, would be sufficient to prove that the sacred day was not of later origin. So many of them are ample to show that it came from the apostles, to whom with one accord they attribute it. A larger number than we have given would burden our pages and prove tiresome to the general reader. Yet, while we have merely scrapped and taken a fraction from the dictionary, we have quoted it as affirming that many more exist not found in its pages. So that, on the whole, the literature of that age is copious and satisfactory in its references to this subject. The fact is established that the Lordian day came out of the apostolic age to the fathers of the church, and they with one accord certify to it. They call it "the Lordian day," too. They do not call it "Lord's day" or "day of the Lord." But their writings are in Greek and they use the adjective, the same as John does in the first chapter of Revelations. They seem to understand that this appellation has a distinctive application to the first day of the week, as it grew into use, (after it had been marked from resurrection to Pentecost), as the day of religious gatherings and worship, at Troas, throughout Galatia, in Corinth, and finally, as mentioned by the apostle, in the church at large. They seem, without doubting its obligation, to be rather inquiring as to what sort of celebration would be most in keeping with its nature. The position in prayer on that day, the propriety of rest from labor, and similar items, are referred to. In our opinion, both scripture and history are eminently satisfactory upon the entire subject.

As to the formal questions proposed above, the testimony is explicit.

1. The Sabbath was not observed as binding upon Christians. It was contrasted with the Lordian day and declared to be abolished.

2. The first day was observed.

3. Its only religious name was "the Lordian day."

4. It was observed because of apostolic authority, in commemoration of the resurrection of the Lord, as a day of joy, religious convocation, partaking of the Lordian supper, alms-giving, and other appropriate exercises, and was gradually taking on, from the recognized propriety of the case independent of the Mosaic law, its sabbatic character, that is, abstinence from secular employments.

The fathers discuss this subject as they do every other that reaches them among institutions inherited from the apostles. What does it mean? What is its object? What is its relation to various parts of the general scheme? What are its points of likeness to anything in the old dispensation? Thus they handle baptism and similar established institutions. They do not question their existence; they examine their nature. They compare scripture, reason, and speculate. Their testimony, therefore, seems incidental and unprejudiced, as it is cumulative and decisive. On any theory that the Lordian day is of post-apostolic origin, or that it was not recognized as binding from the beginning, it would be impossible to explain this mass of patristic testimony. It could not have been manufactured for a purpose, because, first, its nature is entirely contradictory to such a supposition, and second, any theory which it might be supposed to support is of later origin than the testimony itself. Nothing remains, therefore, but to give it full credit as to the question of fact. For anything beyond that we are not inclined to inquire of the fathers. Their time of writing makes them especially valuable as witnesses of facts, and correspondingly weak in the domain of theology.

Some may desire to know more of these writings. They constitute a mass of literature with no very plain distinction drawn between the different kinds of writing or the character and belief of the authors. The pagan or worldly historian, the devout Christian father, the philosopher who reasons in both fields alike with various or varying angles of inclination to the one or the other, the apologist who openly defends the Christian religion or its books against the attacks of their enemies, all add their corroborating testimony. It is a body of literature which could not be read soon if in our own language. Possibly some one who has attempted Eusebius, and found its later Greek quite as difficult to translate as Demosthenes or any earlier author, will be ready to stand sponsor for our statement that very few modern scholars even are likely to explore this field very extensively in the original. The avenues of information open to us are therefore of necessity quotations, extracts, compilations and translations made by numerous different authors at various times and for divers purposes. But combining the labors of original explorers and second-hand copyists and arrangers with such original investigations as time, inclination and ability may lead him to make, the writer of the nineteenth century finds no difficulty in summoning the testimony of the early church, in an intelligent and complete manner, upon any subject upon which it bears.

The fathers of the church! The combination of social and religious veneration is awakened. Though our fathers were possibly in their manhood not wiser than we are in ours, they at least lived in advance of us, and that is no mean thought. The church fathers lived first of all. To them was awarded the privilege of taking up the work when apostles laid it down. It was formed in essential parts to their hands by divine wisdom, but now it devolves upon them to continue it. I have tried to liken this task to anything within present human experience. The effort has failed. The most complicated machinery might be given in the charge of one unskilled in its use. But time, patience, study, would fit him to fill the place of the expert manager. The laws of mechanics involved in its structure are few. They are easily understood. Their action is always alike. Hence it is possible to discover and apply them in the case supposed. One entirely inexperienced in the oversight of a local congregation might suddenly be thrown into the position of responsibility. But this is comparatively a small matter. And there are other congregations which may serve as models of correct procedure. Instruction is found on every hand to supplement and illustrate what the Scriptures contain.

But to have the church, the one grand organization in the world, the living embodiment of all true religion, the realization of all the efforts which God has put forth to purify and save man during the ages from Adam to Christ, now left in the charge of men, inspiration, miracles and apostles withdrawn, it is a fearful thought. Such an idea surpasses beyond conception the imaginary likenesses which we have drawn. It is as though God had left the entire physical universe to man's unaided hand. Unaided? Who said unaided? Who thought unaided? For the task of spiritual upholding is assuredly not less than that of the physical. It was certainly not the meekness of Moses, shrinking from the task of delivering, under God's direction, the Hebrew nation from Egyptian bondage, that inspired the "ruling elder" of the church at Rome to assume the primacy and apostolic succession. It was avarice, ambition, ignorance, wickedness. He could not have realized what he was willing to undertake. The magnitude of such a work, the responsibility of such a primacy at such a time, had it involved all that has been claimed for it, was great enough to overpower any human being. He probably did not care. Visions of preëminence lured him on. But to such feeble agents God had not committed the real fortunes of the church.

We remember the Saviour's parable of the leaven. There is a principle within it which acts by its very nature upon the material of proper kind with which it comes in contact. The woman took and hid it in three measures of meal until the whole was leavened. In like manner, though there were no longer supernatural revelations from a divine source, the truth had been committed to the hearts of men. The Bible in substance, if not as an accepted canon, was given to the race. It must act. It would act. To regenerate the soul was the inevitable consequence, then as now, when men came to apprehend its truths. But it may be men will not read it. They may neglect to preach it, or publish it to others. The world may lie in darkness while the means of its enlightenment are at hand unemployed. There is no lack of faith in the leaven, but the woman is required to place it in the meal. Should man not be disposed to do this necessary work for himself, will salvation in consequence be a failure? Believe it who will.

It is possible that after Christianity has attained its present hold upon the world its inherent divine power may maintain it in existence without further external aid. There is no lack of faith in the gospel to spread from heart to heart and from nation to nation. Like a fire well kindled, it **may** burn on. But to start it, in that the trouble lies. It was perhaps but indifferent material to which the fires of the gospel were first applied, and possibly it is no better now. It is our opinion that he who provides the means with infinite foresight as well as philanthropy, will not abandon them, in such an exigency as this, to any chance of failure. He sees that the good work goes on. He adjusts the circumstances; he provides the agencies; he supplies the missing link which joins agent to object. Whatever is lacking, no more, no less, is furnished. If divine revelation has within itself that power which will sufficiently attract and gain attention as well as work its legitimate effects afterwards, then it will be left alone when once given to the world.

We are of opinion that an overruling providence then as now, but especially then, because more necessary, was presiding over the church. While there was less of sight there was room for greater exercise of faith. When personal divine supervision was not visible, the cultivation of self-reliance made human agencies effective to do their utmost. It was well that a sense of responsibility should attach to the individual Christian, that he should feel that in a large measure the work was committed to his hands, and without his best efforts must fail. A sanctified zeal was enkindled, the energies fully aroused, a love for those whose salvation was committed to his care, thus sprang up permanently in the disciple. But while thoughts like these impress themselves upon us, it is impossible to suppose the divine direction withdrawn. To interpret men's actions, they would appear to think that the larger forces of nature are self-acting, while many of the smaller are under human direction. The Scriptures speak quite a different language. How invariably they ascribe to the all-seeing eye and the omnipotent arm the charge of everything from the least to the greatest. As in nature so in grace. The cry of the young ravens is heard, so likewise the prayer of the righteous.

Consider, then, if you have faith in God, his care directing the early movements of the church, providing for its then present necessities and whatever its future may require. In the institution of the sacred day every step was taken to make it essentially Lordian in all that the term would imply. Coming into use in that natural and appropriate manner which we have seen, no evidence was lacking to connect it unmistakably with the source of legitimate authority. Divine providence presided at the laying of the foundations of patristic testimony, divine foresight secured it, ample in amount, in variety and in unstudied conclusiveness. So that the result gained is a day known in its origin, object and history. Easily traced, clearly defined, exactly adapted to the new era and the new people. Divine in the wisdom of its adjustment and in the authority which it brings, and yet the voluntary tribute of honor by a free people to their Lord and king who has delivered them.

The old day was adapted to the law, this to the gospel. The Sabbath was one of the terrors that emanated from Sinai, the Lordian day that which commemorates the banishment of them all. On this day the yoke of bondage was broken. On this the star of hope rises above the horizon. Exultant millions gather with one accord in the temples that their own free hands have builded; they offer their praises to him that has redeemed them from law and made them the recipients of his wondrous grace. We offer our gratitude to him whose providences have enabled us to look back through the day, as it has been kept in his memory by our brethren of past centuries, up to the morning of the resurrection itself. We thank God for the evidences with which he has surrounded it and made it visible to us.

CHAPTER XIV.

CONSTANTINE AND THE POPES.

The question naturally occurs, what did, or could, Constantine, though surnamed the Great, do to change in any way the validity of either Sabbath or Lordian day, since, at the time of his reign, all inspired lawgivers had completed their work, and left it perfect in the keeping and for the obedience of the church? Christ himself no longer "spake as never man spake." Apostles, through the Spirit, no longer instituted the forms of the church or guided its members in the feeble beginnings of the divine life. Even those who had seen and heard them had long since passed away. The author of this book has as good a right to publish a decree in its pages changing religious forms, as had Constantine, Emperor of Rome.

We should not, therefore, increase the number of pages in this volume by the present chapter, but for the fact that from time to time tracts and books appear asserting, and attempting to prove, that Christians now have no authority for the observance of the first day of the week as the Lordian day, but that of Constantine and the Popes. If this were all, it would be weak indeed, for they are no source of authority of any kind. When, therefore, the question is propounded, "Who changed the Sabbath?" the weakest of all possible answers is, "Constantine and the Popes." Luther, Abraham, George Washington, or Adam, would do just as well. The preceding chapter exposes the absurdity of this position. Have not numerous credible historians been quoted, living and writing many years before Constantine saw the light or a Pope was ever thought of, all declaring that the first day of the week, under the name of Lordian day, was generally observed by Christians in commemoration of the resurrection of our Lord, and that on the other hand the validity of the Sabbath, as a Christian institution, was never recognized or affirmed, but that it was gradually disregarded? In short, we have sufficiently proved that the status of the church at that time, with reference to the day observed, was the same as now.

To one who will think for a moment, it will appear that in the year 324, when Constantine became exclusive Emperor and began his efforts to aid the cause of the Christians, the days of Christ, his apostles and their successors, had long passed. The days of Judaism, too, were numbered. The city of David, of gorgeous temples, the scene of the miracles of time, of the teachings of the Son of God, the crucified Redeemer, where the first fruits of the new covenant came at Pentecost, and the young disciples received their first baptism in the blood of martyrdom, had passed away. Unutterable gloom had presided at its destruction. Those Judaizers who had once assailed Paul, and sought to bind the yoke of bondage upon Gentile Christians, had been humbled till they were no longer to be feared; but pagan persecutions, like those of Nero, had arisen in their stead, bringing greater calamities in their train.

Still the church had prospered. The Redeemer from above was watching its course. The truth could not be crushed out by pagan persecution, or subverted by pagan philosophy. The Spirit dwelt in the heart of the humble believer. We may readily suppose that his simple faith, exemplified by his godly life, was little corrupted by the philosophic reasonings of men, who, like Origen, often with ardent though misguided zeal, mingled the human in unconscious blendings with the divine. Happily, in our days, we can look back to those primitive times, and perceive that most of the dross, which was then mingled with the gold of God-given truth, has been refined away. Happily, too, we find the Lordian day and the Sabbath, each in distinct history, each with its own peculiar purpose and mode of observance, traced clearly before the corruptions came. On this subject there can be no excuse for doubt.

Assuming control of the great empire of the world, into whose expansive bosom the Jewish nation had been engulfed, with few leading traces of its former power remaining, Constantine recognized the growing influence of the Christian Church. Indeed, he was professedly converted to its faith. With how much worldly wisdom on the one hand, or genuine Christian devotion on the other, he arrayed the authority of the empire in its favor, it would here be out of place to inquire. It was at least a stroke of wise policy, such as it is sometimes given, by a guardian instinct if by nothing higher, to rulers to adopt, to bring the most loyal element ever vouchsafed to human government, the honest, industrious, peaceful, moral, Christian hosts, to the earnest support of his standard. The famous decree of Constantine in which the observance of the " venerable day of the sun" is commanded by abstinence from ordinary avocations throughout the empire on that day, can be regarded as nothing more than simply an edict upon a subject in reference to which he considered his authority supreme. Therefore, as a wise ruler, irrespective of his own religious position or possibly inclined by it, he brought this large, influential, loyal portion of his subjects out of their persecuted obscurity and officially recognized their chief day as one of the holidays of the empire.

The attempt to attach some peculiar significance to the phrase "venerable day of the sun," as though there were some recognition with approval of the heathen superstition supposed to be embodied in the name, fails on closer inspection. "Day of the sun" meant nothing more than Sunday. In that form it was used by ordinary writers, some of whom were quoted in the preceding chapter.

While originally, like all the other days, it had a superstitious reference, it was to these people the same simple and harmless term that the more condensed form, Sunday, is to us. Christians using the words were very far from attaching any pagan meaning to them. " Venerable" simply meant worthy of respect because of its religious or Christian associations. " Venerable day of the sun " did not necessarily imply more than *Sunday the religious day* would, employed by a modern writer.

The history of Constantine's conversion may exhibit much of ostentation and absurd claim, as well as superstition, arising from the high station of the convert and the primitive time in which it occurred; but, beyond that, it is impossible, in fairness, to perceive anything more than a simple recognition, both of the Christian religion, and of the day which already by common consent and universal custom had been devoted to its solemn worship.

Although the imperial edict did not originate the day, either as a popular holiday or in its Christian character, it did undoubtedly mark an increase in its Sabbath observance. Hitherto we have found abstinence from labor insisted on as appropriate by some of the fathers of the church, as also made necessary by the assemblies enjoined under apostolic authority, and the exercises of worship and edification allotted to those occasions. But Constantine was the first to require it to be kept strictly as a day of rest by those outside as well as in the church. He gave prominence to one feature of it. But it is impossible to prove, as it is difficult to believe, that he did this contemplating any change of the Sabbath, such as is falsely ascribed to him. We are not informed that the fourth commandment, or any of the law of Moses, was considered by him. We do not know that he regarded himself an apostle or a pope. His character as Emperor is quite sufficient to account for what he did. Those who conceive it necessary to understand exactly the motive which led to his official action, will need to inquire carefully how far he was prompted by worldly and how far by religious considerations. Sovereigns in all ages have been wont to assume spiritual authority. They have arrogated to themselves the headship of the visible church. Claiming supremacy, both spiritual and temporal, he may have issued this edict with a sincere desire to advance the interests of both church and state. He may have mingled with these other reasons. Motives unknown to us may have had more or less influence over him. But of one thing we are certain, the sabbatic aspect of the day already belonged to it. He did not add it or create it. He did not find the Jewish Sabbath by authority of the Mosaic law, bound upon Christians, recognized and observed by them. He did not, therefore, transfer it from the seventh to the first day of the week. He did, however, emphasize and extend that feature of the Lordian day, namely, rest, which could be most readily seized upon for public recognition. Why he required such recognition we may not know with certainty. Prominence was thus given to it so striking as to be suggestive of the Sabbath of Moses. Other than this we find no connection between them. We believe the idea of the Lordian day which makes it the Sabbath, or a Sabbath, changed from that of Moses with or without authority, in any way derived from or likened to it or taking the place of it, is utterly deceptive and false. Still, as indicated by the early fathers, rest from labor must ever be an important feature of its observance. Attention will be specially paid to this point hereafter.

Daniel uses this language in reference to one of the characters in his prophecy (vii. 25): "And he shall speak great words against the Most High, and shall wear out the saints of the Most High, and think to change times and laws; and they shall be given into his hand until a time and times and the dividing of time." Seventh day advocates claim that this passage proves the Catholic church, or rather the popes, to have changed the sabbath from the seventh day to the first. When historic facts have to be established by the mysterious imagery of prophecy, they are far too shadowy to merit attention. For evidence to the proposition that Columbus discovered America in 1492, or that the Declaration of Independence was signed July 4th, 1776, Daniel, Ezekiel and the Apocalypse would be searched instead of the usual records. According to this plan, history might be revised and greatly enlarged, if not improved. It will occur to most minds that a change of the religious day of the week after its occurrence, is not a prophetic, but a historic event easily traceable in the usual way. This legitimate method discloses to us unmistakably the beginning of the church, the epoch of inspired and, consequently, both competent and authorized leaders, as the time when the Lordian came to be the sacred day among Christians.

We are not speaking disparagingly of prophecy, that is, of the more figurative portions, when we say that it is not given to men of the present day to interpret correctly and with certainty any considerable part of it. And this is written in full view of the fact that very many are conscious of understanding it quite well. After having examined impartially, during a number of years, what several of these have published, we are compelled to discount their claims largely. Did we not, it would be safe to say, continuing the commercial phraseology, we should soon be bankrupt in religious intelligence. It occurs to us that time, as it passes, is beclouding some interpretations that were once thought to be clear. Among these, perhaps, may be reckoned a few that have been referred to the Romish hierarchy. It may be unwise to make sweeping statements when there is no opportunity to substantiate them. But to challenge systems of prophetic interpretation, like theories of science, compelling them to establish their truth before they are admitted within the lines which surround and guard the truth, is the prerogative of every sentinel upon religious outposts.

Assurance, fluency, plausibility, are not sufficient indications of what is worthy to be accepted. These may all appear in an advocate or opponent of a protective tariff, for or against the divine origin of the Christian religion, on any side of any question. They will not be accepted, then, as demonstrating that the ready talker upon beasts, horns, trumpets and seals, who mingles correct history, marvelous coincidences and striking facts with the warp and woof of an apparently perfect texture, a system of interpretation of the prophecies, is correct in all, most, or even any of his conclusions. The Bible is the book of time. How many ages hence its precious pages shall be read for the instruction of mortals, we know not. Whether we are in the morning of the Christian age, its high noon, or on the eve of another dispensation, it would be folly to assert. If this be but the early morning, surely all the history of the past and the knowledge of the present combined, will not give us a very complete idea of that which is but just begun. Now there is ever this element of uncertainty in all the prophecy which we apply to current events.

This will appear by illustration. In certain respects the tabernacle in the wilderness, the temple in Jerusalem, and the church now on earth, are alike. It would not be difficult to imagine a prophecy to have been given in advance of either of them, which the Jews under Moses would have regarded as fulfilled by the tabernacle. Afterward, when the temples were built, the worshipers in them would reject the former interpretation because a better fulfillment had appeared. But when at last the church of Christ exhibited in its outward organization, its ordinances and its spiritual fruits, a complete representation, under a new form, of what had before been as dimly prefigured as the candle's light foretells the day, men would see that all previous ideas of the supposed prophecy fell far short of what was intended by it. The ant by the mole-hill may think himself at the foot of a mountain, the animalcule in a drop of water may imagine itself a whale in the ocean, but why should man, with proper use of his reasoning faculties, interpret so confidently, as some do, the prophecies in the book of time, as though referring exclusively to events within their own cognizance.

We have never hesitated to form and hold opinions in regard to these sublime scriptural mysteries. They have been a field in which we have delighted to rove with alert eye. So the hunter traverses in shifting course, with eager eye and beating heart, the grounds where uncertainties and possibilities are greatest. Science sits by a rock with chemicals and hammer. He pounds, he breaks, pulverizes, grinds, melts, assays, mingles with acids and tests in crucibles. What he gets is inert matter, dead as ashes. Does he stop? No, he changes position or varies his methods, and tries again. All worthy results have been thus attained. Here is the most picturesque field in nature. Tell me, wise man, where is its wealth hidden? Is it merely the beauty of its landscape? Is it that its scattered shrubs shall burn for wood, or that its rocks shall be disintegrated to fertilize the cultivated plain? Is its value in the booty of the hunter merely, or in the patches where the humble hermit raises his scanty subsistence? Or, far down in mines unopened are there inestimable treasures, which science, and labor, and capital shall yet unearth?

We envy not the conceit of the man who thinks he understands the prophecies, that is, the more symbolic portions, as well as he does the simple moral precepts in the letters to the churches. We applaud the efforts of the humble, faithful, laborious searcher for the truths therein contained, but despise the cant and rant, brass and egotism of many who go there for the chief support of their crude revolutionary systems. There is some shrewdness in it, but it is superficial. Much truth is employed, but misapplied.

Sound interpretations gathered from reputable sources are made to show on the outside as convincing proofs that all is unassailable, while within is a hidden spring or two which change the entire action of the construction. The letter "n" in the word "never" no more completely revolutionizes an entire complicated proposition, than does some covert assumption or unpretentious statement turn the whole weight of truth into a false channel. The unsuspecting, mayhap uninformed, reader or hearer drifts along with the argument, dazzled with the prodigious learning, delighted with the clearness of explanation, awed with the bold claims, and won by the suavity and zeal of the proselyter, till he is led into the camp of the sabbatarian or the temple of Brigham Young. Thus the comfortable passenger is switched off in a direction and to a destination which he did not intend.

These wayside suggestions are offered as we pass the point most convenient for such a digression, because it is meet that the reader should be forewarned of the emptiness, as well as the brazen pretensions, of the claims which false systems have set up, derived from the more intricate prophecies. At the same time it is foreign to our purpose, in presenting an argument in support of a definite view of the sabbath question, to turn aside very far to combat the affirmative positions of opposing theories.

To return to Daniel (vii. 25). Even the popular supposition among Protestant expositors can not be said to be certainly true, however probable it may appear. A definite period is allotted to the supremacy of this power, wherein occurs one of the chief difficulties in that application. Says Clarke of "until a time and times and the dividing of time": "In prophetic language a time signifies a year, and a prophetic year has a year for each day. Three years and a half will amount to one thousand, two hundred and sixty years, if you reckon thirty days to each month as the Jews do. If we knew precisely when the papal power began to exert itself in the antichristian way, then we could at once fix the time of its destruction." Verily, yes! But if, with the facts of history before us, we can not decide when the papal power began, no very marked event indicating the sudden acquiring of its supremacy, how shall we recognize its overthrow? Will that be any more perceptible than the other? At this writing, the year of our Lord 1884, twelve hundred and sixty years back would bring us to the year 624—certainly a long time after the introduction of most of the corruptions into the Roman Catholic hierarchy. But yet, either at that date the power had not commenced, (in which case it would be hard to tell when it did begin), or it has already been destroyed by limitation of the prophecy, which is equally as difficult to see.

But perhaps some one may be disposed to fix the destruction at some date connected with the career of Martin Luther, since then Protestantism originated. As we have just celebrated his four hundredth anniversary, placing the dates that number of years further back we reach two hundred and twenty-four, about the time when, it must be confessed, departures from the true Christian faith and practice were the most noticeable. They tell us this power actually did change the Sabbath, which they say is the only religious time, from the seventh to the first day of the week. Ignoring the word "think," the plural number of "times," and the added word "laws," in thus giving the passage a strict sabbatic reference, for the prophet says "think to change times and laws," they make it necessary, if the twelve hundred and sixty years began at the time specified, that the Sabbath should be fully and completely restored to the seventh day at Luther's time. On the contrary, since then the first day Sabbath has been more prominent, and that among Protestants, than ever before. "Sabbath, Sabbath, Sabbath," as applied to the first day, under authority, too, of the fourth commandment, has been the reiterated cry of Protestants from the beginning. At least the sabbatic feature in connection with that day has been rigidly adhered to.

On the hypothesis that this is the point had in view by Daniel, history, we have seen, fails to connect its fulfillment with the Catholic church. It would be as reasonable a charge that Thomas Jefferson killed Abraham Lincoln. With other views of the import of the prophetic words there would be greater justice in the application, though even then the limits might give us difficulty. Twelve hundred and sixty years do not seem to apply to that church better than any other period. There is no apparent date when they would begin to agree with the words in an unmistakable manner, so that after just that lapse of time the peculiarities should plainly cease. We have no doubt that popes did "think to change times and laws," for they declare such to be the prerogative of the church. They impose and remove the obligation of days without end and laws without number. This, however, if referring to them, seems to us much more likely to include such matters as modifying the calendar, imposing church festival occasions upon the nations, and assuming temporal power in place of national lawgivers, than anything else. Unmistakably the first day of the week as devoted to the worship of our Lord existed before they began, and shall continue long after, at least with their present assumptions and practices, they shall be finally overthrown.

The distinction between the Sabbath and the Lordian day was clearly made long before Constantine and the popes, the former abolished as a religious day, and the latter instituted as such, in apostolic times. While such observance was certainly recognized by the primitive church, one change must be conceded as referable to a more modern date. The popes and Protestants may settle between themselves as to which is entitled to the credit, or rather discredit, of the unauthorized innovation. Gradually the name belonging to the Mosaic day, the Sabbath, and the law most specifically enforcing it upon the Jews, the fourth commandment, have been taken from that original and only proper application and affixed to the Lordian day, till that commandment, including the name, is quoted for our present Sunday observance. This is misleading; it is wrong. Sabbath or rest may be a proper, even a necessary, feature of true Lordian day observance. It is not the only or chief one, as such a name and authority would indicate. The seventh day was such a rest. Rest was its model, the rest of God at creation; rest was its observance; the gatherer of sticks was put to death; and rest was its glorious antitype, rest for the weary and heavy laden.

Let not the joyful Christian's day, when, with the Saviour just risen from the tomb, he starts out in the delightful activities of a new life, be devoted to rest. Sabbatizing is not the proper idea of the Lordian day. Secular employments should indeed be laid aside, but because they impede Christian work. By every conceivable reason it is the time for "not forsaking the assembling of ourselves together, as the manner of some is," "to exhort one another to love and good works," to "show forth the Lord's death till he come," to "preach the gospel to every creature," to pray, praise and enjoy, teach and learn from the Scriptures. As its chief point of significance is to remember and show forth the Lord as our crucified and risen Redeemer, and as the apostle John and all the primitive Christians called it, not according to Moses and the decalogue, "the Sabbath," but "the Lordian day," why should we not do the same? We verily believe the time will come when the term Sabbath in this use shall be abandoned, and the adjective Lordian exclusively applied, as its Greek equivalent was originally, to the first day of the week when spoken of in a religious sense by Christian people. Since the primitive Christian writers, employing the Greek language, used in this way not only frequently but exclusively the term "Lordian day," following, in that particular, the lead of John on Patmos and clearly indicating the apostolic usage, nothing in consistency is left to us but to do the same.

It remains for those who refer the origin of the present religious day to the popes, to offer the most ridiculous argument possible in proof of the position. A tract page is open before us, which professes to give certain assertions from Catholic authorities on the point involved.

"*Question.*—What warrant have you for keeping the Sunday, preferable to the ancient Sabbath, which was Saturday?

"*Answer.*—We have for it the authority of the Catholic church and apostolic tradition.

. . . .

"*Question.*—Have you any other way of proving that the church has power to institute festivals of precept?

"*Answer.*—Had she not such power, she could not have done that in which all modern religionists agree with her; she could not have substituted the observance of Sunday, the first day of the week, for the observance of Saturday, the seventh day, a change for which there is no scriptural authority."

Ignoring all the writings of the primitive church and all unbiased historians that have collated their testimony, the tract-writer, after quoting these absurd and monstrously false statements from reputed Catholic sources alone, adds this comment: "The above extracts abundantly prove that the Catholic church, or 'man of sin' as Paul calls him, has changed the Sabbath from the seventh to the first day of the week, as the prophecy said he should. Confession is the strongest evidence."

The above is a fair sample of the literature going the rounds in sabbatarian circles, and doing duty as so-called "proof," "evidence" and "argument." We might answer a hundred, and a thousand would follow in their train, equally illogical and ridiculous. The exposure of this shall suffice for the whole. "The Catholic church has changed the Sabbath from the seventh to the first day of the week as the prophecy said he should." The prophecy said no such thing. It said "think to change times and laws" and not one word about the Sabbath, nor is there one particle of reason for supposing that Daniel had any reference to it whatever. Having already shown the abolition of the Jewish Sabbath as a religious institution, and also the establishment of a new and entirely different religious day, under a new and different covenant, for a new and different people, long before popes or Catholic church began, no further argument on our part is necessary.

But behold the statement, "Confession is the strongest evidence." Indeed! Set aside history for the " confessions " of the " man of sin," and this with a little misapplied prophecy, quote as being the veritable history in the case! With this as your stock in hand go forth to deceive the unwary. Bring into disrepute the present general observance of Sunday by the people, by far the best institution in the land. Spread this pernicious falsehood, if you can, till you undermine the faith of some, till you confuse the people as to their practice of rest and a religious day, till the reaper and the factory raise their din and uproar by the door of the church, and the pious worshiper must pass through jeers, oaths, and the noise of traffic, to his Lordian devotions. " Confession is the strongest evidence." Sometimes it is, and sometimes not. Often it is the baldest fabrication. But is this a Catholic confession?

A well dressed man enters a bank in the town of New Castle and says: "I am William H. Vanderbilt of New York. I left home inadvertently without sufficient funds to complete my journey according to the style to which I am accustomed. Be so good as to let me have the use of ten thousand dollars." He carelessly puts the name to a check and takes the money from the confiding cashier. The confidence man goes his way, while the bank officer reports to his superior: " He said he was William H. Vanderbilt, and you know confession is the strongest evidence."

The tract-writer calls the Catholic church the " Man of Sin " of Paul, and with that assertion not yet dry on the paper before him, declares the impudent claim made in the face of history "the strongest evidence" in the case. Why, the assertion of a "man of sin" is no evidence whatever. Least of all can it be when taken in the very line of things in respect to which that epithet was applied. The "confessions" of this character from this source are the most remarkable in history. They are arrogant claims, false and God-dishonoring. With pretenses like this, popes have sat on the highest thrones of earth, and, enriched, have exalted themselves above God himself at the price of the souls of men. Not one of all these hundreds of claims, from that of succession from St. Peter to that of infallibility, has any foundation in truth. And yet it is "the strongest evidence" that Sabbatarians can produce in proof that a change of day was made since apostolic times and without divine authority.

We can not forbear illustrating these characteristic "confessions" by an example taken from a secular paper just at hand. It is one of a thousand not more unreasonable, and a thousand times more worthy of belief than is the "confession" as to the change of the Sabbath, since it does not, like the latter, belie well established history as well as the New Testament itself. Among "the impressive scenes in the monastery at Newark, New Jersey," attending the dedication was this: "In a small sepulcher hollowed out in the center of the altar table, rested the relics of the fourth pope, St. Clement, which had been brought to the monastery by the archbishop. St. Clement is said to be the child whom the Lord blessed when he said : 'Suffer little children to come unto me.'"

CHAPTER XV.

EPOCHS.

There is a special line of consideration which has not seemed germane to the course thus far pursued. The Creation theory implies, necessarily, that in six consecutive days, of twenty-four hours each, God created and made all things, and that on the seventh day, of like duration, he rested. That particular rest day ended, followed of course by six working days, if indeed there was anything left for God to do, but at each successive seventh day, as it returned, he again rested, continuing so to do, making the day in that sense his own holy Sabbath, sanctifying it at creation at the first seventh day, and because of what it was and would be to him, causing all his obedient followers to know which particular day it was, and to observe it, in common with himself, by entire abstinence from all labor; that this day was ever kept by the righteous, and if at any time lost, again revealed to them, until we find it, reckoned by sevens, introduced to the Jews at the giving of the manna, and reinforced in the law on Sinai. It implies that this parceling out of time for God and man, is binding upon the whole human race forever, not for the sake of the utility of such a use of one seventh of the time, but rather for the sacredness of that particular seventh over and above any other seventh. To have at any time lost the reckoning, and afterwards fixed upon Thursday, for example, ever after calling that the seventh day and observing it as the Sabbath, would be an incalculable calamity, since the utility is not in the seventh part of the time devoted to rest, but in the identical seventh upon which God began to rest at creation and has ever since rested.

This ironclad theory, and a variation of it which applies the whole Sabbath to man alone, afford a fine field for the exercise of the reasoning faculties. Let us indulge in a brief diversion of this kind, that it may appear whether either form is safe from difficulties. Assume the limited form, "the Sabbath was made for man," to be correct. Why made for man? For what utility to him was it appointed? For (1) the actual benefits of rest, (2) the typical lesson of a rest in store, or (3) simply the recognition of God as creator and the honoring of him as such? The Sabbath was appointed for man, having these three objects, one or all, in view. But its institution at creation was on the occurrence of the first seventh day. Is not the blessing and sanctifying of it, in the second chapter of Genesis, connected directly with God's seventh day of rest, the first Saturday the world ever knew? And are we not denied, by the supporters of the theory, the privilege of separating the two thus closely connected, by any supposed interval of time?

Well, then, the Sabbath was instituted before the fall of man. But before that event, in their pristine state of glory, Adam and his companion needed not (1) the relaxation of rest to the physical system, which the subsequent cursing of the ground, the condemnation to toil, the eating of bread in the sweat of the face, and the consequent wasting of the physical energies and death, required, nor would (2) the typical lesson of a rest from sin benefit them, since as yet they had not been introduced to it through the agency of the tempter, nor even was there occasion for the day (3) to recognize and honor God as creator, since in Eden they did this to the full extent, deriving complete happiness from it.

To suppose the Sabbath, then, an institution merely for human benefit, in either of these three particulars, is to agree with many popular interpreters, Lightfoot for example, in postponing its origin till the fall of man, since it could not have been of benefit before. Otherwise God is represented as deliberately supposing man's fall and instituting a law based upon that supposition. Sabbatarians tell us that the Sabbath can not be typical because it was instituted before the fall of man. On like consistent ground those who believe it typical must agree that its origin did not precede that event. But this is to introduce a hiatus into the passage in Genesis, which once supposed is as likely, on general principles, to reach to the giving of the manna as to the fall of man, since Moses, the writer of the book in which the record stands, lived late enough for either, and there is no proof to the contrary intervening.

Fall back for a moment to the ironclad theory unmodified. The Sabbath is God's holy day. He observes it himself and imposes it upon all his creatures. The value is not in a seventh part of the time, which might answer the purpose under the limited view, but since God keeps and always has kept the day, we must all observe the same exact twenty-four hours. But this is an absolute impossibility. To the Sabbatarian in Ohio and the Jew in Palestine, from astronomical causes, the Sabbath sun rises many hours apart. We do not and can not keep the same absolute time. How then can we observe a day identical with that of God? It is impossible. There is not and can not be a Sabbath rest at once throughout all the universe of God, when that day is marked by the exposure of revolving planetary bodies to the central sun. Admit that this absolute identity is not important, and you abandon the only feature of the ironclad theory which gives it preference to any other. Those who count it so needful to restore the original Sabbath, were it possible to overcome all chronological difficulties, would then have nothing very definite to return to.

While the Sabbath was declared to have been made for man, this theory seems to regard it as made for God and kept by him for his own refreshment. We confess that the whole idea of rest, as taken or enjoyed by the Divine Being, is entirely foreign to our mind. Can it be supposed that weariness is consequent upon all activity, whether by celestial or terrestrial, spiritual or animal beings? Or, if by all created beings, does it follow that the rest of God is a necessity to him? If weariness, then doubtless sleep, if sleep, inconvenience, pain, and the whole catalogue, stopping hardly short of sin itself. Where is the universe when not upheld by the word of his power? There seems to be such a tendency to dissolution on the part of complex, especially organic bodies, when left to themselves, that it is more than doubtful whether existence and harmony would continue after the hand of the mighty architect were withdrawn. Surely the omnipotent hand can never relax, the omniscient eye never fail.

In an accommodated sense, doubtless, this idea is intended as applied to God. God does not repent, but changes a course of action sometimes very abruptly, from design and doubtless with foreknowledge. He represents himself to man with the qualities that belong to the human soul. Hate, sorrow, repentance, these are applied to God in the Scriptures, and thus bring him within the purview of man's comprehension. This accommodated sense does not require the actual absence of many qualities in the divine nature to which it may apply however by way of modification. These arise from the imperfections of the physical, mental, and spiritual human nature in this state of existence. God, in revelation, condescends to, though he is not bound by them.

Doubtless thus it is that God rests. His cessation from creation, after the completion of that which exists, is styled rest, and even though in one instance the ancient record uses the word " refreshed " in that connection, we hardly know how to apply that term to God, but think it more probable that it was used with especial reference to man. As of man, on completing a great and difficult work, it would be said " he rested and was refreshed," so the same language is used of God (Ex. xxxi. 17), looking, however, more particularly to man's nature, and therefore employing words which he can comprehend. Only by such a use of terms and of ideas as well, can any clear conception of God as approachable by us, be introduced into our minds. There must be a vail before our mental vision, as there was before the physical eyes of the Jews at the mount, else the glory of the Infinite One shall consume us. Such a vail is finite language—our speech; and God uses it to draw near to us, but at the same time it does not and can not present to us the divine perfections. Had we never seen the light but of a densely clouded day, we would have no definite idea of the sun. So God sits away from us, though ever near. We comprehend somewhat of his manifestations, some we see with our natural eyes, some he has spoken to us by our natural language, but all is accommodated to us, so that we may see in part and " know in part," to such extent as may be necessary for us here, of the person and counsels of God.

Nothing is easier than the application of these remarks to the word "day." We are not left to our own conjectures as to time with God. When Jesus used of himself the simple and yet the most wonderful language the Scripture records, " Verily I say unto you, before Abraham was I am," making the divine present precede and include all historic time, when the apostle Peter declares, not as a definite rule, for prophecy, which some few interpreters have very strangely supposed, but with that general and vague meaning, which gives scope for the ages upon ages of God's time, and is in keeping with the reference made generally to him and his attributes, " One day is with the Lord as a thousand years, and a thousand years as one day," the difficulty of determining the length of God's days readily suggests itself. Moreover the Bible distinctly denies this privilege to man. Try Job and the Psalms, and when the inquiry is propounded, " Canst thou by searching find out God ? " the conclusion is everywhere forced upon the mind in whatever form such attempts to reach the attributes and works of the Infinite One are made, " such knowledge is too wonderful for me."

But some one is ready with the suggestion that man's days, by which we mean solar, or such as those to which he is accustomed, are referred to in the first chapter of Genesis. There is no reasonable ground for such a view, except that it is that which suggests itself to an unthinking mind. But we have all learned that as to many matters our first impressions have not been the best. God had created certain things which were to come within the observation, to be largely under the dominion, and to contribute to the necessities of man. He chose, therefore, to reveal himself as the author of these wonderful objects, to the end that man might know and fear him. Such a revelation was the necessary beginning of that course of care and discipline which is required to evoke happiness from misery and holiness from sin. It is God's introduction of himself and the presentation of the credentials of his authority. There is no geology as such and for itself in it, nor science of any kind, nor history. It is simply a great accommodation of infinite, of divine facts to the comprehension of the human race. " In the beginning." " Beginning " is man's word. It conveys an idea to him, sufficient for the purpose, but who shall measure the illimitable reaches, the wonderful import of that word, when, comprehended by adequate intelligence, it fastens upon that to which it refers in the unthinkable duration of God? " Day "—it likewise is man's word. But who shall look into that which God has thereby designated, and tell us in what times and in what ways have occurred the mighty revolutions of the universe, as they have appeared to the earth, and of the earth itself, as out of darkness into light, out of floods into dry land, out of chaos into habitable globe, it has slowly emerged, while things animate and inanimate, myriad in kinds and infinite in number, have come up one after another under the eye and by the power of the great Jehovah himself?

We maintain that here is no ground for dogmatism. He knows most who claims to know least; that is, who is so impressed with the vastness of that which is related as to be conscious of human inability to fathom it. Such a one will never talk of days of twenty-four hours each, nor think of full grown creations springing up as if by magic, where naught had been before. While nature has sometimes illustrated the speed with which dissolution may occur, she has ever declared that organic forms, especially when destined to long life, are slow in their origin; and great changes in the direction of order require long periods in which to be wrought. Now, if the Bible never conformed to nature in such expressions of duration, in instances where no mistakes are possible, it would be more reasonable to interpret the first chapter of Genesis according to the human reckoning. But in all departments of the Bible treating of long and indefinite periods, we are taught to interpret it just the other way. On a principle akin to that which considers creation days only twenty-four hours in length, the early Christians thought the end of the world near at hand, and now, after eighteen centuries have elapsed, Adventists are confidently looking for the same.

In prophecy the element of time is indefinite and uncertain. The so-called "rule" of Peter, "a thousand years are with the Lord as one day" (II. Pet. iii. 8), is no more applicable to prophecy than that of David (Ps. xc. 4), who declares the same to be as a "watch in the night." It depends very much upon what the future event may be. The declaration that the seed of the woman should bruise the serpent's head had its definite fulfillment in Christ after a lapse of four thousand years, while many predictions apparently much more likely to be deferred were fulfilled in a generation. A tale that is told, the grass of the field, whatever is most transient, pictures the life of man, even though it be threescore years and ten—a long time to contemplate in some aspects of the case. We therefore affirm that creation was probably not very rapid, and that in accordance with scriptural usage the days of the account indicated varying and immense periods of duration.

So gradual were the changes, possibly, that had a human life been thrown into the midst, they would not have been perceived. There have been some mighty upheavals, some sudden transformations, but so far as we are able to know, most of the permanent changes are slow. The pointer on the face of the dial that indicates the greater change, moves the slower. There is a lesson of uniformity in nature and of consistency in both it and the Bible which teaches how this creation occurred. There is a rich field before us. We do not think that there is a seed of any kind in its soil. But, behold! when the season opens with the warm sunshine and gentle rain, weeds spring up here and there, and mayhap a shoot which promises a future tree. These bearing seeds within themselves, there is a succession of crops for all the coming years. Had there really been no seeds in the ground at first, the divine fiat supplying the energy to produce the growth, this would have been a true picture of creation. "And the earth brought forth grass, and herb yielding seed after his kind." In this natural way did all things appear at first, in succession, and at such intervals as were necessary to prepare the circumstances suited to each created form. And "the evening and the morning," the beginning and the ending, (in Moses' time evening was put first, because the Jews thus reckoned the day), of this particular part of creation, whether it required a shorter or longer time, God designated a day. There were six such divisions—some of them might have been hundreds, some millions of years in duration—but the "evening and the morning," the beginning and ending of each, constituted God's day for that particular creation. Whenever thus what now appears had assumed its place in the order of the universe, that work ended and the rest day of creation ensued, how long to continue we know not. Who shall say that this is not the correct view? Is there anything in the Bible to contradict it? Is there not much to affirm it, and do not all the voices of the universe speak its truth?

The work of redemption has been slow. Not an uncommon inquiry is made: Why is it that Christ was not given to the world immediately upon the entrance of sin into it? No answer to this question has been made at all satisfactory, except one that involved this principle: God's ways are not as our ways, nor his times as ours. He knows how to send his messengers with infinitely greater speed than the lightning, and he knows also how to wait, while the ages pass by. He employs the processes of water wearing the solid rock, of little insects building great continents, of slow carbonization of the successive vegetable growths of the soil, upon which are imposed formations by equally tardy means; of air and frost disintegrating rugged cliffs, of waters filling up immense basins and scooping out deep channels, of internal fires with occasional eruptions, and cold congealing and contracting solid crusts; in short, agents innumerable, each with unlimited time for its operation, in the great process of world building. He employs, in redemption, the agencies of prophets foretelling events thousands of years before they are to transpire, of providences applied to the training of nations to perform their parts in a foreordained plan, of typical institutions to prefigure with exactness the coming age, of preparatory instruction by inspired teachers at every stage, and finally, after suitable conditions have been evolved and the fullness of time has arrived, the Saviour of Men appears. But his birth, childhood, youth and manhood come in as slow succession as those of others. There is no hurrying, though the fate of millions hangs upon the work of this one. He must become a mature man, and then instruct chiefly but a few, these to continue the work received from him. Thus it has gone on until to-day. There have been reverses, revolutions, paganism, heathenism, false religions, false philosophies, jarring sects, open enemies, but still in one way and another, the nations of earth are coming to the presence of the Great Teacher.

From this there is derived an argument which it is impossible to refute. Creation was a slow work. Else the nature of God has been revolutionized, his plans have been changed, he is varying in his operations. He does not now work in nature as he once did. He does not work in grace as he did in creation. He has suddenly ceased active movements, such as brought all this wonderful arrangement of the universe into being in six working days of twenty-four hours each. Deliberation has succeeded impetuosity. And why? Why think it? Why write it? Because, only, Moses declares that in six days God made the heavens and the earth. And yet everywhere the Bible refers to the days of God as to ages of ours. Because a sabbath of twenty-four hours in length was appointed to man, as founded upon these days of God. But may not man, by keeping twenty-four hours as a sabbath, appropriately commemorate the sabbath of God lasting for twenty-four millions of centuries? Should not God's day and man's day bear some just relation to the power exerted by each, the kind of attributes that belongs to them?

It has been customary in an argument upon this branch of the subject, to refer to the vast time which might intervene between the "beginning" of the first sentence in the Bible and subsequent creation, as assigned to separate days. It is also usual to note the delay of the sun in making its appearance till the fourth day, as evidence that no such days as ours were in existence until then; and finally, it is customary to show that the seventh day of rest from creation did not expire with one diurnal revolution of the earth. To those who may be content with such reasoning as this, we have no objection to offer. It is doubtless conclusive. We prefer, however, to plant ourselves squarely upon the ground of consistency in Bible, nature and God. The sun does not mark days for God. It is but one of the infinite number of time-pieces which he has given out to the different parts of his creation, no two of which are possibly exactly alike, and in the midst of all and without reference to any of which, he accomplishes his own supreme designs. He required none of the sun's light to assist him in creation. He did not cease the creative work of even the fourth, fifth or sixth day when the sun went down. O ye of little faith! Mortals of narrow vision and earth-born thoughts! When will you soar aloft to join in your contemplation the higher intelligences and recognize in the Creator the attributes and methods that belong to him.

Heaven will be an epoch. The highest ambition of the sabbatarian seems to be to divide heaven, earth and hell, time and eternity, the activities of God, angels and men, into periods of twenty-four hours each, six for work and one for rest, in an everlasting inflexible alternation. And this with a fragment of law which was given for a temporary purpose to a temporary people, when the human race was in its infancy, which was thundered in terror from Sinai's peak to a people incapable of gentler wooings or higher conceptions, is to be imposed upon men now as supreme, on the ground that it always has been and always will be the ordinance of God. They have no reasonable hypothesis but to continue it in heaven, also.

The Bible presents heaven to us as another state in which the righteous are to exist, not subject to conditions which surround them here. Whatever may be its revealed or unrevealed peculiarities, it is exhibited as the consummation of all the efforts which are put forth in this probationary state. To attain it is to find rest, deliverance from sin, through the mediation of Christ. It is itself all rest, in the scriptural sense. To it are applied the terms "everlasting," "forever," and all combinations of ideas which imply that it is to be unending. It is, therefore, a period not with such sabbatic divisions as pertain to this state. On the contrary, it is itself all one sabbath which consists in the perfect harmony of the redeemed man and his surroundings, which is therefore complete happiness. Imperfect sabbaths, of which the seventh day is chief, (the Lordian day is not a sabbath), point to this perfect one, as the Jewish and ante-Jewish sacrifices pointed to the slain Redeemer. Each ceased when its superior came.

There may be said to be three periods in contemplation, each of length unknown to us: 1. Creation. 2. Probation. 3. Heaven. Man's continuance in the second is but brief. Of course, any ideas in its representing the other two must be to them as the candle to the sun. Sabbaths are of such a character. Modeled after the immense periods which brought the celestial bodies and the earth into their present state, each in itself an eternity, they must themselves be brief in order to be comprehended, and by repetition thoroughly learned within the earth-life of man. The ordinary day of twenty-four hours is self-evidently the best practical form the lesson could take. But as they sprang out of eternity in creation, so they point to eternity in heaven, both of which extremes are known to the comprehension of God, not to ours. If I could think creation brief, I might think heaven likewise; and the reverse.

We shall not summon an array of geologic authorities, nor make a section of the earth's crust ourselves, to prove the antiquity or the long continuance of the processes that brought our world with its living forms into being. Although there is much strength in such considerations, and devout science is the true handmaid of religion, yet such arguments are neither necessary nor in closest harmony with the mode of investigation in this volume.

The same line of thought which extends the six days indefinitely also protracts the seventh, and, *vice versa,* the scriptural considerations which lengthen the latter, reach, with like effect, upon the former. It has been heretofore suggested that the sabbath does not commemorate creation. The Bible does not so declare, nor by implication teach. How shall inactivity commemorate activity? It would far better perpetuate the idea among men, that God became very weary of works which were arduous to him. Rest was not the most prominent idea in creation, and would not have been selected for use in such a commemorative institution. Some active form would have been chosen for such a purpose. The record declares: "And God said, Let there be light: and there was light." The Psalmist says: "He spake and it was done, He commanded and it stood fast." It is not a picture of weariness and rest, which for its own sake must be impressed upon the mind of man. We can not conceive of the Divine being as hard at work during the creative periods and then having nothing to do. Feeble conceptions would those be of nature which would regard creation as everything and upholding nothing. Does nature tend from disorder to order, from death to life, from destruction to organization, or the reverse? If the Almighty power were withdrawn, what would ensue? If God were to keep strict sabbath, what would become of us all? The man of faith does not believe in a self-existing any more than in a self-creating system of nature.

What, then, was God's rest? No more direct creations. Animate and inanimate, organic and inorganic substances ceased in new forms to come into being by the Divine fiat. They kept their cycles of perpetuation under the laws originally impressed upon them, and the continuance of his exerted power was necessary to that end. Scripture ever holds to our view God's superintending exertions in the continuance of natural forms and phenomena. "He scattereth the hoar frost like ashes," "He bringeth his rain upon the just and the unjust," "He openeth his hand, and satisfieth the desire of every living thing." His rest consisted not in the cessation from labor or even in the diminution, but in the completion of one kind of effort. This is the only possible likeness from God's experience from which to model this institution for man. But, on the contrary, to man rest is necessary. In his fallen estate it is necessary to point out a rest to which he can attain, after this weary life is past. The necessity arises from the fact that he must know it, that he may strive for it and gain it.

But there is no rest in God's experience to which man needs to be pointed for any purpose of benefit to himself. In an accommodated sense, abstracting the idea of the creation of what appears to man from all other forms of God's activity, a model can be obtained, which is used as we have already often indicated. "My Father worketh hitherto and I work." There is nothing in any sabbath to fix, or which has ever set, limits to the activities of God, whether Father or incarnate Son. God's seventh day, filled with unceasing activities, is yet upon us. Thousands of years have past, during which he has given us the same recurrence of seasons, never-failing seed-time and harvest, and in which floods have not destroyed, nor fire consumed, nor comets wrecked, nor spheres collided. I think God would teach us that his days are to ours as his works are above ours. How long the grand period of God now present shall continue we know not, but the time shall come of resurrection, of destruction, of heavens rolling away, of earth melting with fervent heat, of a new heavens and a new earth, and of unrevealed wonders, when this present day of God, these ages upon ages of earth-time shall have passed away.

Tayler Lewis, in the "World Problem," rejecting all scientific authority, and speaking from the Scripture language itself, of which he was an eminent expounder, so closely accords with this view as to merit quotation here:

"Not that the Scriptural writers were ambitious to give us cosmical knowledge, but the manner in which they speak of the great times of God's kingdom—their language of olams and olams of olams, of ages and ages of ages, of eternities in the plural, of great chronological divisions in the past and future, instead of blank continuances after the style of much modern thought—their use of these pluralities and their swelling reduplications, in a manner inconsistent with the narrow bounds into which the historical times of our planet would cramp them—all these produce strongly the conviction that the Bible does not represent our world or olam, as an isolated existence with a cosmical blank before and after, but as connected with an ongoing series of ages stretching immeasurably back as they reach onward to a distance immeasurably future."

The distinction already made between God's days and man's days is the simple thought which will enable one to unravel all the mysteries which may seem to exist in the Scriptures, arising from the different use of the word "day," or any other of like character. "A thousand years are in thy sight but as yesterday when it is passed, and as a watch in the night." With this conception we may look forward to the unfolding of God's purposes, or backward upon his created works, but of our own threescore years and ten, of our recurring Lordian days and work days, the sun with its risings and settings, the winter snows with their comings and goings, are a clear and definite measure.

CHAPTER XVI.

COMMENTS HERE AND THERE.

The Worcester (Mass.) *Spy* recently contained a report of a public meeting by the Seventh Day Adventists, in which questions were proposed and answered :

" 10.—How many annual Sabbaths did the Jews have ? Many voices in the congregation replied seven.

" 11.—How did Moses distinguish between the annual Sabbaths and the weekly Sabbath ? He said that these Sabbaths were beside the Sabbaths of the Lord (Lev. xxiii. 37, 38)."

The word "beside" means here in addition to. The sense of the passage may therefore be expressed thus: You must keep whatever is required in these feasts in addition to all that has been heretofore commanded. The law of the annual feasts is not a temporary substitute for others, but is required over and above them. In other words, double duty was demanded. But these annual sabbaths belonged to the Lord as much as any other. Try the first clause in verse 37 : " These are the feasts of the Lord, which ye shall proclaim to be holy convocations." Or verse 39 : " Ye shall keep a feast unto the Lord seven days, on the first day a Sabbath, and on the eighth day a Sabbath." This attempt to create an immense distinction between the Lord's sabbaths and those of the Jews is a failure.

" 12.—What prediction did Hosea make concerning the annual Sabbaths ? He predicted that they should come to an end (Hosea ii. 11).

" 13.—When was this prediction fulfilled ? It was fulfilled at the cross of Christ (Col. ii. 14, 16)."

The prediction quoted from Hosea was not fulfilled at the cross of Christ. That event did not cause the Jewish feasts to cease. Did the Adventists ever read of the Pentecost, second chapter of Acts of Apostles, seven weeks after the cross? Did the Lord "destroy her vines and her fig-trees" at the cross of Christ? (See next verse in Hosea). It is a vision of destruction and not the abrogation of types by fulfillment.

"14.—What is affirmed of these annual Sabbaths? They are declared to be shadows (Col. ii. 17)."

Yes, and so was the weekly Sabbath, too, according to the same text.

"A shadow simply implies a substance; these Sabbaths were given after the fall of man, and pointed to Christ. The shadowy system ceased at the cross. The weekly Sabbath could not be a shadow, for it was made before the fall of man." A voice in the congregation asked if the Sabbath was in any sense a type. Elder Smith replied, "No, because it is a memorial of creation."

The weekly Sabbath was not made before the fall of man. It was "made for man," and in his pristine state he did not need it and could not comprehend it. Until toil, weariness, pain, sickness, death, sin, he could not appreciate rest, or the prefigured deliverance from sin, or any other idea which attaches to the Sabbath over and above what he already knew. That it was made for man to keep without being for his benefit, is absurd. Moreover, you can not find the Sabbath previous to Israel in the wilderness. Neither is the Sabbath a memorial of creation only incidentally, but it is pre-eminently a type, as we have already abundantly shown.

In a publication by the religious people from whom the above emanated, we observe this among other numbered paragraphs:

"3.—The Sabbath was not a part of the law of Moses."

This statement has reference to the council at Jerusalem and the demand of the Pharisees (Acts xv. 5) in regard to Gentile converts; "it was needful to circumcise them and to command them to keep the law of Moses." Our position as heretofore explained is this: To circumcise them made them Jews; then they should be required to keep the law of Moses, which the Jews as a nation had not abrogated. The law of Moses included the ten commandments and the Sabbath. This last statement is denied in the quotation above. Let the Bible, then, decide between us.

"Remember ye the law of Moses, my servant, which I commanded unto him in Horeb for all Israel, with the statutes and judgments" (Mal. iv. 4). Horeb is Sinai. The law of Moses was given them in Sinai. Turn to the twentieth of Exodus and the fifth of Deuteronomy, and the decalogue is found to be the first thing given in that mount. "The law of Moses with the statutes and judgments." The very next chapter (Ex. xxi.) begins: "Now these are the judgments." The twentieth chapter of Exodus, then, undoubtedly contained the law of Moses or a part of it. "The Lord our God made a covenant with us in Horeb" (Deut. v. 2). The same place, and the covenant was, or at least included, ten commandments (Deut. iv. 13). But should any one suppose that the Lord did not give these commands through Moses but to the people face to face, (ver. 4), the explanation appears in the next verse (5), "I stood between the Lord and you at that time, to show you the word of the Lord: for ye were afraid by reason of the fire, and went not up into the mount." Then follow the ten commandments as the Lord uttered them. The explanation following (ver. 24, etc.) shows that the people had heard the voice of the Lord and were terrified by it though Moses had stood between them and it. They were, therefore, on their request, dismissed to their tents and Moses continued in place, transmitting to them the subsequent commandments and the statutes and judgments, the original ten upon tables of stone. From which narrative it appears that these all constituted what is spoken of by Malachi; and the ten commandments, which the people did not hear themselves but received from Moses, were part of the Law of

Moses. Preceding the above (Deut iv. 13, 14) is a passage showing the ten commandments to correspond with the law of Moses in the description by Malachi. "And he declared unto you his covenant, which he commanded you to perform, even ten commandments; and he wrote them upon two tables of stone. And the Lord commanded me at that time to teach you statutes and judgments, that ye might do them in the land whither ye go over to possess it." Thus while Malachi speaks of the " law of Moses and the statutes and judgments" commanded to Moses for Israel in Horeb, and Moses himself, in both Exodus and Deuteronomy, declares "the ten commandments" (which includes the Sabbath) " and statutes and judgments" (a statement evidently synonymous with that of Malachi) to have thus been given in Horeb, our Adventist authority denies that the Sabbath is any part of the law of Moses.

In the fifth chapter of Matthew (21, 27, 33, 38, 43) Jesus commented upon certain points successively in the old law. "Ye have heard that it has been said by them of old time, 'Thou shalt not kill'" (from the decalogue). "Ye have heard that it was said by them of old time, 'Thou shalt not commit adultery'" (from the dec.). Again, "Ye have heard that it hath been said by them of old time, 'Thou shalt not forswear thyself, but shalt perform unto the Lord thine oaths'" (not from the dec.). " Ye have heard that it hath been said, 'An eye for an eye and a tooth for a tooth'" (not from the dec.). " Ye have heard that it hath been said, 'Thou shalt love thy neighbor and hate thine enemy'" (not from the dec.). This chapter shows that Jesus regarded the decalogue and other passages in the law of Moses as things " said by them of old time," and subject alike to revision by him, instead of one part—the decalogue —being superior to the rest as an everlasting and immutable law according to the theory which assigns it to the creation, or given in the garden of Eden previous to the fall. So when Jesus affirms of a part of the decalogue, " The Son of Man is Lord of the Sabbath," he means that he and, of course, his law and his kingdom are superior to the Sabbath and not subject to it.

"Did not Moses give you the law, and yet none of you keepeth the law? Why go ye about to kill me?" (John vii. 19). Here the law against killing (dec.) is said to be given by Moses. "For the law was given by Moses, but grace and truth came by Jesus Christ" (John i. 17). Here we find the general expression "the law," which meant the decalogue just above, the very form of words which time and again is declared by our opponents to refer to the ten commandments, and this law is said to have been given by Moses. Will it be replied, Moses simply repeated it giving it to the Jews? No, for then with the same reason it might be said that "grace and truth" came second-hand through Jesus Christ. This passage makes a declaration for all time, and teaches the introduction of that to which it refers, the law (the decalogue including the Sabbath) by Moses and the gospel (Titus ii. 11) by Jesus Christ. Moses, too, was the best that the Mosaic age had to offer for salvation. Abraham in the future state is represented as saying (Luke xvi. 29) to one of his descendants who desired to keep his living brethren out of "torment," "they have Moses and the prophets, let them hear them."

"God commands that the seventh day be kept as a memorial of his rest from creation." As the Scriptures do not say that the Sabbath is a memorial, either of the rest of creation, or as usually stated of creation itself, it may be well to consider one of the numerous instances of memorials in the Bible, by way of illustrating their use. Amalek opposed the march of Israel. After Joshua had defeated them, the Lord commands Moses (Ex. xvii. 14) "Write this for a memorial in a book and rehearse it in the ears of Joshua: for I will utterly put out the remembrance of Amalek from under heaven." Many years afterwards when the people had been long in Canaan and Saul was king, there was another conflict between Amalek and Israel. And the Lord said (I. Sam xv. 2): "I remember that which Amalek did to Israel, how he laid wait for him in the way, when he came up from Egypt. Now go and smite Amalek, and utterly destroy all that they have, and spare them not." In this case one circumstance was to be kept in remembrance by a memorial for use at a subsequent time. In this way, and thus only, is the Sabbath used as a memorial of the rest day of creation, that is, to keep the idea of rest alive in the world, until the great promised rest or deliverence from sin. But such is chiefly the idea of it as a type. When, therefore, the proper time came for the introduction of this type in the world, namely, with the Jewish state, the creation of the world by periods was revealed through Moses, and the Sabbath type based in memorial form upon it. Still, the future period of rest was the grand idea imbedded in the sabbatic institutions. Before proceeding to another point we desire to guard against misunderstanding by parenthetically qualifying one statement just made. While there are evidences of extensive revelations to man previous to Moses, the book of Genesis was prepared by him undoubtedly for the use primarily of the Jewish state, and the form of revelation in the account of creation may have been dictated by that purpose. Certainly we do not know that to that extent and in that way the revelation of creation had ever before been made to man.

"Speaking of the state of the pagan world at the advent of Christianity, a late German writer says: 'Roman ladies thronged the synagogues of the despised Jews, and many a Roman observed the Jewish Sabbath in hope of propitiating the great Jehovah'" (Uhlhorn, Conflict of Christianity with Heathenism, p. 63). "This shows that the common notion that the Sabbath was unknown outside of Palestine and the Jews, is wholly incorrect."

There is no such "common notion," for every one knows that since Moses' time, all those nations which have come in contact with the Jews, must have learned of the Sabbath from them. Especially was this true of the Romans, in whose empire the Jews were dispersed everywhere. Seven weeks after the crucifixion of Christ there were at Jerusalem "devout men out of every nation under heaven" (Acts ii. 5), speaking a great variety of languages, and Paul, in his travels, found Jewish synagogues "in every city," in which Moses was read "every Sabbath day." If it is desired to prove that the Sabbath was not exclusively a Jewish institution, it will be necessary to quote either Scripture or authentic history showing its existence prior to Moses or outside of possible derivation from Jewish sources. This the advocates of a universal Sabbath from creation have thus far signally failed to do.

"God commanded the holidays of the old law to be kept in the same way as the Sabbath; and as these were only figures of the Sundays and holidays of the new law, if this was done in the figure, where only temporal benifits were commemorated, much more ought to be done in the substance, which regards the great spiritual benefits of our redemption."

This is quoted from a Catholic work, a favorite source of authority on the Sunday question, by the Sabbath advocates. They delight to parade these claims of the Catholic Church, to have originated by their own rightful authority, what really came from the apostles, and moreover to have the actual prophetic types as authority for their innumerable Romish festivals. It is needless to say that no one outside of this church, and those who thus delight to quote them, ever believed the Jewish Sabbaths and festivals to be typical of any corresponding days under the Christian system.

Jahn, to prove the antiquity of the Sabbath, declares: "As we find by examination of the Mosaic laws, that the greater part of the ordinances which are sanctioned by that legislator, existed in previous times, we have a right to say, the probability is, that this was the case in respect to the Sabbath also."

As an offset, we suggest the following "probability": As we have found that all the Mosaic ordinances known to have had a previous existence, were mentioned in the writings relating to those earlier times, we have a right to suppose that had the Sabbath thus existed, it would have been mentioned also. Jahn gives, as "the whole object of the Mosaic ritual, to preserve the worship of God as the creator and governor of all, till the time when the true religion should be made known to the rest of the world, for which grand end it had been originally committed to Abraham and his posterity." Moses, he declares, "teaches his countrymen that they were bound to devote themselves to God by obligations, which were multiplied and peculiar, since they had received from him such distinguished favors and the promise of others at a future period."

"Numerous sacrifices were insisted on, not, in truth, for any supposed worthiness in the sacrifices themselves, but because they were an indication of a grateful mind, because they presented a symbolic representation of the punishment due to transgressors, and uttered, as it were, an impressive admonition that all sins were to be avoided. Sacrifices, accordingly, and other ceremonies, are never esteemed in themselves considered, of much consequence."

Ceremonies then, according to this view, were "multiplied and peculiar," not because there was anything significant in them; they were required to be observed in the minutest point, not because there was any importance given to the least item, making it like a pin in the frame of a building, in itself of great value. Sacrifices were demanded in most wonderful profusion, to be offered according to precise forms, not because of any specific import or value, such as "without the shedding of blood there is no remission," as Paul informs us, but all simply to show our obligation to obey God. And for that purpose alone, he overloaded the Hebrews with these multiplied and peculiar exactions.

No, indeed, that view of the Mosaic economy, which spans all time and sounds all depths, will reveal reason for everything and arbitrary enactment for nothing. It will show sacrifice as looking Christward; its precise forms and unblemished victims as significant presentations of what man needs to learn in reference to the spotless Lamb of God, and the stainless robes of the redeemed saints. It will appear that while our obligation to obey God may rest upon the fact of his creation and abundant benefactions, his reasons for giving through Moses such laws as he did to the Jews, and by his providence preserving the record of them in the Bible for all time, consist of the valuable lesson or practical use in them. We obey his righteous commands, not his useless forms, because he has created, loved and blessed us.

Looking to service or instruction, separate or combined, as the true objects of whatever God has imposed upon man, it is not difficult to determine why some ordinances preceded Moses while others originated with him. Types have the relation to each other in point of time or order in which the antitypes are to appear. The Jewish nation then being an unmistakable representative of the Church of Christ, the original passover in Egypt prefigures Christ at the cross; and thence onward to the passing of the Red Sea, which delivered in completeness the children of Israel from their aforetime oppressors, may be said to answer for the time which elapsed from the cross until the church was first in completeness, organized, their past sins being forgiven, not as before to the righteous of earth in promise, but in veritable fact the efficient sacrifice now having been slain and the blood of the real (paschal) Lamb of God having been appropriated according to the law of God.

Now observe that the cross comes before the church. For whatever view any one may entertain us to the church beginning in Abraham, he can not suppose it to have existed in the same sense that it did after Pentecost, at which, for the first time, actual deliverance from past transgressions was promised to those who obeyed the word of the apostles. So to the Israelites passing the Red Sea to complete deliverance from their past enemies, the passover preceded. Sacrifice, therefore, in various forms, preceded the Jews, and was typically in order at once after the fall, and among all men down to Christ. In like manner, for example, the distinction between clean and unclean animals was a proper idea to precede the Jews, since instruction to the people as to moral purity and righteousness before God is necessarily in a measure preparatory to the work of bringing them out of the world into the church of his saints. Sacrifice and the distinction referred to belonged to all the world, Jews and Gentiles, from the fall of man to the cross, because all the world before, without, and within the Church of Christ need his atonement. But this side of heaven in the church only, is absolute rest from sin, so among the Jews only after the Red Sea was there any proper Sabbath. We trust this distinction, now repeated, will lead all who are disposed to argue loosely upon the antiquity of various typical institutions, in the style of Jahn, to consider which of them have reasonable ground for such antiquity and which not. It is not Moses, the legislator, gathering up his laws from the usages of the past, but God instituting them at such times as they were suited to his purpose.

Circumcision, as a significant institution, begins at Abraham, but we do not rest the entire argument upon the proof that it was not known by other nations before, nor upon the proof that the week did not precede the Sabbath in the wilderness. It is not proposed to discuss these questions here. As to the week, however, the evidence drawn from the Bible is worthy a moment's consideration that its real fanciful character may appear. Had not the lunar month, which is marked so unmistakably for us in nature, been known actually to exist, we should undoubtedly have had a month of forty days and forty nights proposed on better ground than that which so satisfactorily convinces some minds of the early existence of a week and Sabbath. The ground for such a month would be conclusive. Did it not rain in Noah's time "forty days and forty nights"? Did not the children of Israel eat manna forty years? Did not the spies occupy just forty days (one month) in exploring the land of Canaan? Did not Jonah declare: "Yet forty days and Nineveh shall be overthrown"? Did not the Saviour hunger forty days and forty nights preceding the temptation? And to add largely to the already convincing proof the word forty occurs numerously in the Scriptures, all its uses having an imaginary reference to the length of the month.

The candid reader will observe that there are many peculiarities in the use of numbers in the Scriptures. These were doubtless natural peculiarities belonging to the people and to the times. Among the people now "nine" is a popular number. A child is exposed to the whooping cough or measles, we expect symptoms of the disease within "nine days." A cat has "nine" lives.

> "Bean porridge hot, bean porridge cold,
> Bean porridge best nine days old."

In colloquial style many such uses occur. In primitive times such numeral idiosyncrasies were much more frequent. Seven was perhaps the most noted. But that certain animals entered the ark by sevens, a marriage feast and a funeral lasted seven days, that there were seven years of famine foretold by Joseph in Egypt, proves nothing as to the week or Sabbath.

The anonymous author of a recent work, "Eight

Studies of the Lord's Day," has surpassed all competitors in the effort to prove the existence of a primeval week and sabbath day. The Noachian history (Gen. vii. and viii.) gives but a slender basis to his very imposing structure. The fact has already been noticed that two or three events occurred at intervals of seven days. Now, if you start with these and lay off an indefinite series of weeks, it becomes a pleasant pastime to refer the half dozen other dates of the story to this calendar, so that regular sabbaths, weeks, months and years shall result, after the order of a modern almanac.

Our first objection to the scheme is, that it is purely fanciful; the second lies against the assumption that the events of the entire narrative are of such a religious nature as to be more appropriate to the sacred day than to any other; the third protests against every other number being regarded definite, while the "one hundred and fifty days" are called indefinite, or round numbers for one hundred and forty-seven; the fourth insists that years being reckoned from Noah's life, shows that there was no established calendar, such as a week or sabbath from creation would imply; the fifth suggests that, since months of the year and days of the month are named numerically, by the use of ordinals, we should also have had "seventh day of the week," had the latter been in use; the sixth raises the question why eight or ten events being purposely set apart to the sacred day of the week, such a division of time is itself not mentioned, for in no instance, nor elsewhere in Old Testament history outside of the Jewish nation, is there even a casual intimation of the existence of week or sacred day.

But suppose the calendar, thus brought to light after the manner of the cypher indications of the Baconian authorship of the works attributed to Shakespeare, be correct, there is nothing in it but a peculiar recognition of one day in seven, without explanation or proof of its sacred character. It is quite impossible to believe that Noah himself determined upon the actions or chose the occasions. Hence there is no proof that he attempted to honor a religious day to which he had been accustomed. He did nothing, dared do nothing, of his own will, but in that terrible ordeal implicitly obeyed, in every movement, the command of God.

If among the interpreters of the mysteries imbedded, for the use of future ages, in the form of type and prophecy, one has arisen in these last days, in the person of the author of the "Studies," to discover the true calendar; when revealed it shows only this: God, in that old and wonderful type of the salvation in Christ, has placed the septenary sign of the Christian's rest. This is just what he did afterwards in that other completer type—the Jewish nation. So, after all, the typical theory is the best. The shadow can not be seen out of one or the other of the typical salvations. If we admit that while elaborately wrought out in that of the Jews, it was also dimly foreshadowed, under the divine direction, in the "Salvation by Water," we still can find no trace elsewhere. The world outside had no sabbath, not even a week.

When we introduced the last chapter with the statement of a theory to the effect that God still keeps the seventh day, and the same identical time that man is required to keep, we had in mind, in particular, two opinions that have many adherents: first, that asserted by many Seventh Day Adventists making the creative ordinary solar days in length; second, that often found in writers of "Christian Sabbath" type declaring the Sabbath to have been imposed upon angelic beings previous to the fall of man. Either one of these views necessitates the entire iron-clad theory as there stated, except that the latter class, just mentioned, supposed a change by divine authority to the first day, in which case we suppose it would be held that angels changed their day likewise.

Dr. Lewis, however, a representative writer among the Seventh Day Adventists, in a recent article, made quite a different statement : "When the Bible says that God rested on the seventh day (of the great creative week), and therefore hallowed unto himself the seventh day of the human week, which is the symbol of his, and commanded men to follow his example and hallow the Sabbath according to his law,—men begin the perversion by saying that the seventh day means any seventh part of time. On the contrary, the seventh day necessitates a definite point of beginning at the first day, and so on. Such a beginning God's creative week certainly had, and God ceased and rested on the seventh day of his week. Not on an indefinite seventh part of time. It is illogical and absurd to put such an interpretation on to Gen. ii. 1-3. Man's week is the symbol of God's, but not identical with it. Man's first day was not God's seventh, for God's days were infinite, while man's are brief, measured by the revolutions of the earth. But as the symbol of the creative week, and of the divine resting, man's week must correspond in all particulars, as to order and definiteness."

Of course when Dr. Lewis penned the paragraph quoted, he did not suppose that he was surrendering the entire position. And yet he did so. Sabbatarians have not strenuously opposed, as we have heard some of them do, the epoch theory of creation for nothing. It is one of the keys to their position, and with that understanding we wrote our last chapter. Yet the epoch theory is here admitted by a doctor of divinity and an acknowledged leader. If man's seventh days are not identical with that of the creative week, and they can not be, for twenty-four hours can not be identical with one of God's "infinite" days, nor can a sun-marked day be identical with any definite period of time not thus marked, then we have at least an entering wedge between God's seventh day and man's, absolutely considered. Let us then look at the *symbol* which is now all that is left. The points essential are given by Dr. Lewis in his last sentence, "they must correspond in all particulars, as to order and definiteness." Did then the creative week begin with the commencement of the life of God? If not, need the symbolic week begin with the commencement of the life of man? If it can be proved that God's existence has been divided into weeks made up of "infinite" days, and that God rested from the work of creation on the first seventh day that he ever saw, then there may be some propriety in requiring man to keep up the symbolism by resting on Adam's first seventh day, and on all seventh days thereafter to the end of time. If, however, far on in the existence of God, he undertook the work of creation by epochs, then far on in the existence of man, say at the giving of the manna, the most favorable as well as the most significant time that ever occurred, he might have required the setting off of a symbolic week and on the seventh day thereof instituted the first human Sabbath. The symbolism would be complete under Dr. Lewis' own rules.

The same writer complains of the use of "Jewish Sabbath" for "the Sabbath of the Lord thy God." The objection is groundless, since he admits that God does not keep it himself and can not show that he ever required it to be observed by any human being but a Jew. It is the "Jewish Sabbath" in the sense that it was theirs exclusively to keep, and it is "the Sabbath of the Lord thy God" because it was given by him to them. But it was "made for man," we are informed. Yes, Jews belonged to the human race, and the Sabbath had vastly greater worth to all mankind when assigned typically to that typical people, with a lesson in it of redemption for the world, than it would have had as a mere rest day without any such meaning.

Nevin, in his Biblical Antiquities, page 369, uses this language: "Our Saviour, who was Lord of the Sabbath, caused it to be changed from the seventh to the first day of the week, that it might be, till the end of time, a memorial of his resurrection from the dead; while, being still unaltered in its essential nature, it should continue to answer, also, as before, all the purpose of its original institution."

The manifest objection to this view is that there are no Scripture statements covering it in whole or in any essential part. The fact seems to be that we find the first day of the week now in use as a day of worship under the name and with the character of a "Christian Sabbath," and the above explanation has been contrived to account for it. Yet the historian finding the white man now living in the vicinity of Plymouth Rock, where four centuries ago only the red man could have been seen, might with equal accuracy declare that the red race had been changed to the white. The red have indeed been abolished and disappeared; the white have come upon the scene and remain. The event that brought the one led to the dispersion of the other. So the change in religious dispensation that originated the first day of the week as a memorial day, abolished forever the seventh as a Sabbath. The Sabbath departed as a part of the law, a prominent Jewish institution. It was never changed. But it was abolished as a divine ordinance, just as was every other. The rest element in it was fundamental, both as to the rest of God from which it took its form, and chiefly as to the prefigurement of rest in Christ which was its essential feature. When men discovered that the day was changed from the seventh to the first, why did they not perceive that the "rest" was changed also, since confessedly there is no trace of the sabbatic character attached to it either in apostolic times or the early centuries of the church.

Dr. Potter, an associate of Dr. Lewis, has given us this paragraph: "Thus in our investigation of this question, we find that while the Sunday was, from an early day, observed as a day of worship, it was not claimed to be the Sabbath by people generally till the latter half of the sixteenth century, and then only by the Puritans of Great Britain and America." While this Sabbatarian has confirmed our statement above as to the non-sabbatic character of the Lordian day in primitive times, he has at the same time made an admission of all we ask of his school, namely, that "Sunday was from an early day observed as a day of worship." If as a "day of worship," it is a little singular on his own theory that it was of "pagan origin," and instituted by the "Man of Sin." For both "Pagan" and "Man of Sin," Constantine and the Popes, must have been a little daft to have instituted a day of Christian worship.

But to return to Nevin's view as to the change of the day. Rest from labor on the Lordian day is not memorial, but an act of worship. It is not derived from the Sabbath, for the rest in Christ had already come when that typical institution gave way to the new order. Will the reader ask himself why we all cease labor for a time when a very near relative dies, or a person held in high public esteem? Why do we rest on Thanksgiving day if we keep it at all? Why is the closing of places of business and cessation from the usual avocations an invariable mark of all special occasions? Simply because it is an open recognition and an evident tribute to the purpose which the time marks. A minor idea is that abstinence from labor gives time for actual exercises which may be appropriate. If the Lordian day was originally a day of public worship, there was necessarily some intermission of labor, because worship requires time, even when rest was not itself held to be an item of that worship.

Such we conceive to have been the original character of the Lordian day. As such Scripture and history alike represent it. Along side of it in apostolic times was the Jewish Sabbath, with which every one was perfectly well acquainted. But he knew that the Sabbath was not the Lordian day, and that the Lordian day was not the Sabbath. He knew that the Sabbath had no more binding obligation upon him as an ordinance of God. And yet the Jews still kept it. It was a part of their law. Had such of them as were Christians desired to see it abrogated they could not have effected their purpose. Neither the apostles nor elders at Jerusalem prompted any crusade against it. Under these circumstances it was not surprising that Jews at Jerusalem, as Christians, should even desire to bring all converts into conformity through the initiatory rite of circumcision, with the entire code of Mosaic law, nor that Paul out of the stronghold of such influences should have prudently striven to counteract a tendency which in some Jewish quarters was at this period an unnecessary "yoke of bondage." The Jewish law had no longer anything whatever to do with Christianity, but large bodies of people move slowly and strong prejudices are hard to dispel, so the Jewish law, having no longer religious authority, was as skillfully managed as circumstances would permit.

While Christians at the first did not regard the Lordian day as the Sabbath modified, and the Lordian supper was to them the chief item in its observance, with minor importance attached to various other forms of worship, we are not disposed to doubt that, from the first, abstinence from labor was regarded as certainly a proper method of celebrating this joyful, religious day exactly as it afterwards appears in the writings of the fathers.

Secular occupations will never be engaged in by those who are in the spirit on the Lordian day. Work for the Lord, worship of the Lord, and all the solemn and cheering exercises of the congregation and of private worship will claim its every hour. Its voluntary aspect is one of its most inspiring. The Christian law is one of freedom. A willing people gather around the standard of our Lord. No fourth commandment thundered from Sinai summons them to drop their implements of labor, and either sit in stolid idleness at home or go to church to engage in a spiritless routine of worship. We prefer to bestow a gift upon a friend and not have it exacted of us. The Saviour's injunction, mild as a request, "As often as ye do this do it in memory of me," comes gratefully upon the soul compared with the positive, precise and death-sanctioned edicts of Moses. On such a day, coming to us in such a way, we gather closer around the cross, we sit in loving fellowship with him, consecrated thoughts arise in our hearts, we sit with him at the Lordian supper, as a friend. We are glad when the day arrives that we may commune with him as a friend. Our Lord and our friend! a combination almost as wonderful as God-man! Never did one before thus present himself to us.

Since chapter xi. was written, we observed in the *Christian Standard* an answer to a correspondent in the "Querist's Drawer" in reference to the "Lord's day," in which that phrase is referred to as "being similar in character to the phrases 'the Lord's table,' 'the Lord's supper.'" The *Standard* is correct so far as the English phrases are concerned. But it is in keeping with our purpose, and absolutely essential to the making of necessary distinctions at this point, that we should examine the original Greek. From that we learn that while "the Lordian day" is a similar phrase to "the Lordian supper," there is no other like phrase in the New Testament. It is the table of the Lord, or Lord's table, but not the Lordian table, just as in Acts it is "the great and notable Lord's day," or day of the Lord, and not Lordian day. In other words, the noun and not the adjective is used with table, while the adjective and not the noun is applied to the supper, and the day mentioned by John in Revelations (i. 10). We repeat the distinction, therefore, heretofore fully elaborated. "Lordian," the adjective form, signifies in honor of the Lord; "Lord's," the genitive or possessive case of the noun, signifies belonging to the Lord. "Lordian" applied to only two words, "day" and "supper," in the New Testament, indicates that their use is specifically in honor of the Lord, as such they are employed by man.

In all the vast range of uses of this noun in the genitive case in the New Testament, not one can we discover to have this special meaning. They all apply to such things as are the Lord's rather than devoted to him. Thus the "word," "name," "grace," "coming," "mind" of the Lord. Nor is this distinction at fault in reference to the Lord's table (I. Cor. x. 21). He instituted it, presided at it, took bread, blessed, brake, and said "take, eat, this is my body." He took the cup, blessed, and saying "this is my blood," gave to his disciples. We remarked before of the bread and wine, "This is that of which a man may not take except the Lord shall give." And yet while the emblems were significantly his to give, the institution is significantly ours to keep in his honor. "As often as ye do this do it in memory of me," are the expressive words which make the supper emphatically Lordian. Would it not be well for all Christians to preserve the distinctions which the Spirit has recorded?

CHAPTER XVII.

THE WEEKLY HOLIDAY.

He that would consider many subjects must possess the faculty to withdraw from his own situation to that of others; often, apart from the special surroundings of all parties, to a point of observation where, uninfluenced by any, he can think of all alike and impartially. With such measure of success as we may hope to attain in this direction, the church and the world will be considered with reference to the weekly holiday. On eventful occasions, like the year 1884 in the United States, it is natural to consider the attitude of parties towards each other. But political parties are antagonistic. A desperate conflict is waged between them. Very few have sufficient equipoise of nature to take position upon a neighboring eminence and survey both. Most get their opinions from within the camp of one or the other, with the smoke of battle rising around them. We can not believe many people are fair in their judgment of others politically. Lines are too closely drawn. Men of positive convictions and force are found on either side, but wherever they are, they are decided and firm. Everything which one party advocates is held to be right, all which the other favors is wrong. And very right and very wrong.

We have reason to be thankful that such is not the attitude of the church and the world towards each other. There is rather a predisposition on the part of the latter to admit the claims of religion, to listen to the preaching of the word with interest, and, when duly pressed upon their attention, to accept it. For the most part, unworthy charges are not bandied between them. To "join the church" does not bring odium and petty persecution, insinuations of dishonesty and open abuse, such as is the shame of American politics. Were the church alive to the full use of its abilities and the improvement of its opportunities, results of inconceivable magnitude might be attained.

In this country a large share of non-religious people are favorable to the weekly holiday, as to every other reasonable doctrine and institution of the church. This gives us the advantage in this matter. At the same time, it should not be employed in forcing upon others such extreme measures as do not accord with perfect justice. Upon what basis the civil "sabbath" should rest, and to what extent legislation may impose it upon all the people, is a question upon which all do not agree, and which should be settled, as soon as possible, on equitable principles. Other writers may be depended upon to set these forth more fully than we, still it would not be proper to omit here at least a brief development of the relation which the Lordian day has to the people at large. The fact that the day has not come to us as a modification of the sabbath of the fourth commandment, but as the worship day of the Christian church, will be important in the consideration now proposed.

Nothing is more obvious than that, with relation to our government, all classes of people are equal. The learned and the ignorant, rich and poor, Christian and infidel, claim equal privileges. In view of this, it is often held that Sunday laws are not in harmony with our institutions. Such, however, is a very superficial view of the subject. But before proceeding to examine the true basis and character of such laws, let it be distinctly admitted that they can not be enacted in obedience to the demand of one class only. They rest upon the interests of both. The time, let us hope, will never again come when the church shall attempt to dictate religious legislation on the assumption of its own superior right. Such a course is as fatal to itself as it is subversive of justice to others. Shall it then be admitted that Sunday laws are class legislation? Shall it be said that they are exclusively in the interest of the church, dictated by it, an imposition of religious forms upon others, and therefore partial? A thousand times no. In our judgment there is hardly any subject upon which prudent legislation can subserve the interests of all to a greater extent than in reference to the weekly holiday. No man can afford to have it abandoned.

Undoubtedly, worldly people will keep it quite differently from Christians. They ought not to be, as they can not be, required to attend religious services or to sing and pray. These are voluntary exercises induced by hearty acceptance of the Christian faith. Religious observances of any kind can not be imposed upon them, since religion itself is voluntary, and its obligations are laid upon the individual conscience, by an authority altogether apart from human governments. Nor can they be required to abstain from labor because of any supposed divine law. Even the fourth commandment, if in force, could not be held as part of a national code as with the Jews, but purely divine, and, as such, addressed to the individual wherever found. Were there no other conceivable object except to obey the fourth commandment, then the government should not, on the one hand, interfere with the privilege of any to keep sabbath, nor, on the other, should it exact such service of any. To his God alone should every man be amenable in the matter. For man, in the exercise of governmental functions, to undertake to enforce divine enactments, for no other reason than that they are divine, is presumption. "Who hath required this at your hands?" May not such officiousness be detrimental to the object sought, and displeasing to God himself?

At the same time, if the non-religious can be brought to see that the weekly holiday is of great importance to themselves, that its general secular observance is in reality quite as useful to them as to Christians, that it is to their interest to uphold it in its purity, that it is not strictly a relic of puritanism or of religious bigotry, from whatever source it may have been derived, and that it is as indispensable to them as to the church, and chiefly for the same reasons, they may be brought to its active support, so that the threatening aspect of the country with reference to the day may speedily change. Why, indeed, this widespread idea that the church is imposing her sabbath upon the world, and that as a religious institution only? If such a notion were true, it were better to abolish it at once. The church can get along without it. Christians can keep it, worshiping God still as they did through centuries of pagan and papal persecution, though all the world beside run riot in debauchery and irreligion. Christians are not disposed arbitrarily to rule others for their own convenience or happiness alone. At least they should not be.

Dismissing the idea that it is a special favor yielded to Christians, let every man consider what value the rest day has to all alike. It is needed as a day of relief from labor. A great many people are prone to forget the toiling millions. They are not sufficiently grateful to them, as, in an important sense, the source of innumerable comforts which we enjoy. Next to God himself, we owe most of our favorable physical surroundings to the poor of earth. The men who grade the railroads, excavate the mines, till the soil, weave the fabrics, sail the ships, these are they who deserve our first thoughts. The rich are already provided for, the shrewder wits can care for themselves, the indolent deserve nothing, the laboring poor must be protected. There is a tendency of the rich to get richer, and of the poor to grow comparatively poorer. The chasm between the two classes widens and deepens. The weak are in the power of the strong. If the man who can get but a scanty living from hard work for six days in the week were to toil equally hard for seven, the excess in most cases would soon find its way into the safe of his wealthy employer. If toil were to claim half the night as well as all the day, the laborer would still be poor. Capital and wealth must not be given greater power to oppress labor, but should rather be restrained. Let us then preserve to the poor man his day of rest, his time for home enjoyment. Let us retain such laws upon our statute books, such a uniform and imperious custom in the observance of this one day in seven, that it will never fail to be secure as the poor man's boon. This reason of itself, amplified in a hundred directions and illustrated in a thousand ways, is sufficient to justify the enforcement and the regulation of the weekly holiday by the most rigid laws.

Fill out the line of thought thus begun, trace the positive comforts and advantages that come to all conditions of men from the observance of a Sabbath, and that, too, apart from any religious benefits whatever, open your eyes to what you yourself have seen, read what others have written, and the benign influences of the day of rest will appear with marvelous distinctness. We wish the reader God speed in such an investigation. Were we a legislator with no consideration but such as these admissible to guide our action, we should stand inflexible in the support of Sunday laws, preserving the day, so far as legislation could do so, free from the encroachments of toil and the contaminations of vice.

May we be permitted to suppose that in a series of protracted meditations, involving the lapse of a long time since the last sentence was read, our patient friends have filled out the argument barely introduced in the preceding paragraphs, and are impressed with the weight of the reasons for a weekly holiday founded upon its physical, social, educational, and other similar advantages? If so, they will turn at our bidding and look in a different direction where a picture in miniature opens as it is viewed, into innumerable vistas beyond.

Who shall say what religion has done for the world? What man, not a Christian himself, would discourage it among his neighbors? What professed moralist and philanthropist would venture a step which should turn the masses into infidelity or into the blind rationalism which marked revolutionary France under Robespierre and Marat? What well-wisher for his race would desire to see it under the dominion of sordid ideas only, faithless, sensual, selfish, hopeless? Who, though a pretended disbeliever, would not shudder at the thought that he might waken from his dreaming, and find unbelief absolute and terrible, fastened, not only upon himself, but upon every human being beside? What scoffer at the Bible would sincerely, in his calm moments, wish that it had never been given to the world, that its instruction, its morality, its God, with all the refinement, all the happiness, the unspeakable joys and the unfailing hopes which it has produced, had never been? One might possibly imagine himself complacently beholding such a picture, or even desiring the reality, as a cover for his own depravity, but never when reason or benevolence was enthroned within him. The world in general realizes that Christianity has been its benefactor. Most of all do enlightened Christian nations know it.

A large part of the non-religious people of the country believe that some day they shall become Christians. They do not expect to die without hope in Christ. The executions for the crime of murder show that even the vilest, for the most part, desire to make their peace with God preparatory to death. Many causes of delay have influenced them; some are waiting for one reason and some for another, even of those whose minds are decided; but with very few exceptions, though generally negligent, indifferent, or even open scoffers, men would dislike to see the door of mercy closed forever. Believing, as in reason they must, that their sins have brought them under condemnation before God, in whose presence they must certainly appear, they see no way of escape but that which God has provided, and to remove that would plunge them into utter despair. A blow struck at religion, the hope of the world, is therefore aimed at all alike. Whatever some of us may think, however act, we are all in the same boat together. We may all reach port and home. We really desire to do so. Shall recklessness or indifference on the part of some cause us to omit the necessary precautions? Shall we tear up the sails, split the rudder, or throw the compass overboard, because some of our companions expect no storms, anticipate no danger, enjoy the present floating along on smooth sea under the sunny sky?

If religion be for the general welfare, be relied upon for ultimate security by all, then it may be encouraged by legislation within reasonable limits. To leave the people untrammeled in the exercise of religion, to favor general customs of that nature in which all may be willing to unite, to afford opportunities for peaceful gatherings to the same end, and even to recognize religious institutions in a friendly manner in an impartial way: these are proper lines of governmental action. But if there be one thing connected with this matter, which more than any other comes within the scope of these observations, it is the preservation of Sunday as a religious day. The entire country is accustomed to it. Were there no Christianity, the observance of the day has independent merits sufficient to protect it from abrogation. There is a remarkable unanimity among Christians in its favor. No other day of the week would suit all as well, and one day is a necessity. Besides, of all recognitions of Christianity, this is both the most perfect and the least oppressive or objectionable. It marks the resurrection of Christ, dates back to the origin of the church, and is both a sign and evidence of the divinity of our Lord. Nothing else so simple and yet so powerful, so free from sectarian tendency and so desired by all religious parties, so profitable to the church and so necessary to the world, so instructive in the truth of all truths which it suggests, and at the same time salutary in the outside benefits which it confers. The nation can well afford to preserve this a sacred holiday to all its people. They may justly be prohibited from all active, unseemly avocations, recreations, convocations. The best of order should be required everywhere, and perfect peace and quiet should be assured to the people who are the "salt of the earth," and to the institution which, of them all, is the "light of the world."

No one is more fully aware than we, how meagre are the suggestions here offered. It would be profitable to the people to read an entire book devoted to the true development of this theme. The weekly holiday is an interesting, a practical, a valuable subject. The free-thinkers who contemn, the immoral who desecrate the day, are alike enemies of the republic.

In a chapter which shall be brief, there are yet a few words needed upon Sunday to the Christian. We desire especially to guard against the charge of "no Sabbath," which is the common rejoinder to one who denies either the validity of the Jewish day under the fourth commandment or the change of it to the "Christian Sabbath" under the same law. We emphatically object to the term Sabbath at all, as applied to the day: (1) because it is not the day thus designated in the Scriptures; (2) because that term indicates the very weakest idea connected with our day, though the strongest associated with the other, and (3) because the Scriptures have given us a different name. Paul speaks of being "justified by law and fallen from grace." We can not cling to the Sabbath and rightly appreciate the Lordian day.

And yet there is the Sabbath idea connected with the day hallowed in memory of our Lord. It is a part of the work of hallowing instead of the radical thought of the day itself. Rest was the root idea of the ancient Sabbath. The Lord fixed it in the name. It occupied the leading positions in the thing itself. First, it was fundamental in the object of the day which was a typical institution designed to picture promised rest in Christ. Second, it was chief in the form which was modeled on God's cessation from the work of creation. Third, it was principal in the manner of observance, secular labor being rigidly interdicted, and only a few acts, themselves religious, tolerated. With the Lordian day the case is quite otherwise. First, the main idea is the resurrection of Christ from the dead. That is the great fact of the gospel, the great event of history, the attested promise of eternal life to the world. To continue a typical institution is to deny that the antitype has come. To prefigure rest is to declare that Christ has not already brought it. It is to refuse the call "come unto me and I will give you rest." Typical institutions are all fulfilled in Christ. Since the cross they are as much out of place as a picture of a friend when he is present. How would you like your wife to gaze constantly upon your photograph instead of into your loving face? The New Testament certainly does represent going back to the law as assuming a yoke of bondage and even denying Christ.

Second, the Lordian day is not modeled after any form. It is simply the particular day of the week upon which Christ rose from the dead employed as commemorative of that event. Third, the manner of observing the day is the only one of the three to which the sabbatic idea pertains. And just how it comes in we desire to try to explain. In one sense abandonment of the usual employments is preëminent in the keeping of the day. Look out, around you, on any Sunday, if you live in an ordinary, well conducting community, and this sabbatic feature is the first to meet your observation, and the most noticeable of all. But then there comes up a distinction which an illustration will introduce to us. The eating of food is positively required to sustain the life of the human body. But back of that, equally essential, is work that food may be obtained. And this work, though more remote from the object sought, is that which appears strikingly more prominent to external observation. Possibly, too, a correct analysis of the rest question will show certain other items really nearer to the primary purpose of the Lordian day, while rest, though more remote, shall yet be indispensable and greatly more open to public notice.

What then are the ideas or forms that bring us nearest of all to the object of the day, that is, to the commemoration of the resurrection of our Lord? First, the day itself does it, when separated from others, with that thought in view. Therefore any exercises which contribute to the same end belong most appropriately to that day. But the Lordian supper approaches the specific object even more closely. For, consider that the loaf represents the body of Christ which was slain, the wine his blood which was shed, and lastly, these are both given to his disciples by the living Christ who bids them "take, eat, this is my body." Thus unite in one institution the sacrifice, already completed, effectual to give us life, and the Saviour again living to dispense his blessings to us. Nothing else connected with Christian worship so embodies in its forms the idea of the resurrection as this. No wonder then that the disciples, converted and instructed under the oversight of the apostles, came together to the Lordian supper on the Lordian day as at Troas. Undoubtedly a great many other exercises, less intimately associated with the leading thought, are appropriate to the day. Such are all the forms of worship. Prayer, praise, preaching, exhortation, alms giving, religious assemblies, personal efforts and personal sacrifices for Christ, and others pertaining either to the assembly or to outside Christian conduct. So also is the abandonment of the labor to which men are accustomed and by which they set great store. Not only is this last prominent among these secondary items as being in itself both worshipful and commemorative, but as illustrated above in the relation of work to eating, it is far the most prominent of all in that it furnishes the opportunity and is the necessary antecedent to all. As it was in Troas so it is in Cincinnati, the disciples do not "come together to break bread," and are not willing to spend their time in listening to preaching or in other religious exercises on the Lordian day, unless they are first willing to surrender their profitable employments for that day.

When you combine the thoughts, that this is a mark of respect, hence an item of worship, that it is a sacrifice for a good object, that it is a means of affording opportunity for other good works, that it is the most prominent method of showing our observance of the day, and lastly, that it extends outside of the church as well, conferring inestimable benefits upon all the race, including the most effective agency in gaining their attention, thereby calling them to Christ; then the extent and value of the sabbatic feature of the weekly holiday may begin to be estimated.

Why then are you unwilling to call it a Sabbath, or, if you please, "the Christian Sabbath"? Chiefly for three reasons already given, but also because it is not a Sabbath. All the Sabbaths under the law were alike rest days, and significant entirely of a coming rest. Such is not the Christian's day. Such is not Thanksgiving, though our rulers ask us to cease labor for the proper observance of it. Such is not any holiday, though none of us may work, but surrender the day to its appropriate form of celebration. The Fourth of July is Independence day and not a Sabbath, and so with the rest. You may call the day by its secular name, "Sunday," by its number, "the first day of the week," or by its proper religious title, the "Lordian day," but never, unless you would misrepresent it, call it the Sabbath.

But while we call the day rightly and use it appropriately, we shall have no time for secular employments. All hail! Glad Lordian day! Morn of the blest! Noon of the happy heart. Eve of the tranquil soul. Let every hour be given to thoughts, words, and deeds, such as the Master's short eventful life exemplified, and the Master's welcome plaudit shall approve.

CHAPTER XVIII.

SABBATISMOS.

Though the purposes of God may ripen slowly, there is always the perfect end in view. The great work of redemption, already continued for many centuries, has a consummation yet to be fully reached. In proportion to the time, the effort, the sacrifice, shall be the realization. He in whom concentred the promises, the law, the prophecies, the shadows, of ancient times, when he came, vastly overshadowed them all. There is progression. There is evolution. When the future is wrought out, the present will be transcended by it. The present is greater than the past. God has been at work by himself and through divers agencies. His work has not been in vain. Vast as were the revolutions in creation, when plastic matter assumed its shapely forms, they have been equaled since then in the spiritual world. The throes of nature at the crucifixion, when rocks rent, graves opened, and darkness brooded, were minor events of the scene, waiting on the greater that was then transpiring. Things wonderful to the physical eyes have not been so important as the simple processes which they were intended to aid. The plagues in Egypt were less than the marching forth of the people, the opening of the arm of the sea than their reaching the other shore. So were the miracles of Jesus inferior to his teaching. The incarnation of the Son of God ranks below the partaking of the divine nature by the sons of men, the resurrection of Christ even below that in store for the dead millions of earth.

Such thoughts as these must enter the mind of faith, contemplating the types and the "schoolmaster" of the old dispensation, the probation and the promises of the new. There is a great future to which men are taught to look with the eye of faith. Human life on the earth is now preparatory to that which shall be hereafter. "Now we see through a glass darkly; but then face to face: now I know in part; but then shall I know even as also I am known." The primary idea of such a course of preparation through the ages is advancement. To-day finds us ahead of yesterday, to-morrow will take us still further on. And when one travels, the object of his quest is before instead of behind. Particularly so is it in the spiritual life. The past is irrevocable. We can not amend or erase it. God promises to take care of that, if we obey him and look to the future. While there is instruction in the past, there is no ground for vain regrets. We sorrow not for departed friends as those who have no hope. We obtain pardon for our sins, and they are remembered no more against us forever. But we do need to watch the present; we are under obligations to provide for the coming future. We do this with hope, founded on the divine promises, "as an anchor of the soul, both sure and steadfast, and which entereth into that within the vail." The example of Paul is for us to follow, "forgetting those things which are behind, and reaching forth unto those things which are before, I press toward the mark for the prize of the high calling of God in Christ Jesus." The contest is on us, and the hope before, so that if faithful we may hereafter exult with him, as the crown draws near which is the reward of a well-spent life.

With the overwhelming impression that this is the nature of the work of God on earth, and the spirit of his instructions to men in the Bible, this book, now approaching its termination, has been written. We have been unable to think, for one moment, that the purpose of any great institution, which ran through centuries of time, had branches, reduplications and dependencies, which was remarkably prominent in its recognized importance, sternly protected under the law, and carefully outlined in its history for the benefit of coming generations, could have been anchored in its purpose to the past. Subordinate ones or inferior parts of this might, but the cause for this, the object of it, the lesson in it, is to be sought in advance. Nor is it a mere theory that suggests such a view. The stamp of the thought is indelibly impressed upon the pages of the Bible and can not safely be ignored.

Does this seem to limit the scope of our investigation? Does it appear to any that by our argument we reach its end at the cross of Christ, where the sabbath ceases as an institution bound by law upon men? By no means is this true. Having reached the end of the type, we are extremely interested in the antitype. We earnestly desire to learn what we can of that for which all this was designed in the mind of God, and executed with great care through his providences among men.

There is one passage in the New Testament which, as much as any other, cheers the care and toil-worn Christian pilgrim in this life. It is the only one that points, in the name which it employs and the idea by it represented, to the ultimate complete consummation of what we have somewhat laboriously examined. "There remaineth, therefore, a rest to the people of God" (Heb. iv. 9). There is, then, left a *sabbatismos* to the people of God. The reader will perceive the root of the familiar word "sabbath" in this, and understand that sabbath rest, sabbatizing, keeping sabbath, is the thought conveyed by this unfamiliar word. This is the one place in the New Testament where the fulfillment of the typical sabbath is clearly and unmistakably indicated. The passage declares explicitly, by the word which it employs and by the reasoning of the apostle, that the heavenly rest is the complete antitype of the ancient sabbath.

There are, indeed, other places in which the same heavenly rest is referred to, but not in the use of this expressive word. Thus: "Blessed are the dead which die in the Lord from henceforth; yea, saith the Spirit, that they may rest from their labors; and their works do follow them" (Rev. xiv. 13). And the spiritual, if not the heavenly, is indicated in the invitation of Christ: "Come unto me, all ye that labor and are heavy laden, and I will give you rest" (Matt. xi. 28). In these passages, as in all the others found in Hebrews in the context of the one now under consideration, words are used of which the radical syllable resembles our English word "pause," and means "to cease." The cessation from labor (as God ceased from creation), is the thought which they convey. While there are, in combination with this radical syllable which supplies the primary meaning to these words, certain prepositions intensifying the thought conveyed, so that the cessation from labor is made emphatic and, by implication at least, protracted, yet they all come immeasurably short of sabbatismos in expressiveness.

At least two thoughts are conveyed by this sabbath antitype, not contained in the other words. Cessation from work is negative, while the rest which remaineth to the people of God is positive. In the quotation from Revelation a clause is added which seems to supply, in a measure, what the word itself lacks: "And their works do follow them." There are rewards that come to the faithful laborer when his work is done. When the sabbath was instituted, at the giving of the manna, this lesson was distinctly taught as a part of it. There was no food to be gathered on the seventh day; it was already possessed. It had been provided on the previous day, and the Lord himself preserved it for their use. In the antitypical sabbatismos, then, which remains to the people of God, the Father himself will preserve to his children all that bountiful supply of blessing, and happiness, and life, which the soul shall need. It will come, too, as the result of faithful effort here. Let him, then, who may have reached even the sixth day of these earthly toils and strivings, gather vigorously of the bread of life for the great sabbatismos to come. "Lay up for yourselves treasures in heaven, where neither moth nor rust doth corrupt and where thieves do not break through nor steal" (Matt. vi. 20).

The context (Heb. iii. 11 and iv. 8) shows that the apostle had in contemplation, as a possible rest in store for the ancient people, the Land of Canaan, but dismisses that hypothesis as impossible: "For if Joshua had given them rest, then would he not afterward have spoken of another day." Then follows our text: "There remaineth therefore a rest to the people of God." Now this hypothetical rest was an actual inheritance, a land flowing with milk and honey, rich in the grapes of Eschol, the beautiful country promised to Abraham himself, the faithful patriarch of old. The sabbatismos remaining to the people of God implies, therefore, an inheritance, a "heavenly country," a "city" (Heb. xi. 16), the "new Jerusalem" (Rev. xxi. 2), "new heavens and a new earth wherein dwelleth righteousness" (II. Pet. iii. 13).

But sabbatismos carries with it, in enlarged form and meaning. as the antitype always does from its type, some leading features of the ancient Sabbath. Thus, that institution under the commandment was to be kept holy, and it was, moreover, by way of eminence, styled "the Sabbath of the Lord thy God." From which we may learn the lesson, elsewhere taught, that the future rest is to be holy, a freedom from sin, an enjoyment of the things of God, a new paradise, in short, in which the presence, and blessing, and glory of God shall be freely vouchsafed to His redeemed children. The attachment of Sabbaths to the annual feasts of the Jews, which were in themselves joyous occasions, marking important epochs in their national life or history, would seem, when separately examined, to lead to the thought that the sabbatismos to come would both overflow with the fulness of joy, and derive some of its completeness from such circumstances of the past as may be associable with it.

The second of the thoughts before adverted to, which render this word superior to others likewise translated "rest," refers to the duration implied. Cessation from labor merely, may become irksome. If that then were all which were promised to the Christian, the time might soon arrive when he would wish to resume his work, with all the cares and all the fatigue incident to it. Whenever there is added to the idea of rest, or cessation from labor, the necessary means to continue it, in happiness and cheerful life, men are not desirous to return to former hardships. When God completed creation he ceased that work, and so far as we know, forever. And we do know that that particular creative work sketched in the first chapter of Genesis, namely, the fitting up of this habitable globe, and the arranging of its surroundings to suit the present state in the life of man, was then once for all completed, so that what is indicated by God's rest in that connection was perpetual, and such, we doubt not, is the clear implication as to that rest that remaineth to the people of God. As also Canaan, the hypothetical scene of rest to the Jews was to be a continued inheritance, so the heavenly rest implies an inheritance from which man shall go out no more forever.

Paul, (if we may presume him to have been the author of the Epistle to the Hebrews,) lived at the time when the types had come to an end, and their fulfillment was beginning to be enjoyed in the antitype. Of that fact he appeared wonderfully conscious in writing this epistle. His object throughout is clearly traceable to the present and the future. He would have his brethren, despite their prejudices, habits, and surroundings, forsake the meager and imperfect past for the richness of the favor now enjoyable in Christ. He would unfold and embellish, so far as he might, their present high estate and the greater glory to be revealed hereafter. To the "holy brethren, partakers of the heavenly calling," in parts of the third and fourth chapters, he is both demonstrating the fact that they have a heritage in store, and warning them by well-known examples of the danger of failing to attain it. Whence is his demonstration and warning taken? From the history of their fathers with which the brethren were perfectly familiar. "Harden not your hearts" (iii. 8), "as in the provocation in the day of temptation in the wilderness; When your fathers tempted me, proved me, and saw my works for forty years. Wherefore I was grieved with that generation, and said, they do always err in their heart; and they have not known my ways. So I sware in my wrath they shall not enter into my rest."

Here is the first occurrence of the word "rest." It is used as signifying the cessation from the toils and hardships of their wilderness journey, such as they might expect to enjoy had they chosen to enter the land of Canaan at once. The realization of it was Canaan itself, into which they were forbidden to enter because of their unbelief. The spies, chosen to represent the tribes, after a search through the land for forty days, finding and bringing with them incontestable proofs of its superlative richness, were, with two exceptions, overawed by the military obstacles to be overcome, represented in the giants of Anak, and with their faith in God as a leader at a remarkably low ebb considering what he had already done for the nation, they united with the people at large in clamorously resisting all efforts to go up and possess the land, preferring to choose a captain and return to bondage in Egypt. This was the unbelief, this the disobedience which provoked the wrath of God and caused them to be driven back into the wilderness of wandering, till the unfaithful people had perished, and a new race under Joshua, the son of Nun, were prepared to go forward.

Leaving for the present this provocation in the wilderness, as it is amplified to the end of the third chapter, it will be noticed, at the opening of the fourth, that Paul derives practical instruction from it for his own time, cautioning the Hebrew brethren lest they should in like manner come short of God's rest. To both, the Israelites in the wilderness under Moses, and the Hebrew brethren under the instruction of Paul, the gospel was preached, to one the good news of the promised Canaan, productive as the heart could desire, to the other the good news of a risen Saviour and eternal felicity through Him. As the ancient people had failed by unbelief to enter upon their promised possession, so might these disciples of the Lord himself come short of their promised blessings under the new covenant, from the same cause. For (we who are) believers enter into rest.

Punctuating verse third by a period instead of the first comma, we there enter upon a new thought, and shall run hastily to the end of the entire passage under examination before returning to some peculiarities in the two paragraphs above, which, in connection with our text (ver. 9), complete the required exposition. When God declared that the ancient people should not enter into his rest (vers. 3 and 5). it was not because the preparation had not been made, for the works were finished from the foundation of the world, as was indicated in the record of the seventh day by Moses, namely, that on that day God did rest, having completed *all his works*. As then, from the first, God had prepared a rest for some one to enjoy, and those to whom it was first proclaimed did not enter it, it was necessary that another time should be fixed. Therefore, by David, in the Psalms, speaking prophetically of the gospel age, it is declared: "To-day, if ye will hear his voice, harden not your hearts." For if Joshua had given the promised rest in Canaan, then God, through David, would not afterward have spoken of another day. "There remaineth, therefore, a sabbatical rest for the people of God."

Where, in the Bible, is this promise of God's rest found?

Let this question stand in a paragraph by itself. To answer it is to acknowledge the main position herein assumed. The teaching of Paul, as just examined, with the quotations from former Scriptures, places the promise before himself, before David, before Joshua, before the provocation in the wilderness. This is certainly the clear implication at least. It is, indeed, assumed that God's rest having been prepared from the foundation of the world, and a promise being left of entering into it, some people, at some time, must necessarily be found in whom that promise could be fulfilled. Upon such an assumption Paul's argument is based.

Since this rest is first mentioned with reference to the land of Canaan, at the beginning of the wandering in the wilderness, the promise antedating that event and applying to that inheritance, would seem most naturally to be referred to Abraham, the father of the nation, to whom the country had actually been promised. Now, in the covenant which God made with him (Gen. xii. 2, 3, 7), there were three items of importance: (1) the immense multitude of his posterity, (2) the possession of the land of Canaan, and (3) the blessing through his seed (Christ) of all the families of earth. And no doubt there were involved in these all the great events and promises of both the Mosaic and Christian dispensations. There were various instances in which the whole future was embodied in comprehensive prophetic promises. Thus it was declared that the seed of the woman should bruise the serpent's head, and promised that God would raise up from among the Israelites a prophet like Moses, whom the people would be required to obey. While all these ancient declarations foreshadowed, in various phases, and more or less accurately, the coming times of God's merciful visitation, they fell very far short, even that to Abraham, of supplying the necessary antecedents to the record sketched by Paul in Hebrews, the element of rest being nowhere alluded to in them.

As a result of this futile effort to find a specific, or even a probable indirect promise of the kind sought, we are driven to the types as the last resort. And here in the sabbatic institutions we have the complete answer to every requirement. Whether taken alone or superadded to the promises, it matters not, since the Sabbath was necessary, as a type, too, to furnish the proper premises in the case. It must, in the first instance, have been the weekly Sabbath, since the annual were given to be observed after they should enter the land. Prior to the provocation, however, the people had been keeping the weekly. As it was a typical institution, they, by observing it, had come into possession of the promise of rest which it embodied. Such a type is susceptible of different grades of fulfillment. It was specific as to rest, but not definite as to the kind or degree of it. Thus, though finding its ultimate development in Christ, there were three stages in the progress of events to which, when first given, it might point: (1) Canaan, (2) the church of Christ on earth, and (3) heaven. Hence the provocation, just as they were ready to enter the promised land, caused the declaration from God that they should not enter his rest. But the next generation did enter the land, and they kept the type still pointing ahead to its fuller realization, while Canaan itself became an added type, a further promise more definite and more complete, of the rest to come. In David, therefore, after the height of temporal prosperity had been realized under their greatest king, and nothing more of that nature could be expected, the promise was again declared in force.

We have already found the types to terminate at the cross of Christ. Not that their fulfillment or antitype was in all cases found there, but only the end of their required observance. They were then to give place to other things vastly superior. The antitypical realizations as blessings were to be enjoyed afterwards by the successive generations of men to the end of time, and even in heaven itself. The danger was still that of the provocation which the apostle emphasized, that they should fail through unbelief. Paul said: "We, which have believed, do enter into rest." And further: "There remaineth, therefore, a sabbatic rest to the people of God." Who can doubt that this means heaven, begun in spirit and an earnest of it received on earth, realized hereafter, a state an inheritance like that of Canaan, from which we will not be led away into captivity, which will not be compassed about by enemies, and which new Jerusalem shall never be destroyed like Jerusalem of old.

In the provocation God called it "My" rest, and Paul, in Hebrews, "His" rest. God's rest is perfect and could not be realized by man short of the cross of Christ. Hence any seeming examples of it, as at Canaan, could only have been partial, and the type and promise also, must remain. The thought refers us back to God's rest at creation in Moses' account, also to the entire sabbatic system as God's institution. Man certainly could not enter into God's perfect rest till the work of redemption had been wrought in his heart, his sins pardoned, his desires changed, his hope anchored within the vail, and the Comforter his constant companion. The presupposed promise of rest to man could be found only in the Sabbath considered as a type; much more is that idea of the Sabbath necessary to give us a pledge of participation in God's rest. Observing the Sabbath day, however scrupulously, would not accomplish the promise, for the very Israelites who were excluded from entering the rest, had been long keeping the Sabbath. But if we understand God's Sabbath to be complete rest after a great work wholly accomplished, with that satisfaction which declares at each successive stage "and God saw that it was good," we must look to see man enter God's rest, beyond earthly recurring Sabbaths, to the great work of redemption completed forever, when man can enjoy the unalloyed pleasure of contemplating the past as well done, his Master's commendation "well done" (Matt. xxv. 21), and regard the future with joyful anticipations.

This was the evident intention in the divine mind from the beginning, and all earthly Sabbaths were but embodiments of that purpose and pledge, in lasting and substantial forms as pertains to human institutions, easily kept and easily recognized. How else can the force of sabbatismos in Hebrews be understood? In this view how significant the form of the word becomes. And how else can a reasonable supposition as to the object of the wonderful system of Sabbaths be derived. Finally, it must be observed in this connection, that with this explanation the origin of the Sabbath at the giving of the manna, exactly accords. The sabbatismos mentioned in Hebrews, remains "to the people of God." These are his redeemed people, the church of Christ. Hence its type, the Sabbath, must also have belonged exclusively "to the people of God." in type, as the other in antitype. This typical people was the Jews, as every one who admits a type at all acknowledges. They belonged to God after they were freed from Pharaoh, and it was immediately after this that the Sabbath was instituted and the Mosaic system of laws began to be announced.

An investigation which began at the head of the stream of time, has brought us, in its conclusion, out into the broad boundless sea, where not a hidden rock nor breaking wave threatens the security of the happy voyager. Such is the termination of any just survey of the Word of God, from whatever point of view undertaken. If we may congratulate ourselves on a result, so felicitous, of a mere inquiry, how shall the weary pilgrim from earthly shores exult when the reality of the peaceful prospect unfolds to his vision!

www.ingramcontent.com/pod-product-compliance
Lightning Source LLC
Chambersburg PA
CBHW021957220426
43663CB00007B/856